**Library of Congress Cataloging in Publication Data**

Rouse, Parke, 1915-
A house for a president.

Bibliography: p.
Includes index.
1. College of William and Mary—Presidents—Dwellings—History. I. Title.
LD6051.W534R68 1983 378.755′4252 83-7523
ISBN 0-87517-050-1

Designer: Richard Stinely

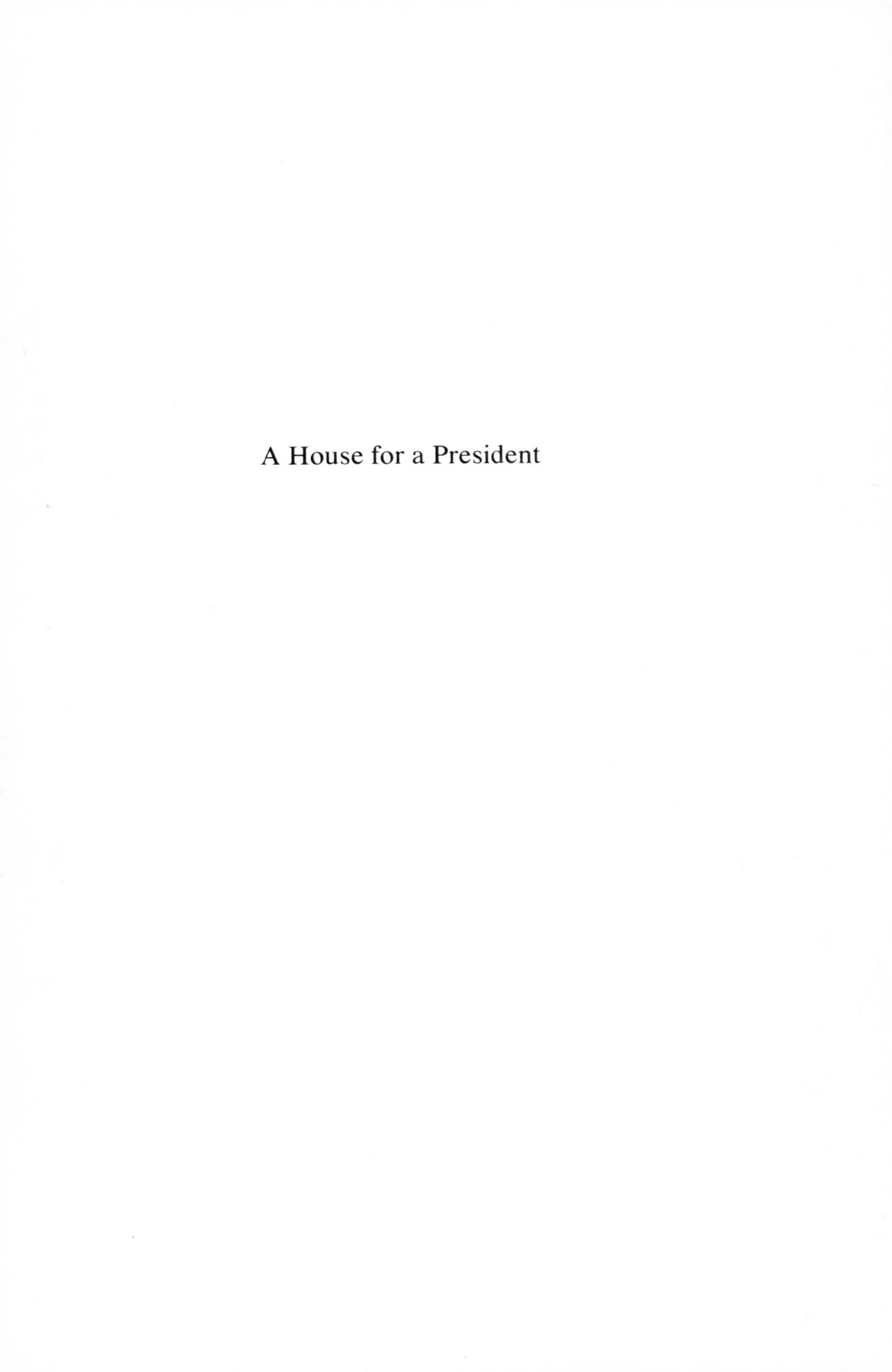

A House for a President

William and Mary College Archives

*The parlors of the President's House at the College of William and Mary are furnished in the Georgian style and have welcomed world leaders.*

# Table of Contents

# Introduction

## *When Two Worlds Met*

IT had never happened before. The ruling monarch of Great Britain had come to see the former colony of Virginia, where a handful of Englishmen in 1607 had planted Britain's flag.

Now Queen Elizabeth II had flown the ocean to trace her countrymen's steps, 350 years after they had stepped ashore at Jamestown—the start of Britain's first successful New World foothold. It was 4:20 on the afternoon of Wednesday, October 16, 1957, when Her Majesty and Prince Philip stepped out of their limousine on Richmond Road at the gate to the President's House of the College of William and Mary.

Cheers arose from the crowd outside the house, as the Queen and her handsome consort mounted the steps to the old house. Sunshine coated the old brick, laid in Flemish bond, amid plantings of boxwood and ivy.

The wide door swung open, admitting the couple to a spacious hallway. There stood Alvin Duke Chandler, president, and his wife, Louise, to offer the hospitality of the house. To Elizabeth and Philip it was a house not unlike others they had known in the English countryside. Wide pine flooring was visible through a scattering of Oriental rugs. Damask curtains enlivened the muted colors of the tall rooms. Walnut and mahogany furniture of Queen Anne and Chippendale design stood between multi-sashed windows. Portraits of early Virginia greats—Blairs and Pages—hung on the walls.

Dressed in a dark blue silk coat with velvet collar and a cloche, the

Queen was friendly but reticent. Prince Philip eased her progress with jaunty informality. Yes, Her Majesty and he would welcome a bit of rest. Then as the college's Board of Visitors and their wives waited unseen in the parlor, the Queen and Prince Philip followed Louise Chandler upstairs for a welcome pause. They had arrived at Patrick Henry Airport in Newport News at 1:30 P.M. and had been driven straight to Jamestown, where the Queen had delivered an address. It gave Her Majesty a chance to change her shoes, supplied from a silk bag by her lady-in-waiting, and to powder her nose before descending to meet the Virginians.

Elizabeth II had read in advance about the College of William and Mary and its link with the Crown. She had also talked of it with her mother, Britain's beloved "Queen Mum," who had visited the college in 1954. Chartered in 1693 by King William and Queen Mary, it had begun in 1694 with a grammar school, teaching to sons of these hard-handed tobacco barons who launched the first families of Virginia. The founders had hoped many students would become clergymen to strengthen the moral fiber of the New World, but most had been drawn into the plantation world and politics of the colony.

Despite later disaffection and American independence, the college had clung doggedly to its royal charter, its coat of arms, and its designation as "Their Majesties' Royal College of William and Mary in Virginia." For over a hundred years it had felt no conflict between its royal origins and its democratic present.

As the Chandlers' guests bowed to Queen Elizabeth and Prince Philip, waiters offered refreshments, with tea sent from England for the occasion, served in English china. "English goods were ever the best," said a guest, echoing Colonial Williamsburg's film *The Story of a Patriot*. Aware of the arduous hours ahead, Philip urged his wife to "Eat a good tea." Of President Chandler, he asked the identity of one of the portraits. "That *can't* be John Paul Jones," he said when it was identified as such.

The Queen told her hosts that her mother remembered many details of her visit to Jamestown and Williamsburg three years earlier. Like her mother, Elizabeth II asked about George Washington, once chancellor of the college, and Thomas Jefferson, who had studied there from 1760 to 1762. Along with Washington and Robert E. Lee, the Queen shared descent through her mother's family from Augustine Warner, a seventeenth-century Gloucester County planter. One of Warner's descendants had returned to Great Britain and linked his family with the Bowes-Lyons, the family of the Queen Mother.

Photograph by Thomas L. Williams

*After tea at the President's House in 1957, Queen Elizabeth II and Prince Philip began a campus tour with Rector James Robertson.*

But time was passing. Outside in the sun a crowd waited for the Queen to walk the hundred yards across campus to the Wren Building, completed in 1695 but badly burned three times before its reconstruction in the 1930s by John D. Rockefeller, Jr., as part of his restoration of Williamsburg. Sir Michael Adeane, the Queen's secretary, strode up to James Robertson, Norfolk attorney and rector of the college, who was to escort her. "Time to leave," said Sir Michael. "Will you tell Her Majesty?"

The Rector led the Queen onto the elm-shaded college yard. Hundreds of people lined the paths, many of them students and professors. With Mrs. Robertson and Prince Philip following, the host led Queen Elizabeth past the statue of Lord Botetourt, a popular Virginia governor before the Revolution. Then they climbed the steps into the Wren Building, the oldest classroom structure in any American college. The procession moved through rooms reminiscent of Oxford and Cambridge. In the group were well-known Britons: the Queen's cousin and assistant secretary Martin Charteris, Foreign Secretary Selwyn Lloyd, Ambassador Sir Harold Caccia, and General Sir Frederick Browning, whose wife was novelist Daphne DuMaruier. They walked on to the Great Hall, where the Colonial Assembly met after the removal of Virginia's seat of government in 1699 from Jamestown to Middle Plantation, later renamed Williamsburg.

Then came the moment for the college's presentation of gifts to the couple. Stepping onto the second story balcony of the Wren Building, the Queen and Prince acknowledged the students' cheers. They stood near the onetime crossroads of Britain's first overseas colony. Ahead of them were the roofs of Duke of Gloucester Street, with the Capitol at the far end and Bruton Parish Church steeple midway. Though it bore the name of an almost forgotten son of Queen Anne, who had reigned from 1702 to 1714, students shortened it to "DOG Street" soon after the street had been laid off. It may well have reminded Prince Philip of the Royal Mile in Edinburgh between Holyrood Palace and St. Giles's Cathedral. Franklin D. Roosevelt called it "the most historic avenue in all America."

The Queen's skirt blew slightly in the October breeze. Escorts were relieved to know that it was weighted by tiny lead pellets, inserted in the hem by the royal dressmaker. "I cherish this link between the Crown and your College," the Queen told the crowd, "because it is a part of our joint histories . . . It also demonstrates the very close association which has always existed between learning, the arts and sciences of our countries . . . It might surprise some of them, but I can say quite sincerely that I am very proud of the fact that this College educated so many founders of this nation. Rarely has any country been able to produce a group of such enlightened and skilled statesmen as those who gathered around George Washington."

Thanking Rector Robertson for the college's gift of drawings of its early buildings, Queen Elizabeth made a gift to the college of a seventeenth-century volume on the Order of the Garter, reading in a clear voice from notes in her gloved hand. Then Prince Philip, chancellor of the University of Edinburgh, recalled the founding of William and Mary by James Blair, an Edinburgh graduate, and presented books from Blair's alma mater.

After a walk from the Wren Building, the Queen was greeted at College Corner by Winthrop Rockefeller, chairman of Colonial Williamsburg. The royal pair then joined Winthrop and Jeanette Rockefeller for a brief tour in a colonial carriage drawn by a pair of handsome horses. They progressed down Duke of Gloucester Street to Palace Green, there to dismount at the Governor's Palace. A liveried coachman and a postilion manned the carriage, while a cordon of soldiers from Fort Knox and peninsula military bases held back thousands of cheering people along the way.

Throughout the day, Philip's wit enlivened the journey and brought laughter from the crowd. A garden reception at the Governor's Palace was attended by several hundred Virginians and gave him a chance to sparkle. When one matron confessed that she felt "so British" in his presence, Philip deadpanned, "But madam, I'm a Greek." When another guest, already introduced to the Queen and Prince, reappeared in the lineup, Philip demurred politely. "We'll be here all night if you keep doing that."

The Queen had been in transit from England via Canada about fifteen hours when she finally appeared, radiant in a jeweled white gown, for the day's last public function. It was to be a dinner for 260 formally dressed guests at the Williamsburg Inn. From tiny, erudite Earl Gregg Swem, historian and librarian ermeritus of William and Mary, she accepted booklets describing the peopling of Virginia and the colony's rise. The next morning, after a night's sleep, the Queen and Prince flew off to Washington to visit President and Mrs. Dwight D. Eisenhower at the White House.

The Queen's visit celebrated the 350th anniversary of the first permanent settlement by Englishmen in the New World, yet her emphasis was toward the future. At thirty-one she had just begun her long reign. "There are many indications today," she had told her audience at Jamestown, "that we are at the beginning of a new age of discovery and exploration in the world of human knowledge and technology. Only a short time ago these unexplored areas seemed as impenetrable as the forests of this continent to the settlers 350 years ago. But they were not deterred. Their example can help us to build another New World, of which our descendants will speak proudly 350 years from now."

When the Queen and Prince departed for the White House the next morning, Williamsburg and Jamestown went back to their workaday world. It had been an occasion packed with drama. Never before had a reigning British monarch visited Virginia, where the global spread of the English had begun. John Smith's landing had opened a new age.

Nowhere was the link between the two cultures so tangible that day as at William and Mary, which proudly keeps its royal name and charter. At College Corner, which had seen many historic events in its three centuries, it was a day to remember. There had been a lot of these days since James Blair and the General Assembly of Virginia had planted Their Majesties' College on that spot.

# *Book One*

Courtesy Colonial Williamsburg Foundation

# The Tumult and the Shouting

## 1693–1777

The foundation of the Presidents house at the College was laid, the President, Mr. Dawson, Mr. Fry, Mr. Stith, and Mr. Fox [Professors and Masters] laying the first five bricks in order, one after another. The reason of the foundations being laid that day was, that Mr. Henry Cary the Undertaker, had appointed his bricklayers to be ready that day, and that they could not proceed till the foundation was laid.

The *College Journal,*
July 31, 1732

# 1

# *When James Blair Lived*

THE house which welcomed Queen Elizabeth II to Williamsburg in 1957 was part of a past that extended back almost to the arrival of the *Susan Constant, Godspeed,* and *Discovery* to Virginia in the spring of 1607. It had known great figures at an early stage of English-American history, for its beginnings went back to the time when Indians and buffalo still roamed parts of Virginia.

After James Blair persuaded King William and Queen Mary to charter a college in Virginia in 1693, he and Governor Francis Nicholson chose a site for it at the junction of the colony's two main roads. One was the great road which led from Jamestown and Green Spring eastward down the peninsula to Point Comfort. The other was the New Kent road, leading northwestward to the interior. In the next century it came to be called Richmond Road, after the village which became Virginia's capital in 1780. These roads merged to pass through the settlement, known since 1633 as Middle Plantation, to continue down the peninsula.

They followed the highest ground between the York and the James rivers, between creeks that drained the forests and growing farmlands. Ravines on the north fed the stream that came to be called Queen's Creek which flowed into the York. Those to the south fed into Archer's Hope Creek, later called College Creek, which emptied into the James. The horse path fronting the college corner was straightened after 1699 and named Duke of Gloucester Street.

The building of the commodious college at this apex began in 1695 and helped to persuade Virginia's governor and Assembly to move the seat of government from Jamestown to Middle Plantation in 1699 after the Jamestown statehouse had burned the year before. The first brick church of Bruton Parish had been built in 1674, near the site where the present larger structure replaced it in 1715. The gaggle of crossroads buildings at Middle Plantation slowly gave way to a tiny "city," directed by Governor Francis Nicholson and laid out by surveyor Theodorick Bland in 1699. Thus the college was largely responsible for the site of the new capital which the Assembly christened "Williamsburgh" in 1699.

Blair and his wife Sarah lived then at Richneck, a plantation off Jamestown Road, a mile from Williamsburg. They had moved there from Varina in 1695, after the Scottish-born cleric had become rector of James City Parish. At first he rented the house and land from Colonel Philip Ludwell I of Green Spring, but in 1699 the clergyman bought one hundred acres of Richneck plantation from the Ludwells. The property was on the south side of Jamestown Road adjoining Raccoon Chase and Ludwell's Millpond (later Jones's Millpond). In the twentieth century the pond was to be ennobled with the name Lake Matoaka.

Virginia's growth in the 1700s was evident in the rise of Williamsburg. Artisans and supplies had to be sent from England for the building of public structures. The colony's builders were kept busy with the projects of governors and general assemblies. They erected a Capitol (1701–1705); a Governor's Palace (1706–1715); a new Bruton Parish Church (1711–1715); a Public Magazine (1715); and a rebuilt college building (1710–1716), after the first had been destroyed by fire in 1705.

The design of the college building, called the Main Building, was attributed to Sir Christopher Wren, then surveyor general for the Crown, by the Reverend Hugh Jones in 1724, and was to have been a quadrangle, as were many colleges of Oxford and Cambridge. However, funds were exhausted after only two sides of the quad had been erected, and the east and north sides were found to be adequate to house the grammar school, Indian school, their masters and students, the president's apartment, and apartments for future faculty. Some college servants and blacks were housed in the Main Building's basement, which also contained facilities for cooking, baking, and brewing.

On its completion, some college rooms were temporarily taken over by the governor and General Assembly until a Williamsburg capitol could be built. Governor Francis Nicholson was briefly quartered in the college, and the Assembly convened in the Great Hall. This use

Photograph by Thomas L. Williams

*The President's House of the College of William and Mary was built in 1732-1733 and has housed twenty-three of the first twenty-four presidents.*

continued until 1704, when the government finally moved into the uncompleted Capitol.

Fire swept through the Main Building the night of October 29, 1705, and destroyed all but its exterior walls. Students and others sleeping in the building escaped with a few belongings, but most books and furnishings were destroyed. Once again the grammar school—the main educational activity thus far—met in the nearby schoolhouse where it had operated from 1694 till the Main Building had been occupied in 1700.

By 1716 the Indian school had found more students, and in 1723 the college erected a building for its use on the Jamestown Road side of the yard. Built with funds left by English scientist Robert Boyle (the money had been invested in Brafferton manor in Yorkshire from which the building takes its name), it was a handsome Georgian structure which has survived these many years. No doubt James Blair and its architect-builder, Henry Cary, Jr., envisioned a similar building across the college yard to balance it.

However, other needs came first. Blair went to London in 1726 and with the help of the Reverend Stephen Fouace, the only other surviving original trustee, and Archbishop William Wake of Canterbury, the college chancellor, drew up statutes to govern the college. The statutes were signed on June 24, 1727, in London. They specified that when funds were available, the president was to get an annual salary of "One Hundred and Fifty Pounds Sterling, with an House and Garden suitable to the Place."

The legal document transferring the college property from founders to faculty was drawn up before Blair returned from London in 1729. As directed by its charter, when the college had its president and six masters or professors, the trustees were to deed all college assets to them, who would become "one body corporate and politic." This could now be done.

When Blair returned from England, he and the Visitors decided to build the third side of the proposed quadrangle, the chapel wing, which was completed and consecrated on June 28, 1732. The time had now come to erect the building to balance the Brafferton, and three days after the consecration of the chapel, Henry Cary, Jr., had the land marked off and ready for the foundation-laying of the President's House.

With due ceremony, on July 31, 1732, Blair and four of the professors and masters laid the first five bricks. They probably wore academic robes, clerical neck bands, and clerical wigs. The *College Journal* for

July 31, 1732, recorded it thus: "The foundation of the Presidents house at the College was laid, the President, Mr. Dawson, Mr. Fry, Mr. Stith, and Mr. Fox, laying the first five bricks in order, one after another. The reason of the foundations being laid that day was, that Mr. Henry Cary the Undertaker, had appointed his bricklayers to be ready that day, and that they could not proceed till the foundation was laid."

It was a memorable year in Virginia. Several months before the chapel had been put to use and the President's House had been started, George Washington had been born on February 22, 1732, at Pope's Creek, a hundred miles north of Williamsburg, in Westmoreland County.

Henry Cary, Jr., one of Virginia's ablest builders, followed closely the lines he had laid down earlier for the Brafferton, but he made the President's House four feet larger in each direction. Following builders' manuals of the day, Cary made it exactly as tall as it was wide: 56 feet from ground to chimney caps.

Blair's second-in-command, the Reverend William Dawson, while writing to the Bishop of London, described it as "a convenient brick house," but it was much more than that. It was built of sand-struck brick, with glazed headers, and laid in the Flemish bond favored in England and Virginia. It was somewhat similar to Cary's own house, Ampthill, which he built in Chesterfield County near Richmond, and also like the house Richard Taliaferro later built on Palace Green for his daughter, Elizabeth, and son-in-law, George Wythe.

Like other structures of its style, the President's House was severely symmetrical. Doors and windows were broad, befitting a house of this size. Though very similar to the Brafferton, as its walls rose, it seemed a small version of the Governor's Palace, minus the cupola and flanking outbuildings. Above a full basement for wine and food storage, it had three floors, the first two with high ceilings.

The house that Cary built was unusually handsome. Its fine proportions and brickwork won the admiration of townspeople and visitors. In modern times, it has been considered one of the most important Georgian houses in the Williamsburg area. Architectural historians Thomas Waterman and John Barrows described it in their *Domestic Colonial Architecture of Tidewater Virginia,* published in 1932:

> The brickwork is especially noteworthy, both in color and elaboration. The walls are laid up in Flemish bond, the stretchers being a soft salmon color, and the headers covered with a silver gray glaze. The arches and jambs of the windows, the string course

Courtesy Colonial Williamsburg Foundation

*James Blair obtained the charter for the College of William and Mary and was its first president. He moved into the President's House in 1733 and died there in 1743.*

> and corners of the building are rubbed brick of a bright vermillion color, emphasizing the architectural features of the structure. The windows are wide, but, being divided into four lights rather than the customary three, create a distinct vertical character which is further emphasized by the dormers occurring over the piers, the steep sweep of the roof, and the location of the T-shaped chimney stacks at the end of the ridge.

Originally the first and second stories of the President's House had four rooms apiece, roughly equal in size, each story being divided by a wide passage or hallway. To these, bathrooms and closets were later added. Before 1732 wealthy Virginians were building wide halls as a means of catching vagrant breezes in the hot Virginia summer.

The third floor was ventilated by dormer windows, and had two rooms which would be used over the years chiefly by house servants or student roomers. The steep roof was a Dutch influence which had come to England around 1660 with the return of Charles II to the throne. It was the most distinctive feature of the Brafferton and the President's House, suggestive of the elegant vertical lines of the Governor's Palace and Westover plantation house, both masterly examples of early eighteenth-century buildings.

The "Garden suitable to the Place," specified in the 1727 college statutes, was an important feature. President Blair and his successors were to depend on the livestock and produce of the college's cultivation, both in the President's House garden and in the larger college garden behind the Main Building. The college overseer and servants were responsible for maintaining both. Like other fine Virginia houses of the era, the President's House had its separate kitchen with second-story servants' quarters, its laundry, privy, and well. All were west of the house, off New Kent Road.

The president at first shared the use of the college stable, carriage house, and garden behind the Main Building with others. However, a separate stable and carriage house for his own use was erected in 1761 on a town lot near the President's House.

For well over a century the house looked westward onto a garden and open land. In 1859 a burying ground called the College Cemetery was laid off at the rear of the president's garden. Here presidents, faculty, their families, and students could be buried. With this exception, the "back campus" remained largely undeveloped into the twentieth century, when President Lyon Gardiner Tyler kept his flock of turkeys there. Indeed, most of the President's House outbuildings, including the kitchen, continued to serve their original purpose until the time of Tyler.

No early drawings of the President's House show any attendant buildings until the "Frenchman's Map" of Williamsburg in 1782, which places two outbuildings west of the house. Privies and wellheads were usually omitted from such plats. An 1853 insurance policy shows the location of the house's wooden kitchen, with an unidentified small building between it and a long building near the Richmond Road edge of the yard. A covered way then linked house and kitchen, probably built in 1848 by President Benjamin Ewell. A similar covered way was added from the Brafferton to its kitchen about the same time.

Despite the elegance of the President's House—handsome mantels, fine mouldings, and imported stone steps—its original cost was only £650, as Professor William Dawson reported to Edmund Gibson, Bishop of London, in 1732. For its size and quality, Henry Cary, Jr., had built it with amazing speed and economy.

Like most of William and Mary in its first fifty years, the President's House was created to the taste of a remarkable man, the Reverend James Blair. He had proposed creation of the college to the governor and General Assembly in 1691, had gone from Virginia to England to obtain its charter from King William and Queen Mary, and had ruled it with an iron hand until he died.

By the time Blair moved into the President's House he was seventy-eight, but he was still firm of step and mind. Although his wife Sarah, daughter of Benjamin Harrison of Wakefield in Surry County, had died twenty years earlier and left him childless, Blair led a full life. His combined roles were as rector of Bruton Parish Church, commissary of the Bishop of London to Anglican Virginia, member of the Governor's Council, and president of the college. Nobody in Virginia but the governor had more power, and even the governor sometimes deferred to James Blair.

Blair probably moved into the house in October of 1733, his plantation foreman and slaves hauling his household goods from Richneck. It was a great convenience for the old man to live in the college yard, at the busiest crossroads in Virginia. Now he could attend to his parish and presidential duties from a centrally located house. Here he could meet with faculty and scholars, receive calls from visiting governors and counselors, and could write out his sermons for Bruton.

Not far away from Blair lived his favorite nephew, the first John Blair, who James loved as a son and who, with his children, would inherit most of Blair's large fortune. With obvious enthusiasm, Blair

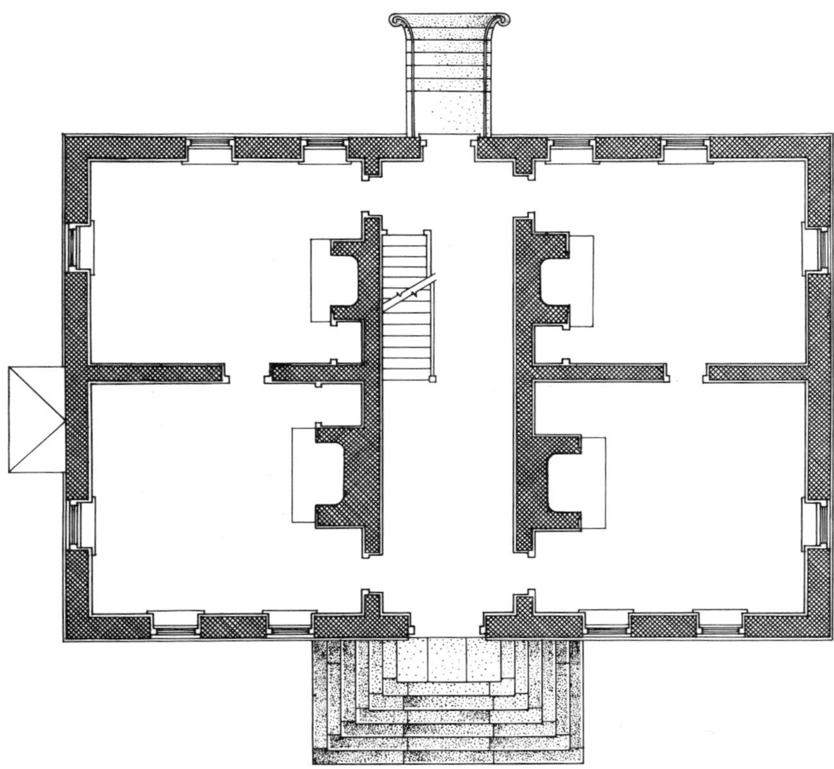

From *The Public Buildings of Williamsburg,* by Marcus Whiffen, Colonial Williamsburg Foundation

*The first floor of the President's House has four rectangular rooms. Rear, at top, looks on Richmond Road and front on the college yard.*

wrote in January 1735 from the President's House to the college Chancellor, Edmund Gibson, Bishop of London, "Our College thrives in reputation, and numbers of Scholars, and handsom Buildings, the chappel and the Presidents house making a great addition to the Conveniency and ornament of it."

The house was well situated for anyone coming to Williamsburg. Though the red-faced Scot was not a sociable man, Blair enjoyed the company of a few old friends like Robert "King" Carter and William Byrd II of Westover, who were fellow members of the Governor's Council. In his early years in politics Byrd had disliked the combative churchman, but in time he had grown to like him. He frequently wrote in his shorthand diary of visits he paid to Blair in the President's House. After a trip from Westover on December 10, 1739, Byrd added this entry. "About 10 Colonel [Robert] Bolling overtook me and came into the chariot and got to Williamsburg about 3. . . I put myself in order and walked to the Commissary's, where I ate a mutton chop and talked till 8, and then returned to my lodgings and put my house in order and prayed."

On April 20, 1740, Byrd recorded his Sunday attendance at Bruton, noting that "After church dined with the Commissary and ate chicken and bacon." Frequently Byrd accepted Blair's invitation to drink coffee or hot chocolate at the President's, as he had done earlier when James and Sarah Blair had lived at Richneck.

On one such visit Byrd "rose at 6 o'clock but neglected to say my prayers because Mr. Commissary kept me to hear a verse he had made for the College." He referred to ceremonial Latin verses which the college was required by charter to present to the governor yearly. Blair especially prided himself on his Latin, and Byrd was one of the Virginia literati who could appreciate it. They read the ancients together by candlelight in the President's House.

Except in the Indian school, only clerics usually taught at the Anglican college in its colonial years, and, though not mentioned in the charter, only the president was permitted to marry. Frequently Blair would ask one of his bachelor professors to absent himself from the Great Hall high table and dine with him in the President's House. His favorite was young William Dawson, who William Wake, Archbishop of Canterbury, had recruited for the William and Mary faculty in 1729 after Dawson had graduated from Queen's College at Oxford and been ordained. Dawson often preached for Blair at Bruton and wrote letters for Blair on college and church affairs to his bishop in London.

But the old man could be harsh with his professors. Informed that one of them was unable to teach after a nocturnal binge, Blair lambasted the miscreant by letter, concluding:

> I understand the same night diversions are designed to be continued, and perhaps your company will be again desired and expected, but for Christ's sake, as you regard the honour of your character, and as you would avoid giving occasion to the Governors of the College to rail against it, employ your good talent of wit and discretion to extricate yourself in time from a practice that will infallibly be attended with such bad consequences.
>
> If I were not very much your friend and had not a just opinion of your candour, it would be so much easier for me to be silent than to venture your displeasure by any freedom of this kind.

The old Scot tempered his reprimand by signing himself as "Dear Sir, your affectionate and most humble servant, James Blair." Then suddenly softening, he added a postscript: "If your health will permit, I shall be very glad of your good company at dinner." James Blair could temper the wind if he thought the shorn lamb deserved it.

An important meeting occurred in the President's House in 1739, when Blair was eighty-four. Now nearly deaf and suffering from a rupture, he received a visit from the Reverend George Whitefield, a young English evangelist and leader of the Calvinistic Methodists, who was preaching in the colonies. A disciple of Charles and John Wesley, Whitefield had been refused some Anglican pulpits. However, Blair invited him to preach at Sunday service in Bruton, and Whitefield wrote in his diary for December 15, 1739:

> Paid my respects to the Rev. Mr. Blair. His Discourse was Savoury, and such as tended to the Use of edifying. He received me with joy, asked me to preach and Wished my Stay was to be longer. Under God he has been chiefly instrumental in raising a beautiful College in Williamsburgh, in which is a Foundation for about eight Scholars, a President, two Masters, and Professors in the several Sciences. Here the Gentlemen of Virginia send their Children; and, as far as I could learn by Enquiry, they are near in the same Order, and under the same Regulation and Discipline, as in our Universities at Home. The present Masters came from Oxford. Two of them I find were my contempories. I rejoice in seeing such a Place in America.

In 1740 Governor William Gooch left Williamsburg to lead in his capacity as commander in chief of the colony Virginia's troops against the Spanish at Cartagena in South America. As senior member of the Council, Blair was automatically entitled to be acting governor in Gooch's absence, and he welcomed it. The old man agreed to serve for the same salary that Gooch received as Virginia's commander. When Gooch returned from Cartagena, Blair was glad to retire from the colony's "Company and business" to the lesser demands of college and church.

The doughty Scot was eighty-eight when his hernia became gangrenous and began poisoning his bloodstream. That was in April of 1743—fifty years after he had journeyed from London to Jamestown with the college charter from the king and queen. He probably lived out his last days in his large bedroom on the second floor of the President's House, his body still fighting for survival.

To the east, James Blair may have gazed through the spring's budding trees down Duke of Gloucester Street. Below, in the college yard, his tired eyes might have made out young men walking to and from classes or to chapel. Among them he might have seen clergy-to-be, aspiring planters, and tomorrow's statesmen—men who in thirty years would raise the cry of liberty. There were Carters, Harrisons, Burwells, Maurys, and Randolphs. Already the college had trained such independent thinkers as Richard Bland and Peyton Randolph. Among its students were many of the Revolution's leaders in the making.

When Dr. George Gilmer, Blair's Scottish physician, stood over him and tried to ease his pain, Gilmer marveled that the old man had fought off death for so long—ten days after the physician thought the end was at hand. At last, on April 18, 1743, with his nephew Johnny Blair at his side, James Blair breathed his last. He had remembered the college he loved in his will, devising his substantial library to it and "500 pounds for a Scholarship, for breeding a Young Divine, successively, for all time to come." He also endowed the college with his fighting, durable spirit.

Five days before Blair died, a child was born in upland Virginia who was to personify the enlightenment that James Blair helped bring to the colonies. He was Thomas Jefferson, and would become the most famous of all of the college's gifts to the world. By the time James Blair died in 1743, William and Mary was training many such men for a new society, freer and more democratic than any the world had known.

# 2

## *A Nest of Preachers*

BY the time James Blair died in 1743 he had set the tone for William and Mary. It was a school administered by Anglican clergymen, and it had the worldly, aristocratic quality that had marked that church since the days of Henry VIII. Though secular students out-numbered its few clerical candidates, it kept its theological tone for many years after Blair's death. Indeed, it continued until 1814 to choose clerics as presidents, despite Jefferson's efforts in 1779 to secularize the college.

True to Blair's hopes, the Board of Visitors chose his favorite faculty member, the Reverend William Dawson, professor of moral philosophy since 1729, as his successor. Dawson was also the popular choice, a man of quiet strength and easy manner. His wife at this time was Mary Stith, the Virginia-born sister of his onetime colleague, the Reverend William Stith, who was to follow Dawson as president.

Compared to Blair's, Dawson's rise to the presidency was easy. After he and his wife moved into the President's House in 1743, it probably looked much as it had when the wealthy James Blair furnished it in the "best taste of the times." For the first time, young children—the family of the William Dawsons—were living in the house. Dawson was thirty-eight when he took office, and obtained two more of the posts that "the Old Combustible" Blair had enjoyed. They were as commissary of the Bishop of London in Virginia and as member of the Governor's Council. However, President Dawson was already serving as rector of the smaller James City Parish Church at Jamestown, to which he had been chosen in 1741, and thus did not follow Blair as rector of Bruton Parish Church. Furthermore, his brother Thomas had been preaching at Bruton for some months before James Blair's death, to the satisfaction of that congregation. Thus Thomas rather than William Dawson became Bruton's rector.

Dawson had obtained his M.A. in 1728 from Queen's College, Oxford, also the alma mater of Governor Gooch and Edmund Gibson, Bishop of London. He had been ordained in 1729 by Dr. John Potter, then Bishop of Oxford and later Archbishop of Canterbury. It was the college's chancellor, William Wake, Archbishop of Canterbury, who had suggested Dawson as professor of philosophy. Dawson thus became the first of a succession of Queen's College scholars who were to impose Oxonian qualities on the college in Virginia.

Another official who befriended William Dawson was Thomas Gooch, Bishop of Norwich in England and brother of Virginia's Governor William Gooch. Governor Gooch sought an honorary doctorate of divinity for Dawson, to be bestowed in Dawson's absence in Virginia. He wrote his bishop brother in England on May 14, 1743:

> Having recommended a Gent*m* from hence to my Lord of London to succeed him [James Blåir] as Comissary, one already chosen by the Visitors [as] President of Wm. & Mary College, I have to request of Your Lordship that if Bishop of London is pleased to appoint him, and it is not worth anybody's while to come hither for £100 a year, for all his other Preferments are disposed of, that Your Lordship would, as my desire, contrive the means to gett him a Doctor's Diploma, which would be of advantage to him in the Exercise of Ecclesiastical authority . . . The Gentleman's name is Wm. Dawson M.A., was nine years at Queen's in Oxford, and as he was ordained Deacon and Priest by his present Grace, [Archbishop Potter of Canterbury] perhaps may be remembered by him. I have a value for Mr. Dawson and hope your Lordship will interest yourself in it with His Grace.

Dawson's degree, his "habit" without sleeves, and his doctoral hood finally arrived from England in August 1747. He wrote friends at Queen's College that the gown was "too warm for this Season" but that he had worn the hood on August 15, "being the Day of our Transfer, wch happened in 1729, the Year of my Arrivall . . ." It was celebrated in chapel with a sermon and sacrament, with "handsome Entertainment" in the Great Hall, a Latin oration by a student, and a faculty party afterward in the "Common Room" where healths were drunk.

Kindly, conciliatory William Dawson never became the "great man" in Williamsburg's governmental hierarchy that Blair had been, but he apparently enjoyed the affection of his fellow teachers and ministers to a greater extent that the Scotsman had. Unlike Blair, Dawson treated them as his equals rather than his inferiors. For nine years he and his family offered the hospitality of the President's House to assemblymen, Visitors, faculty, students, and townspeople.

Especially intimate with the Dawsons were Governor and Lady Gooch, who frequently sought his spiritual counsel and enjoyed the Dawsons' friendship. Once Dawson wrote Gooch in England to ask that Lady Gooch shop for "a compleat Suit fm Head to Foot" for his young daughter, Mary, in order that she might "make a more splendid appearance at the next Birth-Night," referring to the birthday ball held at the Governor's Palace to honor King George II.

William Dawson's literary gifts were evident in his amusing *Poems on Several Occasions By a Gentleman of Virginia,* which William Parks printed at his *Virginia Gazette* press in Williamsburg in 1736. From 1748 to 1749 he suffered from a "very long, dangerous, and expensive Sickness" in the President's House, which caused him to miss some meetings of the Governor's Council. It was probably smallpox, which was then epidemic in Williamsburg.

William Dawson was concerned that Virginia's black slaves should be educated, and he urged the establishment of a school in Williamsburg to teach them reading, writing, and Christian beliefs. He was dismayed to find a shipment of religious tracts for such use in a loft over the President's House kitchen that James Blair had received earlier from London. As Governor Gooch wrote his bishop brother in England, the tracts were "spoilt by the Catts and Rats that were sent him [Blair] by the Bp of London or the Society [for the Propagation of the Gospel] to be dispersed, which he never reported to anyone."

Dawson's wife, Mary Stith, died during his presidency. He later married the well-connected Mrs. Elizabeth Churchill Bassett, widow of wealthy William Bassett, Jr., of Eltham in New Kent. Mr. Bassett had been a member of the House of Burgesses from New Kent County. The wedding on July 10, 1752, would have taken place at the bride's home, followed by a few days of festivities before the couple returned to the President's House. Dawson was stricken by fever and died on July 20, 1752, ten days after his marriage. Governor Robert Dinwiddie wrote to the Bishop of London on July 21, 1752:

> I am very sorry of the Occasion to acquaint You that last Night,

> the Revd Wm Dawson, Yr Lordship's Commissary, & President of Wm and Mary Coledge, in this Colony, died last Night of a violent Fever . . . in low Circumstances, he has left two Children, & a little before his Death, he sent for his Sister, & four Children, which are now here, & had no other Dependence, than the Favour of the late Comissary for their Subsistence, this large Family now must be taken Care of, by Mr. Thomas Dawson.

As the Governor had reported, William Dawson's death created serious problems. Before his death Dawson had brought his brother Thomas to Virginia. Thomas had been ordained in England after studying at William and Mary, and was now master of the Indian school. A second brother, Musgrave, had been educated at Oxford, ordained, and had also come to the colony to take over a Virginia parish. Shortly before his death William had sent to England for his widowed sister and her four children. William Dawson's widow had money of her own, but the future of his son and daughter by his first wife and that of his sister's family was in question.

Writing the Bishop of London after William Dawson's death to urge him to appoint Dawson's brother Thomas as commissary, Governor Dinwiddie and John Blair painted a calamitous picture of the future facing Thomas Dawson, then master of the Indian school. Thomas "will be much straitned in Supporting of them [the Dawson family]," wrote Dinwiddie to the Bishop of London, "unless he has Yr Lordship's Favr in appointing him Commissary."

John Blair made a similar plea. ". . . amidst these Calamitys he [William Dawson] has left behind him a worthy Brother;" he assured the Bishop, "now Senior Master of this College," whom John Blair hoped the Visitors would appoint president. He too urged the Bishop to make Thomas Dawson his commissary.

An advertisement in *The Virginia Gazette* of October 6, 1752, indicates that William Dawson's house had been well-furnished:

> *To be SOLD,*
>
> The personal Estate of Dr. *William Dawson,* deceas'd, consisting of a choice Collection of Books, Plate, Houshold Furniture, a Coach and Horses, &c. Six Months Credit will be allowed, the Purchasers giving Bond and Security, as usual. The Sale will begin on *Tuesday,* the 17th of this Instant, *October,* at *Williamsburg,* and continue until all are sold.
>
> *N.B.* Any Persons, that have any Books belonging to the deceased, are desired to return them.

William and Mary College Archives

*From the campus entrance, the hall of the President's House looks through to Richmond Road rear door. Portraits are of King William III and Queen Mary II.*

Photographs of Blair and Madison from the Virginia Historical Society. Photographs of Smith and Empie by Thomas L. Williams.

*Four early presidents were James Blair, upper left; James Madison, upper right; Adam Empie, bottom left; and John Augustine Smith, bottom right.*

Because all the estate was not sold, a second sale was advertised in *The Virginia Gazette* of December 8, 1752:

> To be SOLD
>
> At Mr. *Wetherburn's*, on *Tuesday* the 12th of this Instant, Three Negroe Slaves. And at the College, on *Wednesday*, the 13th, sundry Houshold Goods, and a choice Collection of Books. Six Months Credit will be allowed, the Purchasers giving Bond and Security.
>
> *N.B.* The Books may be seen, and will be disposed of at a very low Price, at any Time.
>
> Also, to be let, a Negroe House-Wench.
>
> *Thomas Dawson*

The only Dawson household items for which a detailed description has survived were framed engravings William had ordered in 1750 from Benjamin Dod, a print dealer in London. Dod wrote him on March 23, 1751, inquiring as to the "Number wanted [and] whether to furnish one Room or more." He also asked "whether History Portraits Landscapes &c would be more agreeable . . ." He was sending William Dawson "the Battles of Alexander" which he called "the finest Impressions I ever saw, nor do I believe there are 3 such Setts in England."

To the dismay of Thomas Dawson's supporters Governor Dinwiddie and John Blair, the Board of Visitors was divided over the choice of a president to succeed William. By a close vote, they declined his brother Thomas and chose the Reverend William Stith, a Virginian who had attended grammar school at the college, had gone to Queen's College from 1724 to 1730, and been ordained in London. He was master of the college grammar school from 1731 to 1737, resigning to become rector of Henrico Parish. In December 1751 he resigned that position to accept a call to St. Anne's Parish in Albemarle, but when he learned of President Dawson's death he immediately applied for the college presidency. Stith was the brother-in-law of Dawson, for Dawson's first wife had been Stith's sister, Mary.

Though Stith, then forty-five, was sober and conscientious, he had little warmth for friendship. As John Blair wrote the Bishop of London when recommending Thomas Dawson as commissary, "he [Stith] has not that sweet engaging Temper that Mr Dawson has; being, I think, of a too overbearing, Satirical & Domineering Temper (too incident to school-masters); of which I have known many Instances in his Conduct then & Since."

The Stiths probably moved to the President's House in October 1752 from the glebe house of Henrico Parish, where Stith had been serving as rector, fifty miles from Williamsburg at Varina. Stith and his wife Judith, daughter of Thomas and Judith Fleming Randolph of Tuckahoe (and thus her husband's first cousin), whom he had married in 1738, had three daughters. The eldest, also named Judith, was just entering her teens. Her sisters were Mary and Elizabeth. Elizabeth was to marry William Pasteur of Williamsburg, a prominent physician of the town.

Stith's critics on the Board of Visitors, most of them adherents of Thomas Dawson, were unreconciled after his election, but they doubtlessly felt he had some claim to the presidency. He had written the dry but accurate *History of the First Discovery and Settlement of Virginia,* which William Parks had published in 1747 at his *Virginia Gazette* press in Williamsburg. His wife was of the Randolph clan, active at the college since its beginning. In addition, his mother, Mary Randolph Stith, had been the daughter of the remarkable William and Mary Isham Randolph of Turkey Island in Henrico County, whose descendants were numerous and influential in pre-Revolutionary Virginia.

In these years William and Mary was very much a family school. To begin with, the interlocked tobacco clans along the James, the York, and the Rappahannock had combined through their power on the Council and in the House of Burgesses to create the college in 1693. Thereafter, the college educated many of their sons, though some continued to go to England or Scotland for their grammar school and higher education. James Blair's marriage to Sarah Harrison of this planter society had helped assure for the college the support of the planters. Its student body and Visitors were made up year after year of Blands, Braxtons, Burwells, Carters, Carys, Harrisons, Lees, Nelsons, Pages, Randolphs, Tazewells, and Wormeleys.

A little less unanimous patronage of the college came from Northern Neck and Piedmont families, whose sons often learned Latin and Greek from tutors or at grammar schools in England. A few uplanders, like James Madison of Orange and William Henry Lee of Westmoreland, went to the Presbyterian college at Princeton after it was chartered in 1746.

Along with the Blairs, the Randolphs of Henrico County and Williamsburg were one of the most instrumental families in creating the college. The first Virginian to be buried in the crypt beneath the college chapel was Sir John Randolph in 1737. James Blair had persuaded Sir John to join him in England in 1728 to arrange the college's legal transfer from its trustees to its president, masters, and professors. John Randolph returned to Virginia with the document the next year, on the same ship with the Reverend William Dawson, who had come from Oxford to teach at the college. Sir John's sons Peyton, John (who was called "the Tory" for his loyalism), and his grandson Edmund would follow him as students at the college.

The Randolphs produced many lawyers, clerics, and freethinkers, along with a steady stream of planters. The mothers of Thomas Jefferson and John Marshall were also Randolphs.

William Stith had won favor with some of the General Assembly in March 1752 with a sermon to them on "The Sinfulness and Pernicious Nature of Gaming," the Assembly then meeting in the Wren Building. As tobacco money spread, it had stimulated horse racing, cockfighting, and gambling, which were conspicuous in Williamsburg by mid-century.

As soon as he moved into the President's House, Stith acted to control student betting. No scholar "of wt [what] Age, Rank, or Quality, soever," he declared, could keep a racehorse in town or engage "in backing, or abetting" those who did. None could "be anyway concern'd in keeping or fighting" cocks, and none could bring to college "any Cards, or Dice, or other Implement of Gaming." Any miscreant convicted "of ye Crime of Gaming" would be punished.

Unlike Blair and William Dawson, Stith was not named Commissary to the Bishop of London, as he had hoped to be. He had aroused the ire of Governor Dinwiddie by opposing Dinwiddie's proposed pistole fee—a tax on land grants—and the governor had opposed his appointment. The Bishop instead named Thomas Dawson as commissary. Stith was then chosen by fellow Virginians as chaplain to the House of Burgesses.

Like Blair and William Dawson, William Stith was often visited in the President's House by councilors and burgesses. This was especially true after the Capitol burned in 1747 and until the completion of its replacement in 1753. In those years the General Assembly met in the Great Hall of the Main Building, as had the first Williamsburg assemblies from 1700 to 1704. There were no meetings of the Assembly in Stith's brief presidency.

In the study of the President's House Stith wrote letters, lectures, and sermons for chapel services, which continued to be held on weekdays at 7:00 each morning and 5:00 each afternoon.

Stith's presidency lasted three years. He died suddenly at forty-eight on September 19, 1755, probably at his wife's family's house, Tuckahoe plantation, in Goochland County. Notice of his death did not appear in Williamsburg's newspaper, *The Virginia Gazette,* until fourteen days later, on October 3, suggesting that he had been away from Williamsburg when he died. "Friday Se'nnight died the Rev. *William Stith,* A.M. and President of *William & Mary* College, a Gentleman of great Learning and Abilities, universally beloved by his Friends and Acquaintances. and whose Death is greatly lamented."

Unlike James Blair or William Dawson, President Stith lived so briefly in the President's House that he left little record. However, in a letter to the Bishop of London on August 13, 1755, introducing a William and Mary student for ordination, the president intimated that the college was not peaceful. He promised to write the bishop "a full Account" of the "real Estate of Affairs" but did not live to do so. Stith's successor, Thomas Dawson, was to inherit them in his presidency from 1755 to 1760. In the struggles between faculty and Visitors and the oncoming contest between England and the colonies, Dawson was an early victim. Among the college's presidents, none was to have a sadder fate than he.

# 3

# *When Williamsburg Was Young*

SMALL as it was, the college drew a remarkable group of students in its early years. It was a time to challenge young men. Virginia had prospered since the 1690s, and tobacco wealth had created the outlines of a planter class along the James and York. By the mid-eighteenth century the tide of settlers had rolled inland and upland, beyond the fall line, through Piedmont and northern Virginia. Instead of the twenty-two counties that made up Virginia when the college began, it had thirty-seven by 1743, the year James Blair died and William Dawson took over the President's House.

The college fared better after Lieutenant Governor Alexander Spotswood—Blair's last major obstruction—left the Governor's Palace in 1722, to be succeeded by Lieutenant Governor Hugh Drysdale. After Blair's other major opponent, ex-Governor Francis Nicholson, died in England in 1728, the college was able to move more confidently. Now old, Blair was never to be seriously challenged after Nicholson's death. Fathers who might earlier have sent sons to England to be educated were more apt to enroll them in the college by the 1730s. With powerful trustees and Visitors like "King" Carter, William Byrd II, and the Randolph brothers, William, Jr., and Sir John, the college seemed bound to succeed.

Besides, in the age of reason learning was becoming more essential to planters' sons. Once it had been primarily for clergymen, schoolmasters, and lawyers. Now, with European scholars creating a new world of science, a gentleman could not afford to be ignorant. Writers like John Locke, Adam Smith, Lord Coke, and Montesquieu found receptive minds in America. Locke's theory of the natural rights of man became the gospel of thoughtful colonists.

Only three colonies—Massachusetts, Virginia, and Maryland—had founded colleges in the seventeenth century, but by the year 1755 four others—Connecticut, Pennsylvania, New Jersey, and New York—had joined them. There were also private academies and free schools in most of the colonies. Graduates of such academies often went on to college or studied law with an attorney already in practice.

By mid-century William and Mary was drawing students from a wider orbit, and some were fine scholars. When the Reverend Hugh Jones had come from Oxford to teach math in 1716, the college was only a grammar and Indian school. Jones wrote that some were "sent to England" for education, adding that "Virginians being naturally of good parts . . . neither require nor admire as much learning as we do in Britain." He said students had "good natural notions, and will soon learn arts and sciences; but are generally diverted by business or inclination from profound study, and prying into the depths of things . . ." He mentioned their "quick apprehension" and "fluency of tongue." Jones found the "habits, life, customs, computations, etc. of the Virginians" were "much the same as about London, which they esteem their home . . ."

A twelve-year-old entering the grammar school at Williamsburg would arrive on campus at the beginning of the term, to be received by the president and masters, and assigned lodgings, usually in dormitory rooms on the third floor of the Main Building. The masters' rooms were on the second floor, assuring a modicum of faculty supervision. On the first floor were the Great Hall, grammar school, and other classrooms. The chapel was added in 1732. Besides two-room apartments for professors and masters, the second floor housed the convocation or Blue Room for faculty and Visitors' meetings, the library and "philosophic [scientific] apparatus," a common room for the use of the faculty, and later, in the nineteenth century, rooms of the Philomatheon and Phoenix literary societies.

Dormitory rooms were provided with chamber pots, for the building had no plumbing. A privy at the rear of the Main Building was known to collegians at one time as "Egypt" or "Purgatory," the latter in contrast to the "Paradise" of the Main Building.

The Great Hall in the Main Building, where the Virginia Assembly had met from 1700 to 1704 and from 1747 to 1752, was the social hub of the college. It was there that students and faculty dined. As in the colleges at Oxford and Cambridge, the room was an all-purpose "commons," and at William and Mary it also served as a chapel until 1732. Students occasionally danced and staged plays in the Great Hall. At meals, professors, masters, and older students sat at its "high table," from which food was blessed and discipline imposed. Younger students sat at lower tables, in descending order of age and rank.

The college grammar school was roughly analogous to the high school of today, though it offered a far more thorough classical education, being largely restricted to teaching Greek, Latin, and mathematics. Penmanship was also taught, but English grammar in the early years was presumed to be absorbed through study of classical languages, the fundamentals having been learned before entering grammar school.

Grammar scholars could be taught only from textbooks approved by the president. No master could teach any author "as insinuates any thing against Religion and good Morals," according to the 1727 and 1758 statutes of the college. In language study, the statutes decreed that "nothing contributes so much . . . as dayly Diologues, and familiar Speaking together in the languages they are learning." The teacher was to impart "the Colloquies of Corderius and Erasmus."

In the four years required to complete grammar school the grammar master taught the older boys and the usher, or assistant, taught the younger. The usher also taught new boys to write and to repeat the Anglican catechism in "the vulgar Tongue," or English; the older boys learned to say it in Latin. On Saturday and the day preceding a holy day, a sacred lesson was prescribed.

As in Great Britain, school terms were based on the Christian year. The first term began on the Monday after Epiphany, which was January 6; the second on the Monday after the first Sunday after Easter; and the third on the Monday after Trinity Sunday, with substantial holidays between each term. The longest holiday came at Christmas and lasted about three weeks. The summer recess ran from July 25 through October 18.

On the college level William and Mary followed the curriculum of Oxford and Cambridge. The Statutes of 1727 and 1758 both noted that progress had been made since "Aristotle's Logick and Politics reigned alone in the Schools," and the professors in the philosophy school could teach what systems they thought fit. William and Mary's graduates were versed in John Locke, Montesquieu, and Rousseau. Soon they would also reflect the teachings of Adam Smith and the Scottish "common sense" philosophers.

According to the Statutes of 1758, the college required four years for its bachelor of arts degree and seven for its master's, according to the "Form and Institution of the Two famous Universities [Oxford and Cambridge] in England." When the Reverend George Whitefield of England visited the college in 1739, he noted that most of the professors were Oxford alumni like him, and that it was "near in the same Order, and under the same Regulation and Discipline, as our Universities at Home."

Many colonial Virginians continued to go to Britain for grammar school, and to obtain their degrees and study medicine and law, attending the English and Scottish universities, and furthering their knowledge of law at the Inns of Court in London. Among Virginia youths attending such institutions—some of whom were first at William and Mary—were Amblers, Armisteads, Blands, Beverleys, Blairs, Baylors, Brookes, Balls, Byrds, Burwells, Carters, Corbins, Carys, Fauntleroys, Fitzhughs, Gilmers, Griffins, Grymes, Lees, Meades, McClurgs, Nelsons, Pages, Randolphs, Robinsons, Skipwiths, Spotswoods, Scotts, Tayloes, Tuckers, Washingtons, Wormeleys, Warners, and Yateses.

What seems to have been the first chair of natural philosophy in the British colonies was established at William and Mary in 1711. It was held by the Reverend Tanaquil LeFevre, who was licensed to Virginia on June 19, 1709, but did not appear till later because of his entanglement with an "idle hussy," according to Governor Spotswood. LeFevre and his "hussy" got to Virginia before April 17, 1711, when he called on William Byrd II at Westover. Byrd found him "a French gentleman of great learning." At a meeting of the Board of Visitors on April 25, 1711, LeFevre was named "professor of philosophy and mathematics with a salary of £80 a year," but he was turned out nine months later for "Excessive conviviality" and because of the "hussy."

In 1729 there were two divinity professors to assist postulants with Biblical analyses, Anglican theology, and the study of the Bible in the "Oriental languages." One divinity professor taught Hebrew and was required to "critically expound the literal Sense of the Holy Scripture." The other was to "explain the common Places of Divinity, and the Controversies with Hereticks" and to debate these with students. Disputation—the effort to reach truth through philosophic debate—was highly valued.

To the Church of England's regret, comparatively few students enrolled in theology, a fact which also must have disappointed James Blair and the bishops who befriended the college. Except for William Stith, Thomas Dawson, and James Madison—all of whom studied theology at the college and later became president—only about thirty-five graduates went to England for ordination and returned to Virginia parishes from 1731 to 1775.

One of these was theology graduate Reverend James Maury, a Virginian of Huguenot ancestry who received the King's Bounty to go to London in 1742 to be ordained by his bishop, as the Church of England required. Maury served a long ministry in Louisa County and is remembered as the grammar school teacher of Jefferson, Jefferson's cousin, Dabney Carr, and of the Reverend James Madison, who would become the college's eighth president. Though Anglican officials praised the caliber of Williamsburg-trained clerics, the Visitors came to feel by 1776 that the divinity school did not justify its cost. It was abolished in 1779.

Grammar students at William and Mary in its early years were waked at sunup and required to go to bed not long after sundown. They were expected to attend chapel, held at 6:00 A.M. in summer, 7:00 A.M. in the winter, and again at 5:00 in the afternoon. After attending classes and completing their required reading, they had time to fish, hunt, skate in season, or to ride the horses that some had brought to college. Games like quoits were probably played in the college yard and in the clearing behind the Main Building. In winter students skated on ice in local ponds. Like other colleges prior to the Civil War, William and Mary had no organized or inter-collegiate athletics.

Emulating planters who came to town at Public Times, older collegians drank in local taverns and bet on races at the quarterpath track east of town. It was such betting that had led President William Stith to ban any form of gambling in 1752. But high living continued.

A few young scholars were even accompanied to college by a black manservant from the family plantation. The practice recurred now and then until the twentieth century.

Faculty patience was often exhausted trying to control indulgent young men. Small as it was, eighteenth-century Williamsburg had nearly two dozen inns, taverns, and ordinaries. The tippling, gaming, and wenching which went on among their male patrons were recorded by William Byrd II, who noted his own trangressions in his diary. At a faculty meeting on August 2, 1766, the president and masters decreed "that the Keeper[s] of the Publick Houses in Town be desir'd not to entertain any of the Students hereafter; if they do, the President & Master will apply the proper Authority to take away their Licence for the same."

Tippling attracted even beardless boys in the lower grades. In 1766 the faculty ordered "that the Boys in the Grammar School who were guilty of the same offense [drinking] be punished at the President's Discretion." Minutes of William Yates's presidency for 1761–1764 record frequent punishment for drunkenness or for brawling. Three students were "rusticated," or sent home for a month by Yates in 1763 for their "injurious Behaviour . . . to a family in Town." In Jefferson's letter to John Page of October 7, 1763, three others, Lewis Burwell, Warner Lewis, and William Thompson, "fled to escape flagellation." Burwell and Lewis came back to face the music, but Thompson never did. In December 1763 the faculty banished him from the college in absentia:

> Whereas William Thompson, lately a Student of This College, some time since in Company with other[s] was concern'd in an act of no small Violence and Outrage in this Town, and for this apprehensive of the Punishment he so justly deserv'd desert'd the College, and his Duty therein, and ever since refuses to return and submit himself to the Discipline the President & Masters thought proper to direct; We, in order to discourage and prevent as much as lies in our Power such very bad Behaviour in others for the Future, do in this publick Manner expel the said Thompson from our Society, and strictly forbid all our Young Gentlemen from entertaining, or associating with, him, under Pain of a most severe animadversion & Punishment.

As a student at William and Mary, the teenaged Jefferson joined in revelries with his peers, but he left no hint of any excess. From his room in the Market Square Tavern, where he stayed while reading law under George Wythe, he occasionally strode up Palace Green to enjoy an evening with Governor Fauquier in the Governor's Palace or with the college students in taverns on Duke of Gloucester Street. Enamored with the beauteous Rebecca Burwell of Gloucester, who he privately called "Belinda," he wrote his former fellow student John Page on October 7, 1763 in a low state of mind from Williamsburg. "Last night, as merry as agreeable company and dancing with Belinda in the Apollo [room of Raleigh Tavern] could make me, I never could have thought the succeeding sun would have seen me so wretched as I now am!" Ardent as it was at that moment, Jefferson's romance with

"Belinda" was born and died in his years as a law student in Williamsburg, which in his 1764 letters to John Page he called "Devilsburg."

In an age which exalted its seniors and expected them to set a good example, the president of the college mixed with students outside of class as well as within. This occurred at "commons" in the Great Hall, at annual oral examinations, graduation exercises, and at social events.

In the case of exceptional students like Thomas Jefferson and John Page, even Governor Fauquier is recorded as dispensing hospitality at the Governor's Palace. Jefferson was also an occasional guest of his Randolph cousins, Peyton, on Nicholson Street and John, on the other side of town. He was often at the home of his friend and teacher, George Wythe, who lived on Palace Green. Williamsburgers were known for their hospitality to students.

Much later when William Taylor Barry, who was to be a cabinet member under President Andrew Jackson, came to college he was struck by the town's hospitality as others had been before. "They still continue to be distinguished for their hospitality and attention to strangers. This I believe proceeds in some manner from a kind of family pride, of which the citizens of this place, particularly the old people, are pretty full."

Life at College Corner in the eighteenth century could also be thoughtful as well as social. Students joined philosophical societies to debate, and literary societies to read their essays and poetry. In 1750 several young men banded together to form the F. H. C. Society, presumably standing for Fraternitas, Hilaritas, Cognitoque (Friendship, Good Living, and Knowledge). It was the first secret society on an American campus and the forerunner of fraternities. Its aim was "that youth may perfect the cultivation of virtue and invigorate learning in order to become a great ornament and support of affairs both general and particular . . . That due rewards may not be withheld from those who have borne themselves with becoming modesty and sobriety, who have shown themselves well mannered, God fearing, and cultured friends."

Alas, the F. H. C. soon slid from this high resolve to become a drinking club. However, the Phi Beta Kappa society, begun by students twenty-six years later in the Raleigh Tavern, was more enduring. It was created in 1776 for "that freedom of inquiry . . . which ever dispells the clouds of falsehood." Although it was to die out in Williamsburg in 1781, when the college closed during the Revolution, it was renewed in 1779 and carried north by Elisha Parmelee, a student from Connecticut, and planted at Harvard and Yale. In the nineteenth century it spread through many institutions, becoming the preeminent academic society in the nation. It was revived at its place of birth in 1849, William Short, the society's 1779 president, having survived to sign the order for its renewal.

Williamsburg and its college remained small, but they planted ideas which grew big. Wrote historian Vernon Louis Parrington in his intellectual history, *The Romantic Revolution in America,*

> Between the older colonial America and later industrial America stand the ideals of the Old Dominion, more humane and generous than either, disseminating the principles of French romantic philosophy, and instilling into the provincial American mind, static and stagnant in the grip of English colonialism, the ideal of democratic equalitarianism and the hope of humane progress. The nineteenth century first entered America by way of the James River.

Much of the credit for that change belonged to the College of William and Mary.

# 4

# *The Damnation of Thomas Dawson*

WHEN William Stith died in 1755, after three years as president, Thomas Dawson was an easy choice to succeed him. Like his brother, William, he had been born at Aspatria in Cumberland Shire, England, and had completed classical school and possibly some studies at Oxford before he reached William and Mary. He planned to preach and teach, as his older brother had before him.

Thomas had arrived in Williamsburg in 1735 when he was about twenty years old. His brother William was a professor during this time and was one of Thomas's teachers. After serving as usher of the grammar school Thomas was named in June 1738 as master of the Indian school. In these years he had studied divinity, and in 1740-1741 he briefly interrupted his Indian school service to return to England for ordination to the priesthood, traveling with a grant of £20 from "the King's Bounty."

When James Blair died in 1743, Thomas Dawson was elected by the Bruton Parish vestry as rector. Vestry minutes of May 6, 1743, recorded that he had "for some time officiated for Mr. Commissary, in which he hath acquitted himself to the Universal good liking of this Parish." He also produced a "letter from the Honble. the Governour, strongly recommending him to the Choice of the Vestry . . ."

As a popular minister and professor, Thomas was quickly nominated upon his brother William's death in 1752 to be president of William and

Mary. Though he lost by a few votes to William Stith, he was appointed by the Bishop of London as his commissary. Thus for a while young Thomas was doing well.

On his brother's death Thomas assumed heavy family responsibilities, not only helping to care for his brother's two young children but also helping to support his widowed sister and her four young ones. He had earlier declined offers from ex-governor Sir William Gooch to provide a parish for him in England, writing to Gooch in June 1751 that, though he might "frequently repent" not coming to England, he was "now for ever destined for Virginia." That decision was reinforced on September 12, 1751, when Thomas Dawson married Priscilla Bassett, the daughter of William and Elizabeth Churchill Bassett of Eltham plantation in New Kent. Gooch died in 1751.

In 1752 Dawson's older brother, William, a widower, married his brother's mother-in-law, Mrs. Elizabeth Churchill Bassett. When William died shortly thereafter in 1752 without a will, Thomas had the responsibility of settling his estate to the best advantage of William's widow and children.

For a time after William's death, Thomas Dawson seemed crushed. He had depended on his older brother for strength. He wrote Lady Gooch in England that he was "confined at Home by Grief, by the Distresses of the Family, & by Funeral Service." Though Governor Dinwiddie and Councilor John Blair both assured him of their help in succeeding to William's offices and perquisites, he felt "cool and indifferent at first . . . as to all these Places."

He lost the college presidency by a few votes at that time, but he was appointed by the Bishop of London as commissary, the best paid clerical office in Virginia. There was "not one Clergyman in this Colony better Qualified" to be Commissary, wrote Governor Dinwiddie. When Dinwiddie offered to get him appointed to the Governor's Council, Thomas declined, asserting that he had enough responsibility to keep him busy.

Even so, the Governor insisted that "it was absolutely necessary he should be one of that Body, on many Accts.," and Thomas accordingly took his seat in that august body on May 1, 1753. He performed his duties with zeal during a period of many tensions.

The presidency of the college finally came to Thomas Dawson in 1755 after William Stith's death in September of that year. Dawson took his oath of office at a faculty meeting on November 1, 1755. As master of the Indian school, he and his wife had been living in the Brafferton building, since the little dormitory space and the classroom needed by the handful of Indian students (only eight in 1754–1755) left most of the three-story house for the use of the master.

After Thomas's election as president of William and Mary in November 1755, the Dawsons simply moved across the college yard from the Brafferton to the President's House.

Dawson's presidency began well enough. Three of his four masters and professors, the Reverend Thomas Robinson, the Reverend William Preston, and the Reverend Richard Graham, were alumni of Queen's College. The fourth, the Reverend Emmanuel Jones, Jr., was a Virginian, having succeeded Thomas as master of the Indian school in 1755. Jones's father, Emmanuel Jones, Sr., was a graduate of Oriel College at Oxford and had served as rector of Petsworth Parish in Gloucester from 1700 until his death in 1739. He had also been a Visitor of the college from 1723 until his death.

The newly-elected President Dawson soon learned that Benjamin Franklin, already famous for his writings and experiments, was coming from Philadelphia to Williamsburg in the spring of 1756 to confer with William Hunter. Hunter had succeeded William Parks as editor of *The Virginia Gazette* and also as owner of what was then Virginia's only printing press. Franklin and Hunter had been named by the Crown as joint "Deputy Postmasters and Managers of all His Majesty's Provinces and Dominions on the Continent of North America." At Dawson's behest, William and Mary's faculty voted to give the visiting Pennsylvanian its first known honorary degree, the master of arts.

No doubt Franklin was entertained at the President's House, for he spent almost a month in Virginia, working with William Hunter on details of postal routes. The M.A. "diploma" signed by Dawson and others, was dated April 2, 1756, but evidently it was conferred eighteen days later, if an account of the award in *The Pennsylvania Gazette* was accurate. Franklin found Virginia "a pleasant Country, now in full Spring; the People extreamly obliging and polite." As president of the College and Academy of Pennsylvania (later the University of Pennsylvania), he was understandably interested in Virginia's college.

While in Williamsburg Franklin heard an anecdote about William and Mary's founding which he recorded for posterity. As he put it, when James Blair was visiting London in 1691 he proposed a college for the sake of Virginians' souls. One crusty courtier had exploded. "Damn their souls! Let them make tobacco!"

Besides his wife and three children, Billy, Rebecca, and Thomas, Thomas Dawson admitted as a roomer in the President's House the thirteen-year-old John Page of Gloucester County. Young Page had entered the grammar school, but his father asked President Dawson to give him extra tutelage. Years later, after serving in the Revolution and as governor of Virginia, Page wrote that he was "far better" educated "in Latin than many of the boys much older." He recalled that Thomas Dawson "was proud to introduce his pupil to the particular attention, first of Governor Dinwiddie, an old Scotch gentleman, who was fond of appearing a patron of learning, and secondly to Governor Fauquier, to whose much greater learning and judgement my ever to be beloved Professor, Mr. [William] Small had held me up as worthy of his attention."

In 1756, during Dawson's occupancy, repairs to the President's House were made by architect-contractor Richard Taliaferro. Taliaferro had built a plantation house for himself in James City County called Powhatan and also a townhouse on Palace Green, about 1755, occupied by his daughter Elizabeth and son-in-law George Wythe. The house was subsequently known as the Wythe house. Taliaferro was engaged by the faculty to "repair ye President's House in a proper Manner," and to erect a paling fence around the college yard. Taliaferro repaired the house, but it remained basically as when it was built in 1732-1733.

Thomas Dawson's downfall resulted from contention between the clergy and Virginia Assembly over the so-called Two-Penny Acts. The first act was passed in 1755 by the Assembly to permit the cash payment by parishes of clergy salaries at the rate of two pence a pound rather than in tobacco, the usual currency, which had climbed in value after a bad harvest to the high price of six pence a pound. The clergy felt themselves cheated by the Assembly's action and most of them opposed the measure.

The issue put the faculty of clergymen at odds with the Board of Visitors, many of whom had been members of the Assembly which had passed the acts. The breach widened when the Visitors questioned faculty expulsion of two grammar school boys and an usher—a decision which by college statutes was entirely in the hands of the president and faculty. The Visitors then proceeded to dismiss the grammar master, the Reverend Thomas Robinson, because of alleged "bodily Infirmities" and ordered President Dawson to ask the college's chancellor, Thomas Sherlock, Bishop of London, to send over a layman in his place. The Visitors brashly declared that a clergyman "often proved a Means of the School's being neglected" because of his "frequent Avocations as a Minister." It was clearly a blow at faculty clergymen.

Faculty resistance finally led the Board of Visitors to decree on

November 11, 1757, "That Mr Camm, Mr Graham and Mr Jones be removed on Wednesday the 14th of next Month; and that other Masters be provided in their Room, who will submit the Reasons of their Conduct to the Consideration of this Visitation . . ."

Governor Dinwiddie, siding with the Visitors, had in 1757 written the Bishop of London, Dr. Sherlock, that the Visitors had for "many years been dissatisfied" with the behavior of the Reverend Richard Graham, professor of moral philosophy, and of the Reverend Thomas Robinson, grammar master, charging them with "Intemperance & Irregularity." They "had married and contrary to all rule of seats of learning kept their wives, children & servants in the college which must occasion much confusion and disturbance . . . about a year ago they removed them into the Town and since that time they have lived much at home, and negligently attended their duty in College . . . They have quite ruined this Seminary of Learning . . . & many have already sent their children to Philadelphia for education which is 300 miles from this . . ."

In this case, as in others, the Visitors overstepped their authority as spelled out in the statutes of 1727 and 1758. Such conflict over the respective powers of faculty and Visitors was to continue for many years, impeding college progress.

After his return to London in 1758, ex-Governor Dinwiddie wrote to President Dawson of the very "infirm" state of Bishop Sherlock of London. However, he added that the Bishop and he concluded that President Dawson was at fault because of his mild and inadequate discipline. Dawson had not properly exerted his "Authority over Professors . . . as they have been so refractory & unmannerly to the Visitors . . . by disputing their Authority." In a strong letter, Dinwiddie admonished Dawson that since the college would soon "have all new Professors," he not let his "good nature allow them too much familiarity, but keep them to their duties." However, it was not Dawson's nature to dominate his faculty, and the situation worsened.

Faculty replacements arrived from England, but some were soon in the bad graces of the Visitors. In the spring of 1760 the board accused the Reverend Goronwy Owen, the new Welsh grammar master, and the Reverend Jacob Rowe, professor of moral philosophy, of being "scandalously drunk in the College, and in the public Streets of Williamsburgh and York." They had also been heard to "utter horrid Oaths and Execrations in their common Conversation." The two were dismissed by the Visitors.

To escape conflicts which he was unable to control in these years, Thomas Dawson took to drinking in the privacy of the President's

House. At one embarrassing meeting, the Visitors accused him of "habitual Drunkenness." Dawson admitted drinking, but the new Governor, Francis Fauquier, defended him as being "teazed by a contrariety of opinions" between himself and the clergy "into the loss of his Spirits." Fauquier declared it was no wonder Dawson "should apply for consolation to spirituous Liquors." The president was thereupon pardoned by the Visitors, but his dilemma remained.

Dawson's spirits continued to wither, and he died in the President's House on November 29, 1760, after just five years in office. *The Virginia Gazette* issues for this period are missing, but *The Maryland Gazette* of January 15, 1761, carried this notice, headed "Williamsburg, December 5":

> On Saturday last died the Honourable and Reverend THOMAS DAWSON, one of his Majesty's Honourable Council, Commissary for the Lord-Bishop of London, President of the College of William and Mary, and Minister of the Parish of Bruton; a Man eminently endowed with Moderation, Meakness, Forgiveness, Patience and Long-Suffering, of a most extensive and unlimited Benevolence and Charity: These Virtues rendered him beloved by his Friends in his Life, and regretted in his Death; and if it is possible that these great Qualifications could be carried to an Excess, that may be said to be the fundamental Error of his Life. Yet this amiable Disposition, this noble Life of truly Christian Talents, could not be secure from the Attacks of Enemies. for, it is much feared, he fell a Victim to the repeated Marks of Ingratitude and Malice, which he, unhappy Man! too frequently experienced in his Passage through his State of Probation.

It was a sad end for a conscientious teacher who had devoted twenty-five years to William and Mary, but it was not the last time that a president would be caught between a conflicting board and faculty. Indeed, for several incumbents, the President's House was to prove a heartbreak house. In the case of Thomas Dawson, even his burial place is unknown, though it is believed to be in Bruton Parish Church or churchyard, inasmuch as he had been Bruton's rector. However, it could have been in the cemetery of his wife's family, the Bassetts, at Eltham plantation. No stone has survived at either place, and burial registers for that period of Bruton history are missing.

# 5

# *Living in the President's House*

FROM James Blair's presidency until today the President's House of William and Mary has been important to our nation's story. After 250 years of use, it can look back on the longest career of any college residence in the nation. That includes Harvard, founded in 1636, whose president's house of 1644-1645 has been replaced by five later ones.

The routine of life changed as William and Mary has grown older, but the house has been a center of hospitality since Blair moved into it late in 1733, there to spend his last ten years. Each of the college's twenty-four presidents except Robert Saunders, who served from 1846 to 1848, lived there. Several children have been born in its bedrooms. Several presidents, including James Blair, William and Thomas Dawson, and James Madison have died in the house.

It was usual for the president to have his office in the house from 1733 until the twentieth century. There the president read his mail, wrote lectures, and conferred with teachers and students. Clergymen presidents composed sermons there, writing them in longhand.

Of all the early presidents, James Blair left the most complete record of his life in the house. Although his wife Sarah had died twenty years before he moved in, the Scotsman led a full life there until his death in 1743. As president in his last years of the Virginia Council, and as commissary of the church in Virginia, he had responsibilities that added to his collegiate ones. Governors and members of the Governor's

Council dined at his table, and he entertained visiting Virginia clergymen and evangelists from England like the Reverend George Keith and the Reverend George Whitefield, traveling in the American colonies.

Among Blair's frequent guests was Sir John Randolph of Williamsburg, son of William and Mary Isham Randolph of Turkey Island, who attended the college, had studied law at Gray's Inn in London, and was later knighted for his work promoting conciliation between the Crown and Virginia planters in 1732. Another was Robert Carter of Corotoman, known for his wealth and power as "King" Carter, the most influential planter of his day. One of his most frequent visitors, other than his nephew John Blair, Jr., was William Byrd II of Westover. Byrd's secret diaries, deciphered two centuries after his death, record many visits to Blair in the President's House to drink coffee or chocolate, or to eat "boiled beef," roast turkey, or minced chicken.

Two of Blair's early allies were his influential brothers-in-law, both men of affairs but both dead by the time he moved into the President's House. One was Benjamin Harrison III of Berkeley, who served as the colony's attorney general. The other was Philip Ludwell II of Green Spring, who had wed Hannah Harrison, the sister of Blair's wife, Sarah. Ludwell and Harrison were in the group which Governor Spotswood castigated during his governorship as "the Ludwell faction," opposed to Spotswood's rule.

From its beginning in 1695 the college owned slaves to help maintain its buildings and its farm and to cook and serve in its Great Hall "commons." These worked as needed and assigned under the steward, the matron, the cook, the gardener, and other college employees.

The president's servants usually lived on the President's House premises, in rooms over the kitchen and other outbuildings. Sometimes a nurse for the children stayed on the third floor of the house. Sometimes the president's servants were a married couple, the husband serving as butler and coachman while the wife—and possibly another servant or two—cleaned house, cooked, and cared for the children.

Some such arrangement persisted from Blair's presidency through the nineteenth-century presidency of Colonel Benjamin Ewell, whose black manservant, Malachi Gardner, was his coachman and the college's bell ringer. Through all these years the cook brought dishes for each meal from the outdoor kitchen through the basement of the President's House, where they were sent up by dumbwaiter to the president's dining room. Outside kitchens were usual in Virginia as a means of avoiding house fires.

During the eighty-one years when Williamsburg was Virginia's capital, it became the scene of much entertaining during the Assembly, and the spring and fall meetings of the General Court in the Capitol, called Public Times. In those gala weeks the town of a thousand souls swelled to many more as legislators, litigants, lawyers, and itinerant peddlers, actors, and racetrack followers poured in.

The president of the college and his wife were apt to take part in these seasonal festivities for they were members of Williamsburg society at its highest level. There they mingled with planters, lawyers, physicians, merchants, and colonial officials who made up the ruling element of the colony.

Inventories surviving for many of the Williamsburg households in the colonial period reveal that they were equipped to serve large dinners. Fine china, glass, silver, and linen were among possessions of the town's planters and professional men. Twentieth-century excavations around the President's House confirm the popularity through the years of tea, coffee, and chocolate as social rituals. Countless fragments of fine Chinese and European porcelain and others of Delft, English creamware, and of queens ware have been uncovered.

Some planters had large libraries, and books from England or printed in Williamsburg were often advertised in *The Virginia Gazette*. The prevalence of Bibles and prayer books in Virginia indicated that family prayers were observed. Card tables frequently stood in parlors, for card games like whist and loo were popular, along with chess and backgammon.

Most furniture used by early presidents and their families was English in origin. Incoming presidents brought some to the house with them and ordered more as needed. Furniture and other imported furnishings and clothing were unloaded from British ships at wharves near Williamsburg. Virginia plantation society, to which most early presidents were connected by birth or marriage, continued to follow the customary trade pattern until the Revolution. They bought articles of British make in exchange for the credit received for their tobacco shipped to British agents. Such agents were responsible for obtaining and shipping the orders which Virginians requested.

Because James Blair was a partner in a large Williamsburg mercantile business, regularly trading with Britain, it is probable that his household effects were almost completely British. Later presidents may have purchased a few furnishings from vessels plying the coastal trade from New England, New York, and Pennsylvania. A rather small amount of colonial-made furniture entered Virginia on such vessels, some of them returning to their home port with a supply of Virginia furniture woods—especially walnut—in their cargo.

For lesser furniture, early presidents probably bought some locally-made Williamsburg pieces for the President's House. However, England made it so advantageous for planters to exchange their tobacco for British manufactures that English furniture predominated in Virginia houses. Royal governors encouraged this exchange and reported on it frequently to the London Board of Trade.

British imports discouraged many Virginia artisans. To survive, Williamsburg cabinetmakers supplemented their work with repairing, upholstering, installing cabinetwork in buildings, making coffins, or undertaking. Some gave it up entirely as did one who became the keeper of the Raleigh Tavern. Cabinetmakers in the north fared better, and those in Philadelphia, Boston, and other cities were thought to do finer work.

British scholars coming to the college to teach brought furnishings with them or purchased them from departing teachers. After Professor William Small returned from Williamsburg to London in 1764, he informed a prospective master that the two-room faculty apartments in the Main Building were "by no means elegant" but that he could "buy Furniture there, all except bedding & blankets, which you must carry over—Chairs & Tables rather Cheaper than in England." An English cleric who returned to London in 1770 termed Virginia furniture "incredibly mean," but he added that homes of "many of the eminent planters" were "pretty well furnished" with items from Britain.

Walls of the President's House would have been hung with prints and maps, which were common in colonial inventories and that were advertised by *The Virginia Gazette* printing office. In 1750 President William Dawson sent to a dealer in London for prints to hang in the house. Professor Samuel Henley, a loyalist who returned to England from the college in 1775, wrote of "mahogany tables, chairs, bureaus, bookcases, desk, library table, bed, etc." that he was forced to leave, plus a collection of "scarce and Valuable editions" of books and "engravings, etchings, and mezzotints by the greatest masters." After loyalists' possessions had been sequestered by Virginia in 1777, Jefferson bought most of Henley's books. President Madison tried to save other possessions for his friend in the President's House, only to see them destroyed when the house burned in 1781.

The college owned few portraits until the twentieth century. In 1859 it had only six, all of which were saved when the Main Building burned.

The second floor of the President's House contained a master bedroom for the president and his lady, with three smaller ones for family or guests. Infants usually slept in their parents' bedroom. As they grew older, boys were usually put in one room and girls in another. A nurse might sleep in a child's room or on a pallet in the hall outside it.

Records of the college indicate that presidents occasionally rented their two third-story rooms to students, usually to youngsters in the grammar school. Each room could accommodate at least two double beds, affording abundant sleeping space. However, presidents with families seldom took in more than one or two students. During the presidency of Bishop James Madison, a British visitor to the President's House, Isaac Weld, wrote of dining with the president in the 1790s, apparently in the President's House. Weld wrote: "The Bishop of Virginia is President of the College, and has apartments in the buildings. Half a dozen or more of the students, the eldest about twelve years of age, dined at his table one day while I was there; some were without shoes or stockings, others without coats. During the dinner, they constantly rose to help themselves at the sideboard. A couple of dishes of salted meat and some oyster soup formed the above dinner. I only mention this, as it may convey some idea of American colleges and American dignitaries."

Through the 250 years of the life of the President's House, many sons and daughters have been reared within its walls. Their education remained much the same through the eighteenth and most of the nineteenth centuries, until public schools were created in Virginia in the 1870s. Before public schools, children of presidents were taught reading, writing, and arithmetic either at home by a member of the family, by private tutors, or at small local schools. Williamsburg had many such schools in the eighteenth century, including free schools and private ones. Between 1716 and 1776, seven dancing schools and four music schools existed. There were also fencing masters in Williamsburg.

Girls' schooling did not usually go far beyond elementary levels. Although most girls were taught dancing, fewer of them were instructed in music, painting, and French. Most girls learned sewing, embroidery, and other fancy work.

In the eighteenth and nineteenth centuries, small schools were operated in Williamsburg both for girls alone and for girls and boys together. The retired actress Sarah Hallam had a girls' boarding school after the Revolution. Mrs. Mariah Clopton conducted a school for girls at the Raleigh Tavern before it was destroyed by fire in 1859. Miss Gabriella "Gibbie" Galt taught boys and girls in a house on Francis

Street, now known as the Griffin house. From 1840 until about 1865, when it was discontinued, the Williamsburg Female Academy operated on the site of the Capitol.

Boys in the president's family usually followed their primary education by attending grammar school at the college. When this was discontinued, from 1780 to 1792, some attended classes given by the Reverend John Bracken, former master of the college grammar school before its discontinuance. These were held in Bracken's residence on Francis Street, now known as the Lightfoot house. In 1784 Walker Maury conducted a grammar school in the Capitol building, which was taken over by John Bracken in 1787. Bracken returned as grammar master at the college in 1792.

The most enduring school in Williamsburg was begun with a free school founded by Mrs. Mary Whaley in 1706 in memory of her son Matthew, who had died in 1705. It first stood on the east side of Queen Mary's Road, a little beyond Waller Street, and included a schoolhouse, master's house, and stable. Mrs. Whaley moved to London where she died in 1742, leaving a considerable legacy to the school. Her executors had altercations with the church wardens of Bruton, who had been overseers of the school, and the legacy was held up for years in English chancery court.

After an English attorney had called attention to the unfulfilled legacy in 1859, the College of William and Mary agreed to discharge Mrs. Whaley's trust. It obtained the legacy and in 1867 erected a brick schoolhouse near the Palace site, known first as The Grammar and Matty School and later as The Matthew Whaley Observation and Practice School. It became a Williamsburg public school and its name was memorialized in a large, modern building erected near the Palace in 1931, during the town's restoration.

The president of William and Mary often moved his family to a farm or plantation in summer, when the college was closed. James Blair had set this pattern when he continued to live on his farm at nearby Richneck in James City County, even after a presidential apartment had been set aside for him when the Main Building was erected in 1700. Presidents John Bracken and Benjamin Ewell also acquired nearby plantations, Bracken's in York and Ewell's in James City County. The plantation house built by Ewell in 1858–1859, known as Ewell Hall, is still standing.

With the growth of interest in the President's House in the 1980s, further research began on its architectural history, its occupants, its furnishings, and on the archeology of the college yard surrounding the house, where the president's garden and a succession of outbuildings have stood. A few early furnishings of the house have been located, and one or two have been given to the college. However, substantial knowledge of the furnishings and decor of the President's House dates from the administration of President Lyon Gardiner Tyler, who took office in 1888. The testimony of Tyler descendants and of subsequent presidential families is being collected.

The impetus to revive the college and to preserve its history was greatly accelerated by restoration of the three original college buildings in the years 1928–1932 as the first step in the Rockefellers' revival of Williamsburg. Through research and archeology, architects were able to re-create the original exterior of the buildings. Their most important aid was the discovery in 1929 in the Bodleian library at Oxford University of a copper engraving known as the "Bodleian plate." It shows the college yard from Duke of Gloucester Street, in about 1733 to 1747, along with other Williamsburg buildings. Included is a rear view of the Main Building after the chapel had been added.

Efforts since that time have brought to light many other details of the college. However, much has been lost in fires that have swept the institution and in the burning of James City County's records in 1865 in Richmond, where they had been taken at the outbreak of the Civil War for safekeeping. With these county records were included inventories of the estates of most William and Mary presidents before the Civil War, listing furniture, furnishings, and books. Much more would be known of the early contents of the President's House had the records survived, but existing inventories of comparable Virginian houses of the period can be of help to researchers.

Efforts to collect college records were intensified by Earl Gregg Swem, librarian and archivist of the college from 1920 to 1944. Subsequently, the Colonial Williamsburg Foundation, through Mrs. Mary Randolph Mordecai Goodwin, assembled and indexed all early data on the college and its affairs. Even so, much remains to be learned about the first 250 years of the President's House.

# 6

## *The Struggle for the College*

FOR twenty-five years, from the death of William Dawson in 1752 until the inauguration of James Madison in 1777, William and Mary was torn by quarrels between its whiggish Visitors and its more loyalist professors, who were usually English-born and Oxford-educated. It was a foretaste of the Revolution.

The issue was usually professors' behavior, but the larger implication was Virginia's resistance to imperial policies, especially to any British attempt to tax Virginians. Though Governors Gooch, Dinwiddie, Fauquier (who advised against the Stamp Act, which was repealed in his governorship), and Lord Botetourt (who was faced with the British Revenue Acts) all tried to make the royal will palatable to dissatisfied Virginians, some clergymen on the faculty were less sensitive to the growing unrest of the colonies.

The immediate cause of friction between Visitors and faculty was the Two-Penny Acts passed by the Virginia Assembly with the assent of Governors Dinwiddie and Fauquier. These were finally repealed by the Crown, but not before they had stirred bitter resentment between the Assembly and the Virginia clergy, including most of the faculty.

As the power of the Assembly in eighteenth-century Virginia grew, the college's Board of Visitors came to demand virtual independence in its control of the institution. Although after the 1729 transfer the president and faculty owned the college property and held full responsibility for the "ordinary running" of the institution, the Visitors increasingly usurped those powers.

As a result, every president from William Stith's time until the Revolution was caught in a struggle between the Visitors and faculty. Backed up by the charter, the statutes of 1727 and 1758, and the 1729 transfer, the faculty fought back at the Visitors, embroiling the president. Professors wrote complaints to the commissary and he wrote to the college's chancellor in England. Some were fired. Some resigned.

At the President's House, candles often burned late as professors voiced complaints. Such problems drove gentle Thomas Dawson to an unhappy death at 46, and they may have hastened the end of others. Certainly a string of presidents died young: William Dawson at 47, William Stith at 48, Thomas Dawson at 45, William Yates at 43, and James Horrocks at 38. The President's House was not a happy place.

To succeed Thomas Dawson on his death in 1760, the Visitors in 1761 turned to a born-and-bred Virginian in hopes of unanimity. He was William Yates, a forty-one-year-old cleric who had been educated at the college, sent to England by President William Dawson for ordination, and had served as rector of Abingdon Parish in Gloucester for about nine years. Yates's wife was the former Elizabeth Randolph, granddaughter of William and Mary Isham Randolph of Turkey Island, who have been called "the Adam and Eve of Virginia's first families."

Mrs. Yates was also a cousin of both William Stith and his wife, Judith Randolph Stith, who had occupied the President's House from 1752 to 1755. The Randolphs were everywhere!

Yates was acceptable as president to the Visitors because he had not been involved in the conflicts at the college. Moreover, he had a good academic background. Beyond his own record at the college stood that of his father, Bartholomew Yates, Sr., who had come to Virginia in 1701 and held two parishes before he served as rector of Christ Church Parish in Middlesex County for thirty-one years. The elder Yates had been a graduate of Brasenose College at Oxford and had become professor of divinity at William and Mary in 1729. He was also a member of the Board of Visitors from about 1723 until his death in 1734.

William and Elizabeth Yates brought three children with them to the President's House in 1761: Edward Randolph, Sarah, and William. Yates also brought experience, having conducted a grammar school for boys in his Abingdon Parish glebe house in Gloucester. There he had taught several students who later enrolled at William and Mary, including John Page who had come to the college grammar school as a teenager and had lodged with the Thomas Dawsons in the President's House.

Yates was elected rector of Bruton Parish soon after he became president, but for the role of commissary the Bishop of London preferred another man. He was the Reverend William Robinson, minister of Stratton Major Parish in King and Queen County. That created another potential conflict, this time between the Visitors and Commissary Robinson, who was also a member of the Board.

Yates found his faculty in turmoil. The irate Visitors had dismissed three faculty members in November 1757, leaving their places unfilled. Only two masters, the Reverend Emmanuel Jones, Jr., and William Small, professor of natural philosophy and mathematics, were present at Yates's first faculty meeting. In 1761 the Reverend Richard Graham, who had been dismissed in 1757, was reemployed as professor of moral philosophy and in 1763 the Privy Council in England reappointed all three to their former positions.

A new grammar master, The Reverend James Horrocks—the first Cambridge University graduate to join the faculty—was named in 1762. On a campus of about 100 students, the six professors and masters appear to have been kept busy.

The unhappy state of the college which Yates inherited was reported by Commissary Robinson to the Bishop of London: "My Lord, there have been within these four years at this little College, two Professors worried into a Resignation, and five deprived. Out of these, one was early restored to his Place, and another lately prefer'd to a fresh Professorship. And after all the College, as to the behaviour of the Students, is at this time . . . in as bad if not worse condition than ever. Facts, which might teach the Visitors, that the Blame . . . does not lie upon the Professors . . ."

Despite these wrangles, the college prospered. Demand for tobacco and Virginia's growth in wealth were reflected in the building of handsome plantation houses. The college could afford a new stable and carriage house — built on a town lot — for the president's horses, and Yates added other outbuildings to make life more livable.

During Yates's administration the President's House knew some remarkable personalities. One was William Small, at first professor of natural philosophy and later of moral philosophy, who inspired his students as no teacher before until he returned to England in 1764. Another was the scholar and lawyer George Wythe, a resident of Williamsburg. A third was the Albemarle youth, Thomas Jefferson, who attended college from 1760 to 1762 and then spent time in Williamsburg studying law under Wythe.

Jefferson's two years at college stimulated friendships with Professor Small, George Wythe, and with several students, including John Page,

Photo from The Colonial Williamsburg Foundation

*Austenaco, center, a Cherokee chief from western Virginia, was a guest of President James Horrocks in the President's House in 1765.*

with whom he corresponded voluminously. His first serious romance, with young Rebecca Burwell of Gloucester County, began and ended in Williamsburg, which he called "Devilsburg" in letters to Page because of his romantic frustrations there.

In his old age Jefferson did not always speak well of "Devilsburg," but he retained a warm lifelong affection for his teachers Small and Wythe, and for schoolmates John Page and Dabney Carr.

President Yates died only three years after taking office, at age forty-three. His term was too brief to breed conflicts, but he left serious problems for James Horrocks, the grammar master who succeeded him in 1764. From the outset, the Visitors' choice of Horrocks was disliked by the faculty, who had preferred the Reverend Richard Graham, the senior professor, once fired and then reemployed by the Visitors. Soon it was Visitors versus faculty all over again.

Horrocks alienated his colleagues in the very beginning by swearing obedience to a new statute of the Visitors, "depriving" any of the presidents and faculty of their positions "at pleasure." By this statute the Visitors had usurped faculty prerogatives granted in the original statutes, and the faculty resented Horrocks's acceptance of the oath of office. Horrocks weakly explained that without taking the oath he could not become president.

Commissary Robinson protested to the college's chancellor, the Bishop of London, that by his cowardly act Horrocks had reduced the "Authority of the President and Masters to a mere Shadow" and had also undermined "his own Peace and future Security." The judgment unhappily proved correct.

Horrocks's chief disadvantage in the President's House was his youth and inexperience. He was barely thirty, and his wife, Frances, was eleven years younger. Before receiving his master of arts from Trinity College at Cambridge in 1758, he had taught at the well-known Wakefield School in Yorkshire, where Richard Henry Lee and five other Virginians had gone for their grammar schooling in the 1750s. Horrocks had come to Williamsburg in 1762 to succeed Goronwy Owen, the alcoholic Welsh clergyman-poet who had been forced to resign as master of the grammar school in 1760, after a brief and hectic tenure.

Loudest among Horrocks's critics was Commissary Robinson, a member of the Board of Visitors and Horrocks's rival for leadership in the Virginia religious establishment. Robinson had favored the Reverend Richard Graham for the presidency and wrote his bishop in 1764 that: "Mr. Horrocks, a young clergyman, after having been master of the Grammar School two or three years, has found means of carrying the Presidentship of the college against Mr. Graham, a clergyman of unexceptional character & Generally esteemed, who has been Professor of Mathematics at the college near twenty years."

Robinson attributed Horrocks's selection to his ambition and his cultivation of the Governor and Visitors, a judgment with which the faculty concurred. Even so, Horrocks was a man of ability. As the gap between Visitors and faculty widened throughout his seven-year tenure, Horrocks soon swung to the faculty side. When Edward Hawtrey arrived in 1765 to become grammar school master, he found an encouraging enrollment of sixty-four grammar school students, although he was impelled to write the Bishop of London that: ". . . these unhappy differences which at present subsist between one or two of the Professors & the Visitors of the College make me cautiously avoid enquiring into them for fear of being insensibly drawn in, to interest myself too warmly on either side. The President is so worthy a man &

so well respected by all the Gentlemen in the country, that I shall by all means endeavour to keep upon good terms with him, especially as it was your Lordship's particular advice to me before I left England."

From the Bishop of London's Palace at Fulham, Richard Terrick, who was chancellor from 1764 to 1776, wrote hotly to the Board of Visitors that, because of them, it had become almost impossible to fill vacancies in the college. The "Power which the Visitors seem'd desirous of exerting in displacing at their Pleasure the Professors and Masters" made it no "easy Matter to prevail on any Person to enter upon so precarious a Situation," he scolded. The Visitors replied in a letter by Rector Dudley Digges, excoriating faculty treatment of every president since William Dawson.

When Horrocks saw Digges' letter, he wrote Terrick to deplore Digges' inaccurate, "even malicious Representation," which was "as full of improper Praise of the Deceased as of injust, illiberal Abuse of the Living . . . ," and to brand the Visitors "a set of Illiterate, ignorant, & intemperate Men totally unqualifyed for the Purposes of directing & governing a Society established for the Purposes of propagating Religion and Learning."

Concerned by Virginia's growing protests of British policy, King George III in 1768 appointed the courtly Norborne Berkeley, Baron de Botetourt, as governor of Virginia to succeed Francis Fauquier, who had died at the Governor's Palace. The Stamp Act had been repealed in Fauquier's administration, but the Townshend Act had been enacted in its place. In his two years in the Governor's Palace, Lord Botetourt effected some conciliation, and he warmly befriended the college. He frequented its chapel services, gave annual gold medals for its best scholars in the classics and in science, and mediated between Visitors and faculty.

As an older friend and adviser to the disillusioned Horrocks, he was probably often in the President's House until his death after brief illness in the Governor's Palace in 1770. He was buried with awesome pomp after elaborate services at Bruton, his body being placed in a vault under the college chapel.

Worn out by contention, James and Frances Horrocks decided to sail for his native England in 1771 for a rest. Like his predecessors, the young president felt the bitterness of colonial dissatisfaction, now threatening revolution. In an effort to hearten his clergy, Horrocks called them into convention at the college before he sailed to draw up a request to the Crown to name a bishop for the colonies. But nothing came of this.

Like his late ally, Lord Botetourt, James Horrocks frequently invited faculty and clergy to his house in hopes of restoring colonial tranquility. But Patrick Henry and Richard Henry Lee were beginning to talk of independence, and the future was clouding.

Horrocks's tenure acquainted him with many talented students, including Edmund Randolph, grandson of Sir John and nephew of Peyton Randolph, the alumnus soon to be chosen first president of the Continental Congress. An unusual visitor to the President's House in Horrocks's term was the exotically dressed Austenaco, chief of the Cherokees of western Virginia. Clad in robe and moccasins, he had come to appeal Virginia's moving his tribesmen from the mountains to a reservation in North Carolina.

Militia Lieutenant Henry Timberlake described the chief's visit to the President's House:

> A few days before they [the Cherokees] were to depart for their own Country, Mr Horrocks invited Ostenaco and myself to sup with him at the College, where, among other curiosities, he shewed him the picture of his present Majesty [King George III]. The chief viewed it a long time . . . Then, turning to me, "Long," he said, "have I wished to see the King my father; this is his resemblance, but I am determined to see himself; I am now near the sea, and never will I depart from it till I have obtained my desires." He asked the Governor next day, who tho' at first refused, on Ostenaco's insisting so strongly upon it, gave his consent.

James Horrocks left the President's House seven years after he had moved in. *The Virginia Gazette* of June 20, 1771, reported that "This Day the Reverend and Honourable the Commissary, with his Lady, took Shipping for England on Board the Savannah la Mar, Captain Tomlinson, for the Recovery of their Healths. In his Absence, the Reverend Mr. Willie is to act as Commissary, and the Reverend Mr. Camm as President of the College; and the Reverend Mr. Henley officiates as minister of Bruton Parish."

Horrocks never returned. He died in Oporto, Portugal, on October 8, 1771, nine months after he had sailed. Reporting his death, *The Virginia Gazette* called him "a Gentleman well versed in several Branches of sound Learning, particularly the Mathematicks, and eminently possessed of those Virtues which increase in Value as they are farthest from Ostentation." But Richard Bland, an elder statesman who had attended William and Mary and served it as a Visitor, had a harsher judgment.

> I acknowledge, for I will do him all justice, he made a tolerable Pedagogue in the Grammar School of our College. Here he ought to have continued, but unfortunately for his reputation, as well as for the College, he was removed from the only place he had ability to fill to be President of the College. This laid the foundation for his other exaltations, & by a Sycophantic Behavior he has accumulated upon him the Rectorship of Bruton Parish, the office of Bishop's Commissary, of a councillor, of a judge of the General Court, and of Ordinary of Newgate, all of which offices he now possesses except that of attending the condemned criminals in the Public Gaol, which he resigned upon his leaving the colony. Was his Sincerity and abilities equal to his good Fortune, he would be one of the most accomplished men amongst us.

The president's widow, Frances Horrocks, returned to Williamsburg after her husband's death and died there in December 1773 "in the 26th year of her age." She had been the daughter of Thomas Everard, clerk of York County Court and auditor of Virginia, clerk of the General Court, and twice mayor of Williamsburg. *The Virginia Gazette* declared her to be "adorned with every truly feminine virtue, unaffected piety, filial affection, and conjugal fidelity." Shortly before her death, an advertisement in *The Virginia Gazette* offered for sale "THE LIBRARY of the late COMMISSARY, consisting of a Variety of valuable Books, and a Number of Sermons by the most celebrated Authors," the collection being "lodged for Sale at Mr. William Pearce's Store," in Williamsburg.

As with other occupants of the President's House, the Horrocks family's furnishings were disposed of without surviving record. Only a little about the couple is still known, the minutiae of their lives having disappeared amid the fragments left by the wars and fires that swept Williamsburg and Virginia so often.

# 7

## *The World of College Corner*

As a result of faculty rifts and Visitors' blasts, life in the President's House on the eve of the Revolution grew more troubled. Yet this was a time of colonial growth, fed by British expansion in the western world. The empire's victories in Europe's endless wars were costly, but they were exhilarating. They reached their climax after the British under General Wolfe defeated the French at Quebec in 1759. Montreal also fell to the British, and London became the world's most powerful capital since ancient Rome.

As the nerve center of Britain's oldest overseas dominion, Williamsburg felt the surge of British power. By 1770 the Virginia settlement had grown to 750,000 people—larger than any other British colony. Its settlers stretched westward from the Eastern Shore to Botetourt County in the Valley of Virginia, and it claimed land as far west as the Mississippi River. In these years buckskinned frontiersmen rubbed elbows with Tidewater grandees when the House of Burgesses gathered at the Capitol.

Williamsburg now offered greater diversity of entertainment. During Public Times, when the General Court met at the Capitol twice yearly, in April and October, Courthouse Green and Market Square offered livestock sales, auctions, and the bucolic pleasures of a country fair. The spring fair was held on St. George's Day, April 23, and honored England's patron saint. Visiting troupes performed Shakespeare and other plays in a theater on Waller Street. Horse races and card games fed the thirst for betting.

In Anglican Virginia the president of the college and his family joined fully in most diversions, for Tidewater had little of the Calvinist austerity of the Presbyterian uplands or of Puritan New England. Tea parties and dinners enlivened the President's House. As in London, Anglican clergy took part in ceremonies of government and in entertainments.

You might see the governor's carriage draw up near the President's House. Similarly, the president and faculty went to the Governor's Palace for such functions as royal birthdays and anniversaries of royal accessions. The mayor, recorder, aldermen, and common council of Williamsburg met annually on St. Andrew's Day, November 30, honoring the patron saint of Scotland, to elect a mayor from among the aldermen for the ensuing year.

Now and then a William and Mary professor was elected mayor, an office invested with pomp and held by a succession of Williamsburg's leading men.

Some Virginians thought the college's professors and students lived too riotously in these years. A few miscreants gave them good cause. Tutor Philip Fithian reported in his diary a conversation with Robert Carter of Nomini Hall in 1774. The Carters had lived in Williamsburg, occupying a house on Palace Green from 1761 to 1772. Carter told Fithian that the college was "in such confusion at present, & so badly directed" that he could not "send his Children with propriety there for Improvement & useful Education—That he has known the Professors to play all Night at Cards in publick Houses in the City, and has often seen them drunken in the Street! . . ." But the debauches of poor Goronwy Owen, who had left the faculty in 1760, were hardly typical.

The British governors in Williamsburg befriended the college as evidence of Crown support for religion and learning. After James Blair's last major adversary, Governor Spotswood, had left the Palace in 1722, relations between governors and presidents of the college were generally amicable. This was true of successive governors Hugh Drysdale, William Gooch, Robert Dinwiddie, Francis Fauquier, Lord Botetourt, and even of the hapless Lord Dunmore, who held office before the Revolution and sent his sons to William and Mary. Dunmore served on the Board of Visitors, as had most governors.

Sir William Gooch, an Oxonian, gave the Burgesses an endorsement which was typical of governors' support in these years: "If I tell you that there is not in any Part of the World, a College, where good Order,

Decency and Discipline are better maintain'd, where God Almighty is more constantly and devoutly worshipp'd, and where greater Care is taken to train up young Students in the Rudiments of Religion, Loyalty, Science, good Manners, and carrying them on towards Perfection, than in This, I am sure I should speak without Artifice or Flattery, and I dare say, within the Bounds of Truth."

The college took its lead in morals and manners from the president, who was required by charter to be a cleric and by the 1727 statutes to be "a Man of Gravity, that is in Holy Orders, of an unblemished Life, and good Reputation, and not under Thirty Years of Age." He must also be "skilful in Business" and "diligently inspect into the Revenues and Expences" of the college, keep a "watchful Eye over the other Masters and Professors," and give "a Theological Lecture once a Week in the Explication of Scripture . . ." Not an easy job!

In the 1758 statutes, the president's salary, then £150, was raised to £200 per annum and his "Theological Lectures" reduced to four a year. As before, he continued to enjoy the benefit of "an House and Garden, suitable to the Place," as in Blair's day.

The ability of eighteenth-century professors to shift from one branch of learning to another, as was required of the small faculty, indicates their breadth. Surviving writings also attest their literary facility. Thomas Jefferson wrote of the college in 1788, "I know of no place in the world, while the present professors remain, where I would as soon place a son."

Most of its early records were lost in fires, but a sense of the college's life survives in its statutes, which Blair and the Reverend Stephen Fouace had drawn up in London in 1727, with the help of the chancellor, Archbishop William Wake. After transfer of the college from its founding trustees to its president and faculty took place in 1729, these statutes governed operations of the college. The changes between 1727 and 1758 were incorporated in a new printing, in Latin and English, of the *Charter, Transfer, and Statutes,* published by William Hunter in 1758, to supersede the William Parks printing of 1736.

The statutes set forth an idealistic curriculum, followed until the college's reorganization in 1779, which centered on philosophy and religion. Greek and Latin were its underpinnings. Four years of study were prescribed for the bachelor of arts and seven for the master's, following the "Form and Institution of the Two famous Universities in England," Oxford and Cambridge.

The 1727 and 1758 statutes referred to the "dark days" when "Aristotle's Logick and Physicks" reigned "alone in the Schools," and prescribed a far broader course. At William and Mary, the two philosophy professors were to "teach what Systems of Logick, Physicks, Ethicks, and Mathematicks" they thought preferable. One of the two, the professor of moral philosophy, was to teach "Rhetorick, Logick, and Ethics." The other, in natural philosophy, was to teach "Physicks, Metaphysicks, and Mathematicks." Besides such ancients as Plato, Socrates, Demosthenes, Tacitus, Aristotle, and Epictetus, students were to study more recent works such as Montaigne, Bacon, Spinoza, Boyle, Locke, Newton, Voltaire, Rousseau, Adam Smith, and others. Contemporary textbooks used in classes were sold at the printing office in town and advertised in *The Virginia Gazette*.

The 1727 statutes also directed that students were to be "exercised in Declamations and Themes on various Subjects," except from the Bible. These were left to divinity students.

"Disputations," or debates, were called for by statute, for they were commonly used in British universities to develop forensic skill and to deepen the students' grasp of logic, philosophy, and history. Such disputations were often held before an invited audience, with one student "propugning" a thesis and another "conpugning" it. Such debates were later taken over by the two college literary societies, the Phoenix and the Philomathean, which met in quarters in the Main Building in the nineteenth century.

At commencement each summer, degree applicants would declaim in the Great Hall or chapel, and medals and prizes were awarded for superior performance. Such experience proved useful in molding many of William and Mary's early students who were to distinguish themselves in political debate or in courtroom argument.

In eighteenth-century Williamsburg, collegians bestrode the town in academic gowns worn rakishly over their clothes, as in British schools. They occasionally went to debates in the House of Burgesses or sat in on cases being heard in the General Court. Seasonal races at the quarterpath racetrack near the Capitol on the outskirts of Williamsburg attracted some, while theatrical evenings in the playhouse first on Palace Green, and later on Waller Street appealed to others.

The pre-Revolutionary years saw many musical performances in town and college, for the baroque composers of Europe were becoming popular in the American colonies. Thomas Jefferson and his cousin, John Randolph, later called "the Tory," played the violin at small gatherings. Works by Mozart, Vivaldi, Haydn, and Handel were heard with enthusiasm at functions at the Governor's Palace, the Capitol, the theater and at Bruton Parish Church.

Music and dancing had been important to Williamsburg from its beginning. Between 1716 and 1776, seven teachers giving lessons in dance and five in music advertised in *The Virginia Gazette*. Instruction was available in violin, organ, harpsichord, spinet, German and common flutes, French horn, hautboy (oboe), and guitar. One teacher was Cuthbert Ogle, who owned several instruments and much music. Another was Peter Pelham, who came from New England, installed the first organ in Bruton in 1755, and became its first organist. He was a stepbrother of Boston portraitist John Singleton Copley. He also kept the public jail.

The college in the mid-1700s increasingly admitted lay teachers to its faculty. One who came early was Joshua Fry, a graduate of Wadham College, Oxford, a grammar master from about 1729 to 1731 and professor of natural philosophy from 1732 to 1737. He obtained his surveyor's license for Albemarle County from the college. Fry and Peter Jefferson, father of Thomas, created the widely used Fry and Jefferson map of Virginia, published in London in 1751 and updated several times.

Another lay professor was scientist William Small, a graduate of Aberdeen University, who arrived from England in 1758 to be professor of natural philosophy and mathematics. Thomas Jefferson and John Page, two of his students, credited Small with unexcelled teaching and were his lifelong admirers. Small frequented Governor Fauquier's philosophical and musical evenings at the Governor's Palace along with George Wythe and students Jefferson and Page.

Small taught during the presidencies of Thomas Dawson and William Yates, managing to stay out of most conflicts that embroiled the faculty. When Professor Graham, fired in 1757 and re-hired in 1761 as professor of moral philosophy, was reinstated to his original professorship in 1763 by the Privy Council, he and Small exchanged professorships. Returning to England in 1764 on a leave of absence, Small purchased an elaborate philosophical apparatus for the college in 1767, paying £332 4s. 05d. for it and receiving a fee of £50 from the college for his trouble.

Deciding to remain in England, Small settled in Birmingham, becoming a friend of engineer James Watt and of scientist Erasmus Darwin, grandfather of Charles. It was a great loss to the college.

William and Mary sometimes appeared to contemporaries as more grammar school than college, for its twelve- to fifteen-year-old preparatory boys outnumbered collegians. In 1779 Jefferson urged the Visitors to close the grammar school, writing in his *Notes on the State of Virginia* in 1781-1782, "The admission of the learners of Latin and

Greek filled the college with children. This rendering it disagreeable and degrading to young gentlemen already prepared for entering on the sciences, they were discouraged from resorting to it [the college], and thus the schools for mathematics and moral philosophy, which might have been of some service, became of very little."

In spite of Jefferson's objection, the college's grammar school was essential in the early years, providing preparation for boys to enter college. Such instruction was then given by relatively few schools in the colonies. As colleges were rare before the Revolution and as few young men could afford to attend them, drilling in Latin and Greek grammar, which the grammar schools offered, was in limited demand.

Some sixteen grammar schools operated in Virginia before the Revolution, all except the college's being conducted by individual clerics on a short-term basis. Twelve of these were run by Anglican clergymen, usually at glebe houses in tidewater or piedmont parishes. Four dissenting ministers—three Presbyterians and one German Lutheran—also had schools in the Valley of Virginia. A few girls' schools also operated in this period, their courses offering more artistic and domestic subjects.

An important duty of William and Mary's president was to keep order among his faculty and students. Under the president, the grammar master was responsible for the behavior of grammar students. The statutes of 1727 and 1758 forbade lying, cursing, swearing, obscene talk, fighting, gambling, or drinking. To prevent these and "anything that is contrary to good Manners," the master was to "chuse some of the most trusty Scholars for public Observators, to give him an Account of all such Transgressions." A student accused of "heinous" error was brought before the president and faculty in the Blue Room. The control and discipline of older collegians was under the president and professors. They enjoyed wider latitude than the younger boys.

Another concern of William and Mary's president was housekeeping, especially in the dining hall. For a brief time Mrs. Clayton, the sister President William Dawson brought over from England shortly before he died, was housekeeper at the college. She was mentioned as being present in February 1758 when President Thomas Dawson was trying to oust the Reverend Messrs. Robinson, Camm, and Graham from their apartments in the college, at the orders of the Visitors. The Reverend Goronwy Owen arrived in the spring of 1758 to replace Mr. Robinson as grammar master and, his first wife having died on the voyage, he married Mrs. Clayton, who survived only a short time as Mrs. Owen. The faculty minutes for August 28, 1759, appointed Mrs.

Martha Bryan housekeeper "in the place of Mrs. Owen deceas'd." In August 1761 Mrs. Martha Bryan resigned, was given the unanimous thanks of the faculty "for the faithful discharge of her Office," and was replaced by Mrs. Isabella Cocke. Mrs. Cocke served such wretched food that it became gossip throughout the country. The faculty prepared a set of instructions for her, including the following orders concerning food.

> That there be always be both fresh, and salt Meat for Dinner; and twice in the Week, as well as on Sunday in particular, that there be either Puddings or Pies beside; that there be always Plenty of Victuals; that Breakfast Dinner and Supper be serv'd up in the cleanest, and neatest Manner possible; and for this Reason the Society faculty not only allow, but desire You to get a cook; that the Boy's Suppers be not as usual made up of different Scraps, but that there be at each Table the same Sort: and when there is cold fresh Meat enough, that it be often hash'd for them . . .

When Isabella Cocke failed to keep this commandment, the college fired her and hired "a Man capable of managing the Housekeeper's Business." He proved no more acceptable. Thus it went.

In the nepotistic world of the college, Vistors and faculty often awarded jobs to needy widows, sisters, or other kinsmen. This accounted for the presence of a Mrs. Stith (nee Randolph), a Mrs. Digges, and a Mrs. Cocke among the matrons or housekeepers of early years. Other widows of Visitors or professors kept boardinghouses or rooming houses near the college.

The world of College Corner was a small one, but it produced many people Americans would remember.

# 8

## *The Pot Boils Over*

WHEN Lord Botetourt died in the Governor's Palace in October 1770, hope of reconciliation between England and Virginia faded. A gloomy prospect faced President Horrocks and his wife as their ship, *Savanna la Mar,* sailed through the Capes in June 1771 enroute to England, "for the Recovery of their Healths."

What lay ahead for Virginia, where Britain had invested so much effort? The times called for forbearance by officials at Whitehall and in Williamsburg, but it was not forthcoming. Both Governor Botetourt and President Horrocks would be succeeded by uncompromising men who did little to avert the coming disaster.

Botetourt's successor was John Murray, Earl of Dunmore, who arrived in September 1771 to receive the warm welcome that Virginia accorded royal governors. Horrocks's successor was John Camm, whom he had designated as acting president before he had sailed from Virginia. After news of Horrocks's shocking death in Portugal, on March 20, 1772, had reached Williamsburg, the Visitors elected John Camm president on July 30, 1772.

It was an act of pure folly, for Camm's prior eighteen years as a professor had shown his independence of the Visitors. Born in England's North Country, John Camm had gone from Yorkshire to Trinity College at Cambridge in 1738. After graduation and ordination to the priesthood, he came to Virginia as minister in Isle of Wight County. In

1749 he became rector of York-Hampton Parish, whose principal church was at Yorktown and was appointed in September of that year as professor of divinity at the college. Though he first lived at the parish glebe farm between Felgate and King's creeks in York County, he was forced in 1755 to move to rooms on the second floor of the college in response to the dictates of the Visitors.

John Camm triggered the Visitors' ire in 1757 when he and others of Thomas Dawson's faculty had refused to give the Visitors their reasons for dismissing an usher—an act within their prerogative. They believed—and they were later upheld by the Privy Council—that they would relinquish faculty rights under the Charter and the 1729 Transfer if they gave in. Camm and Professor Graham had been dismissed by the Visitors, but they had refused to surrender keys to their quarters and classrooms to President Dawson.

The Virginia clergy subsequently elected Camm to take their case against the Two-Penny Acts to the Privy Council in England. Camm left Virginia in 1758 and remained in England until the spring of 1760, having enlisted Archbishop Thomas Secker and the Bishop of London to obtain a hearing by the Privy Council. He notified fellow Virginia clerics by letter of his success in having the acts repealed, but he took his time returning to Williamsburg. In 1763 the Privy Council reinstated Camm and Graham to their 1757 professorships, Camm to teach divinity and Graham natural philosophy and mathematics.

Governor Fauquier was furious with Camm for not having notified him of the Privy Council's disallowance of the Two-Penny Acts until months after its issuance and five months after Camm had notified others in Virginia of it. Fauquier also resented the minister's inordinate delay in returning to Virginia and his failure to come to the Governor's Palace to present the disallowance until a week after he reached Virginia, on June 20, 1760.

Thus, when Camm finally walked into the Palace to present the papers, the normally agreeable Fauquier launched into a tirade against him. As Commissary William Robinson described the scene,

> The Governor shew'd Dr. Camm the door & bad him come there no more. Mr. Camm obey'd and retired but before he had descended the steps was commanded to stop. He halted accordingly, & the Governor bawled out for "Westmore." . . . The Governor cried out to him, "Call all my negroes." When His Honour thus was pleased to address himself to them, "Look at this gentleman,' pointing to Mr. Camm, "Look at this gentleman that you may know him again & if he ever attempt to come hither do not suffer him to enter my gates."

To see a gentleman so humiliated before servants shocked Robinson, who added, "There was something peculiar in this last indignity, for it is the greatest affront that can be put upon a free man here [in Virginia] to give orders concerning him to the slaves, it is what a white servant would not endure with any patience."

The Governor demanded that Commissary Robinson break off his acquaintance with Camm, but Robinson wrote Bishop Sherlock in London that "there had been an intimate acquaintance between Mr Camm and Myself for this fourteen Years past, in all which time I never knew or heard he had been guilty of one mean unworthy Action." However, Fauquier called Camm "a Turbulent Factious one" and wrote the Bishop of London that Camm's "Delight" was "to raise a Flame and live in it."

Camm, who was reinstated to his professorship of divinity by the Privy Council in 1763, did not cease his attacks on the Two-Penny Acts. Although the acts had finally been rescinded, he believed some proponents were avoiding paying the Virginia clergy the back salaries they felt they were entitled to. To answer "calumnies" and "falsehoods" published about him in *The Virginia Gazette* during his absence in England, Camm responded with a critical pamphlet, printed in 1763 in Annapolis.

This prompted the angry colonels, Richard Bland of Prince George and Landon Carter of Richmond County, his bitterest critics, to write rebuttals. They were issued in pamphlet form by Joseph Royle at his *Virginia Gazette* press in 1764. Undaunted, Camm resumed the exchange with another pamphlet, printed by Royle the same year.

John and Betsey Camm—Camm had baptized Betsey as an infant—moved into the President's House soon after his surprising election by the Visitors in 1772. Camm was also appointed commissary to the Bishop of London and took his seat on the Council in October 1772. It seemed a complete vindication for a man once out of favor with Virginia's leaders.

The new president and his wife were an odd couple, indeed. He was 51 and she only 16 or 17. He married her in July, 1769, when he was treasurer of the college and rector of York-Hampton Parish and she was Betsey Hansford of York County. The John-and-Priscilla romance was the talk of Tidewater. The bachelor clergyman had gone to Betsey's father to offer the marriage proposal of a young man of his parish, but Betsey interrupted and told the minister to "go home and look at 2 Samuel xii, 7." It read: "Thou art the man."

Because of the Board of Visitors' rules, he gave up his apartment in the college after his marriage and moved into a house.

Camm's marriage in 1769 was described by Martha Goosley of Yorktown in a letter to a friend in London: "Mr Camms Marriage has made a great noise here but Pray why may not an old Man afflicted with the Gout have the Pleasure of a fine hand to rub his feet and warm his flannells[,] comfortable amusement[,] you will say for a girl of fifteen but She is to have a Chariot and there is to be no Padlock put upon her mind."

An inventory of the Camms' possessions, made after their deaths, lists furnishings they probably used in the President's House. It included a canopied bed, several corner cupboards, many books and bookcases, a number of black walnut tables and chairs, and a magic lantern with pictures. They also had glass, porcelain, silver, and other items to a value of £7,258 Virginia Currency.

The college grew in attendance in the 1765-1770 period, reaching almost 100 students. So encouraged was the Board of Visitors that it decided in 1772 to enlarge the Main Building and to complete the quadrangle originally intended. This would create a building like many at Oxford and Cambridge. Governor Dunmore, a Visitor like his predecessors in the Palace, asked Thomas Jefferson to draw up architectural plans, which the young man readily did. Building supplies were ordered and excavations made for the foundations, only to be halted by the outbreak of the Revolution. The materials were sold after 1782 and removed from the college yard.

Two new Oxonians and one Virginia-bred clergyman had joined the faculty in 1770, during Horrocks's presidency. The Reverend Thomas Gwatkin taught natural philosophy and mathematics, and the Reverend Samuel Henley, moral philosophy. The Reverend John Dixon, educated at the college and rector of Kingston Parish in Gloucester, was appointed professor of divinity.

James Madison, another Virginia-born scholar, became writing master in May 1772, before he received his degree from the college that August. According to *The Virginia Gazette,* he was appointed mathematics professor in 1773 while still a student. He probably studied divinity between 1773-1775 before departing for England in the latter year to be ordained by the Bishop of London, and to study chemistry and anatomy while there. He was later to prove one of the most influential figures in the life of the college.

Williamsburg was dividing into warring camps in the years when John and Betsey Camm occupied the President's House. With disaffected Virginians meeting off and on in Williamsburg to protest taxes, it was hard for a boy to keep his mind on ancient languages or mathematics. Governor Dunmore, who was increasingly disliked for the policies he defended, informed Camm and his faculty on April 3, 1775, that he was resigning as a Visitor. The Governor was urged by the faculty to reconsider, but after British marines on his orders removed gunpowder from the colony's Magazine several weeks later, hostilities finally broke out in Williamsburg.

About this time news of the battles of Lexington and Concord arrived in Virginia, being circulated in a printed broadside on April 29, 1775, and confirmed fears that war had come at last. Dunmore pulled his sons out of college and sent them home to England with his wife. Professors Henley and Gwatkin, who had arrived from England only in 1770, also chose to return, all sailing in June 1775.

Though the college was rapidly losing faculty and students, Camm kept it open, chiefly for its grammar school boys. In September 1775, Patrick Henry, commander in chief of Virginia forces, arrived in town, and a camp was laid out "behind the College." Troops from the "different Counties" were now "on the March." In early 1776 the newly proclaimed Commonwealth of Virginia considered emptying the Main Building to serve as a barracks or hospital, but that was resisted. Alumnus John Page protested by letter to Major General Charles Lee, who was in charge of Virginia's defense: ". . . as the College is the only place in the Country where our youth can be tolerably educated it seems highly improper to debar ourselves from that invaluable advantage, and indeed as it is the freehold of the President & Professors, we fear it will look like a violation of private property. . . ."

President Camm did not return to England, but he was suspected of loyalism, and his days as president were numbered. No record of his departure from the college survives, but he ceased to be president in mid-1777. A later president, Lyon Gardiner Tyler, wrote that Camm was an "ardent tory" and would not accept the idea of American independence. Camm was succeeded in October 1777 by the remarkable young James Madison, recently ordained in London, where he had also gathered some "Knowledge in the Chemical & Anatomical Field." Madison's election was the more remarkable because he was two years below the legal presidential age of thirty.

A New York publisher, Ebenezer Hazard, who had been chosen by Congress as Surveyor General of the Continental Post Office, visited Williamsburg in 1777. He found the college devoid of theological students and most collegians. Hazard wrote that the Main Building

> . . . is badly contrived, and the Inside of it is shabby; it is 2 ½

> Stories high, has Wings & dormer Windows. At each End of the East Front is a two Story brick House, one for the President, the other is for an Indian School . . . At this Front of the College is a large Court Yard, ornamented with Gravel Walks, Trees cut into different Forms, & Grass. The Wings are on the West Front, between them is a covered Parade, which reaches from the one to the other; the Portico is supported by Stone Pillars: opposite to this Parade is a Court Yard & a large Kitchen Garden:—There is also the Foundation of a new Building which was intended for an Addition to the College, but has been discontinued on Account of the present Troubles;—at the South End of the Parade is a small Chapel for the Use of the Students . . . at the North End is a Room allotted for a Divinity-School, but there have been no Students in it for several Years; there are but 18 Students belonging to the College, & about 30 Grammar Scholars: the College has been on the Decline for some Years.

On leaving the college, John and Betsey Camm moved to his farm in York County. Both died in 1779, leaving five small children: Anne, a girl of nine, who would later marry Robert Hall Waller of Williamsburg, and Thomas, Robert, John, and Elizabeth. Camm's books and scientific instruments were put in custody of a new professor and rector of Bruton Parish, the Reverend John Bracken, who advertised them for sale for the children's benefit on May 10, 1779. They were described in *The Virginia Gazette* as "the very valuable Library & Philosophical Apparatus of the Rev. John Camm, deceased."

John Camm left a sizable estate. His personal property was valued at £7,258 10s. 0d. in Virginia currency, a goodly sum by today's standards. The inventory in York County indicates that the Camms lived well in the President's House, for they had fine furniture, silver, linens, and pictures. Camm's York County farm had thirty-nine cattle, seven horses, and some hogs and sheep. His ten slaves—four men, two women, and four children—included some who served at the President's House.

Virginia's break with the mother country cut off revenues which had sustained the college since it had been chartered. The colony's action also ended control of the college by the Church of England, including the last British chancellor, Bishop of London Richard Terrick, who had been college spokesman at court. Furthermore, the act forfeited Robert Boyle's endowment of the Indian school and other British legacies.

Nevertheless, the Commonwealth was determined to keep its proud college, whose Visitors were a self-perpetuating corporation. Besides, it had powerful friends in such Revolutionary leaders as Jefferson, Wythe, the Randolphs, Benjamin Harrison, John Page, the two Madisons, and others.

The departure of Henley, Gwatkin, and finally of Camm left President Madison with a faculty of four. The Reverend John Bracken was now master of the grammar school, Emmanuel Jones, Jr., of the Indian School, and the Reverend John Dixon taught theology. Madison himself taught natural philosophy and mathematics. It was a small faculty, but students were few.

Like his predecessors, James Madison as president also continued to serve the church. In 1777 he became rector of James City Parish. The old church at Jamestown was by this time in ruins, so he preached at the new "Church on the Main," near Green Spring, which succeeded it. In 1777 he was also appointed chaplain to the General Assembly, and in the same year Governor Patrick Henry and the Council named him captain of a "Company of Militia formed out of the Students of the College."

Prospects of independence lifted American spirits, but few except President Madison and Governor Jefferson appear to have given much thought of what would become of the college. Even they were to prove unequal to the sad adversities which lay in store for it.

# *Book Two*

William and Mary College Archives

## The Captains and the Kings

### 1777–1846

The sick and wounded of the Army, which my Necessities have compelled me to trouble you with, shall be removed as soon as Circumstances will permit, An Event which will be as pleasing to me, as agreeable to you.

George Washington, commander in chief, to "The President and Professors of the University of William and Mary," October 27, 1781

Courtesy The Newport News Daily Press

*For nearly 200 years the President's House had few neighboring structures, as this 20th-century photograph shows.*

# 9

# *Jefferson Offers a Plan*

WHEN young James Madison became president of the college in September 1777, he faced a succession of wartime problems. He apparently discussed the college's future at length with Governor Thomas Jefferson, almost six years his elder, who occupied the Governor's Palace from his election in mid-1779 until he moved with the seat of government to Richmond in the spring of 1780.

Like his British predecessors in the Palace, Jefferson became a member of the college's Board of Visitors when he became governor. He had given thought to the role of the institution in the new Commonwealth, and especially to the need for legal and medical training to replace that which had been cut off in England and Scotland.

Accordingly, Jefferson in 1779 proposed a radical reorganization of the college which the Visitors adopted on December 4 of that year. It was designed to remake the college into a more diverse university. He later wrote that he

> . . . effected during my residence at Williamsburg that year [1779], a change in the organization of that institution by abolishing the Grammar school, and the two professorships of Divinity and Oriental languages, and substituting a professorship of Law & Police, one of Anatomy Medicine and Chemistry, and one of Modern languages; and the charter confining us to six professorships, we added the law of Nature & Nations, & the Fine Arts to

> the duties of the Moral professors, and Natural history to those of the professor of Mathematics and Natural philosophy.

At the first meeting of the new faculty on December 29, 1779, Madison and the Reverend Robert Andrews were the only holdovers. Madison continued to teach natural philosophy (science) and mathematics, while Andrews—a graduate of the college at Philadelphia and an Anglican clergyman—handled moral philosophy, "the Laws of Nature & of Nations" (political science and economics), and "Fine Arts."

There were three new professors. One was George Wythe, who taught "Law & Police" under the college's aegis, having previously taught the classics and law at his house on Palace Green. Dr. James McClurg, an alumnus of William and Mary who had studied medicine at Edinburgh, London, and Paris and who had settled in Williamsburg by 1777, joined the faculty to teach "Anatomy & Medicine." In 1777 McClurg was associated with Virginia's public apothecary shop in Williamsburg and served troop hospitals there and in Yorktown, Hampton, and Portsmouth. He had become a member of the prestigious American Philosophical Society in 1774.

Charles Bellini, an Italian who had arrived in Virgina in 1773 to assist Jefferson in his wine experiments, taught modern languages. Bellini spoke several languages including Italian and French and interpreted for Virginia's Council in its wartime dealings with the French.

The college in 1779 closed its grammar school and dining room in the Great Hall in response to Jefferson's recommendations. Although they could room in the Main Building, students boarded with families in town. Professors could live where they pleased. *The Virginia Gazette* for January 8, 1780, advertised that "a person near the college, and well qualified to give satisfaction," had arranged "to furnish breakfast and dinner to any number of students, not exceeding twenty, at the rate of 3000 pounds of tobacco per annum, and at the rate of 2500 pounds, if the number be greater." Inflation had arrived! In 1762 a student had paid £13 per annum for "Board Wood Candles Washing & Tuition," which President Yates said had actually cost the college about £20 for each student per year—the college funds paying the difference.

Jefferson's university plan also clarified the respective powers of Visitors and faculty, which recently had created such animosity. From the President's House, where he was visiting his cousin while serving as a member of Governor Jefferson's council, James Madison, Jr., future President of the United States, wrote his father on December 8,

1779, that by ". . . A New Arrangement of the College here nothing is in future to be taught but the higher & rarer branches of Science. The preliminary studies must therefore be pursued in private Schools or Academies."

President Madison of the college wrote Ezra Stiles at Yale on August 1, 1780, that ". . . The Professorship of Divinity is also abolished. It was formerly instituted for the Purpose of the Church of England, wh[ich] was here established, but it is now thought that Establishment in Favr of any particular Sect are incompatible with the Freedom of a Republic . . ." Despite the disclaimer, Madison's priestly orders and his elevation in 1790 as first Episcopal bishop of Virginia continued to give the college an ecclesiastical character.

The most radical changes in 1779 were the abandonment of required Greek and Latin and the provision of elective courses. The college also made class attendance optional and eliminated residence requirements for degrees. As Madison wrote Yale's Ezra Stiles in August 1780:

> The Doors of the University are open to all, nor is even a knowledge of the Ant. Languages a previous Requisite for Entrance. The Students have the Liberty of attending whom they please . . . The lectures continue from October until April, & from May until August.
>
> The Time of taking Degrees was formerly the same as in Cambridge, but now depends upon the Qualifications of the Candidate.
>
> The number of students is more considerable than heretofore and encreases daily.
>
> We have a well chosen Apparatus wh[ich] cost 500£ Stg. [pounds sterling] made by the best hands in London. Our library may be considered as a good foundation to improve upon. Before this unnatural War, we had formed a Plan of importing annually some of the best modern Books, and among others the Publications of the different Philosophical Societies in Europe, wh[ich] we shall resume whenever it is practical.

The university that Jefferson envisoned included several important educational innovations, but it largely ignored the crucial problem of governmental funds to replace the support of the Crown. In his letter of August 1, 1780, to President Stiles, Madison wrote: "Since the Revolution, its [the college's] former Resources have been almost annihilated. From a Revenue of 5 or 6000£ Stg a year, wc[h] arose principally from Duties on Articles of Commerce, it now depends for its support upon the rent of 2200 acres of land, wc[h] in Time will become considerable, but at present does not afford more than 500£ Sterlg—There is indeed also an Income from Surveys, but not very considerable . . ."

On October 29, 1780, a student wrote that the college was "entirely deserted by every Studt but one or two who are Sick"; President Madison was "talking of resigning his Professorship, & the Studts all turned Soldiers . . ." Virginia was beginning to feel the effects of the war.

On January 18, 1781 after turncoat General Benedict Arnold had begun his southern march, to be joined later by General Cornwallis, the college's Madison wrote his cousin, now attending the Continental Congress in Philadelphia, that "The University is a Desart," its teachers and students "entirely dispersed." He even began reading law under George Wythe with a view to changing his profession. However, Cornwallis's invasion of Williamsburg in June while pursuing General Lafayette's Virginia forces soon interrupted Madison's law studies.

About June 25, 1781 Cornwallis took over the President's House as his headquarters, forcing the Madisons to move to rooms in the Main Building. The Britisher lived in the house about ten days before defeating Lafayette in the battle of Green Spring and moving his army to the British base at Portsmouth and finally to Yorktown. Colonel St. George Tucker wrote from Williamsburg to his wife on July 11, 1781:

> Here [in Williamsburg] they [the British] remained for some Days, and with them Pestilence and Famine took root, and Poverty brought up the Rear. Instead of attempting a florid Description of the Horrors of this Place, I will endeavour to give you an Account of the Situations of a few Individuals with whom you are acquainted. Our Friend Madison and his Lady (they have lost their Son) were turned out of their House to make Room for Lord Cornwallis. Happily the College afforded them an Asylum. They were refused the small Privilege of drawing Water from their own Well. A contemptuous Treatment, with the Danger of Starving were the only Evils he recounted, as none of his Servants left him. The Case was otherwise with Mr. McClurg . . . But that is not all. The Smallpox, which the hellish Polling [plundering] of these infamous Wretches has spread in every Place through which they have passed has now obtained a Crisis throughout the Place so that there is scarcely a Person to be found to nurse those who are most afflicted by it . . . Among the Plagues the British left in Williamsburg, that of Flies is inconceivable. It is impossible to eat, drink, sleep, write, sit still or even walk about in Peace on account of their confounded stings.

In 1778 Madison had an observatory erected at the college for his study of astronomy. Some of his scientific instruments were lost during the British occupation. He later wrote to Jefferson, "I wish we had a barometer, but there is no possibility of getting one here at present. The British robbed me of my Ther & Bar."

Once Williamsburg was in the combat zone, Madison felt the need to move his young family to a safer place. He wrote his brother William, sheriff of Botetourt County, on July 21, 1781: "I find I must at Length remove from this Place. The College is entirely broke up, all Business in my Way at an End, & of course not a Farthing to be made . . ." He left Professor Bellini in charge, observing later that the Italian had "withstood all the Calamities which surrounded him with a Fortitude worthy of an old Roman Descent."

When General Washington reached Williamsburg on September 14 in pursuit of the British, accompanied by General Rochambeau and one or two more officers, French troops were already encamped and waiting for them. Together, the two great armies marched to Yorktown on September 29 and laid siege. The British surrendered on October 19, 1781, but before the surrender Washington found it necessary to requisition use of the college for wounded French soldiers. The Main Building, except for "the Library, the Apparatus Room, & the Rooms of Mr. Bellini," were to be used for enlisted men and the President's House for officers.

When John Blair Jr., rector of the Board of Visitors, replied to Washington's requisition, the American commander wrote from "Camp before York" on October 7, 1781, two days before Cornwallis's surrender:

> You may be assured Sir that nothing but absolute Necessity could induce me to desire to occupy the College with its adjoing Buildings for Military Purposes—I am very sorry to say that the Number of our Sick & Wounded are increasing so fast that Room cannot be found for their Cover & Convenience—In these circumstances I am persuaded, that Mr Bellini will be ready to give up the House you mention . . . I flatter myself also that the good People of this Part of the Country will the more readily submit to a partial & temporary Inconvenience, when they have Reason to hope, that the close of our present Operations will place them in a State of Quiet & Security—which I trust will be lasting.

As first president of the United States, Washington later would appoint John Blair, Jr. to be a justice of the United States Supreme Court.

It was fortunate that Professor Bellini remained on campus, for he was able to negotiate in French with the college's new tenants. "All the French officers went to call on him," one officer wrote, impressed with Bellini's command of "French, Italian, Spanish, and German, besides having a perfect knowledge of English."

While twenty-two French officers were hospitalized there, the President's House burned the night of November 22-23, 1781, a few weeks after Rochambeau had begun to winter his army near Williamsburg, following Cornwallis's surrender. Patients in the house were moved "elsewhere without any accident and lost only a few goods," a contemporary wrote, but President Madison and his wife lost all their household furnishings. Madison lost "every Book and Paper which I had," he wrote Yale's President Stiles.

By June 1782 the treasury of France had provided bills of exchange for "the destruction of the President's House," amounting to £1542 13s. 6d. However, the extensive repairs did not begin until 1784.

The fire left the thick exterior walls still standing, as well as some of the interior, for the lathing was later both replaced and repaired, as was the plastering, according to 1786 accounts left by the contractor who did the work. Some £616 10s. was spent for bricklaying, £774 for carpentry, £124 for "Articles imported," £27 12s. for painting and glazing, which, with nails, paint and oils, grates, and "other sundries" totaled £1579 11s. 8d.

President Madison returned to the college from Botetourt County in the spring of 1782 to be "a Spectator of Misery & Ruin," as he wrote his cousin in Philadelphia. "Our Friend Bellini . . . affords me now Asylum to write you a few Lines, otherwise I know not that I could here scarce find a place." Bellini penned a postscript to "Dearest Mr. James," noting that despite all he had suffered with regard to his friends, and especially "the President and the poor Univeristy, I have not hanged myself."

The college soon rented for its homeless president a frame house on Nicholson Street that had been built by Dr. Archibald Blair, brother of James Blair, and later acquired by Archibald's grandson, John Blair II. There the Madisons remained nearly four years, until the President's house was rebuilt in 1786.

Virginia's Attorney General Edmund Randolph, a son of John Randolph the Tory, reported in July 1782 to James Madison, Jr., at Congress in Philadelphia, that his cousin "was paid very handsomely for his library." Randolph added that citizens of Williamsburg "almost universally" regretted the departure of the French from the town in the summer of 1782. "Such condescension [affability] in commanders, and good order in soldiers were never yet known in any army," he observed.

Although the college remained closed and its Main Building occupied by French enlisted men, four professors nevertheless met on March 17, 1782, and voted an honorary degree of "Doctor of Civil Laws" to General Chastellux, one of Rochambeau's staff who was about to depart on a tour which resulted in his *Travels in North America, 1781-1782,* published in Paris in 1786. Chastellux described William and Mary as:

> a noble establishment which embellishes Williamsburgh, and does honour to Virginia. The beauty of the edifice is surpassed by the richness of its library, and that, still farther, by the distinguished merit of several of the Professors, such as the Doctors Maddison, Wythe, Bellini &c., who may be regarded as living books, at once affording precepts and examples. I must add that the zeal of these Professors has been crowned with the most distinguished success, and that they have already formed many distinguished characters, ready to serve their country in the various departments of government.

Before Rochambeau led his army to Philadelphia in July of 1782 to bid farewell to Congress, he was roundly praised by town and college. The tribute in French from the "Universite" assured "le Cte de Rochambeau" of "la sincere affection" of that institution, the address probably written and presented by Bellini.

From his temporary quarters at the Archibald Blair house, William and Mary's Madison wrote to President Stiles on June 19, 1782 acknowledging two letters from him.

> I have at length returned (about a month past), though with little prospect as yet of re-establishing our ruined affairs . . . It is with great satisfaction that I find the muses still frequent your college and that science will flourish at Yale, though it seems to have deserted us . . . The college is still an hospital and has been such ever since the arrival of the French army, as it was entirely evacuated both by professors and students when the Britons took possession of this part of the country . . . I shd have been able to have given you an acct of several Auroras—but for an Accident which I shall always regret, for the House destined to the use of the President has unfortunately been consumed last winter, and with it every Book and Paper that I had.

After the French departed Madison began preparations to reopen the college. He advertised in Richmond's *Virginia Gazette, or American Advertiser* under the dateline William and Mary, 9 August 1782:

> THE PUBLIC are hereby informed, That the University of William & Mary is now open for the reception of Students: The Commencement of Public Lectures is postponed until the first Monday in October, in order to afford time for those to assemble who wish to profit by them: But the Professors will give instructions privately to those who attend before the above-mentioned time. Many respectable families in town will board Students upon reasonable terms. The inconveniences which have been formerly felt make it necessary to inform the Public that the usual fee will be expected upon entrance.

Preceding the reopening, Rector John Blair, Jr., convened the Visitors on September 2, 1782, "to take under consideration a variety of business, which the situation of the country for some time past has not been permitted to attend to." He referred to the need for money. The bursary was bare, and funds from debts due were needed to repair buildings. Madison published an appeal in James Hayes's Richmond *Virginia Gazette* of August 20, 1782, declaring that "the present situation of the College indispensably" required "a speedy and general collection of what is owed to it." Little money came in, however.

Hard as Virginia had been hit, the revival of the college still seemed possible to Madison and to Rector Blair. The experience of Yale, less affected by the war, showed it could be done. In October 1782 the Connecticut college had more than 200 students. An announcement of the reopening of William and Mary came on August 9, 1782, and on September 7, a writer who signed himself "Senex" wrote in William Hayes's *Virginia Gazette* in Richmond urging Virginians to support it:

> Rouse, then, I beseech you, from these slumbers of ignominy & disgrace. Behold the examples of some of your sister States. Catch from them at least the example you ought to follow. Consider the lost reputation of the once respected Virginia. Reflect deeply on the cause. The remedy lies on your own doors. Resolve liberally to bestow upon your children that institution which your situations will admit & which the nature of your government requires. Ignorance and the want of virtue will render your country despicable and unhappy, whilst with the opposite qualities she may become the wonder, the envy of the whole world.
>
> . . . I see that the University [William and Mary] is soon again to

> renew a course of instruction, which, before the interruptions of the enemy, promised most solid advantages to the country; and therefore I esteem it the duty of every citizen to give all possible encouragement to so valuable an institution. It is with joy that I am preparing my remaining sons for that place, with the anxious hope that I may yet live to enjoy the greatest of all rewards, that of seeing them return, a comfort to myself, and an ornament to their country. SENEX

However, bankrupt Virginia needed more time. Few students and little money came the college's way during the first years of its reopening. Bursar Robert Andrews took to *The Virginia Gazette* in 1782 to urge surveyors to pay their required fees and ex-students to pay debts, "the current Situation of the College indispensibly requiring a speedy and general collection of what is owed."

The faculty advertised for sale two houses between the Main Building and the college barn behind it, along with unused lumber after building of the college quadrangle had been abandoned. It also sold "Negroes not employed about the College" and rented Brafferton Hall for £50 a year.

President and Mrs. Madison entertained young Isaac Stiles, son of Yale's president, who was considering a career in "some one of the Southern States," while living in their rented Archibald Blair house in the fall of 1783. At that time the college had a student body of eighty, a faculty of five, and courses in law, medicine, languages, philosophy, science, and mathematics.

Madison wrote that the war had fortunately spared the college's library of "ancient Authors." At the request of the Marquis de Chastellux, King Louis XVI had sent 200 books "in beautiful Editions" from France. However, Madison wrote to Jefferson in 1785 that many of these "were ruined before they came to us," but the college "did not beg for more."

After the reopening, the faculty remained briefly as it had been recruited for Jefferson's university in 1779: Madison, Wythe, Andrews, Bellini, and McClurg. Thus it stood in 1782 when the president and professors bestowed the degree of doctor of laws upon Jefferson. Sometime between 1783 and 1784 a German traveler wrote of William and Mary as:

> . . . the only College in all the Southern colonies at this time and has a corp of Professors, teaching Theology, [sic. no theology] Law, Medicine, languages, Philosophy, and Mathematics. The

> Professor of the Medical school is Dr. Maclurg, author of a valuable treatise on the Gall. The present number of students is about 50. Some of them lodge in comfortable rooms in the College, while the rest lodge and board in the city for from 36 to 40 Virg. pounds per annum. The total annual expenses of students, including lectures need not to exceed 100 Virg. Pounds (333 Spanish Dollars). Doctor degrees of all the various schools are awarded here, yet most young men after having ended their course of studies here, prefer finishing their education at some English or Scottish University and there to graduate with high honours.

Unfortunately the faculty was soon depleted, along with some of the new curriculum. Dr. McClurg moved to Richmond in 1783 or 1784, where he was several times mayor and in 1787 replaced another Virginia delegate to the Constitutional Convention in Philadelphia. Edmund Randolph, writing a friend about the college in 1792, explained that "the emoluments" were "too low to invite men of genius to the different chairs." He noted that McClurg "was the lecturer in anatomy and the theory and practice of physic, but the office had not pecuniary allurements to detain such uncommon abilities in the functions of mere, abstract science." He added that he ventured "to challenge the United States with the talents of bishop Madison, the president, as a natural philosopher. But he lingers at college for very peculiar reasons, and cannot be replaced by any successor, whose literary merit would not be questionable."

The aging Wythe quit as law professor and moved to Richmond in 1789 after becoming chancellor of Virginia's High Court of Chancery there. Jefferson wrote that "Mr. Wythe has abandoned the College of Wm & Mary disgusted with some conduct of the professors, & particularly of the ex-professor Bracken, & perhaps too with himself for having suffered himself to be too much irritated with that. The Visitors will try to condemn what gave him offense & press him to return: otherwise it is over with the College."

No professor of medicine was hired in McClurg's place, and the medical instruction begun at Jefferson's behest in 1779 abruptly ended. However, St. George Tucker succeeded Wythe as law teacher in 1791, continuing the college's most popular course. Thanks to the law professorship, the college from Revolution to Civil War was distinguished by outstanding graduates who entered public life. Jefferson pointed this out when he wrote of the college from Paris in August 1785 as ". . . the place where are collected together all the young men (of Virginia) under preparation for public life. They are under the direction (most of them) of a Mr. Wythe, one of the most virtuous of characters, and whose sentiments on the subject of [opposition to] slavery are unequivocal." Similarly, when the Reverend Jedidiah Morse of Massachusetts described the collegians in a letter of 1786 to President Stiles of Yale, he wrote that "most of them are Law Students." Concerning William and Mary, Samuel Miller declared in *A Retrospect of the Eighteenth Century,* published in New York in 1803, that ". . . there is probably no College in the United States in which political science is studied with so much ardour, and in which it is considered so preeminently a favourite object, as in this."

The "ardour" that Miller observed was the ambition of men aspiring to public life, as evidenced by Richard Bland, Dabney Carr, Peyton Randolph, Thomas Jefferson, James Monroe, and other William and Mary alumni. In the sixty years after the college began teaching law in 1779, eighteen of Virginia's thirty governors had attended William and Mary, most studying law. The most conspicuous was John Tyler, who became President of the United States. "They were the pick of Virginia," wrote Tyler's son, Lyon Gardiner Tyler, "and there were very few among them who did not make name and fame."

Lyon Tyler also pointed out that William and Mary in Madison's presidency was the first American college to "establish the elective and honor systems"—innovations criticized in their early years by some northern observers, but later to become widespread.

Madison and his faculty attracted students from a wide area, including western Virginia, North Carolina, Maryland, and Kentucky. Some of them were privileged to view the cosmos through Madison's observatory, which he had built in 1778 and reopened after the Revolution. "The night before last I did not go to bed at all, being with Mr. Madison at College viewing through the Telescope an Eclipse of the moon," wrote George Blow in 1804 to his father in Norfolk.

One explanation of Madison's success as a college president and teacher was clearly his close relationship with his students. John Tyler, once a Madison scholar, wrote that "He lived on terms of close intimacy with his students. His manner to the inmates of the College was kind and parental, and his reproof was uttered in the gentlest of terms."

More than any other man, the gentle, philosophic Madison kept the college alive through the Revolution and beyond.

# 10

# *The Irreplaceable James Madison*

THE imprint of William and Mary lay on many Virginians who helped to win the American Revolution. Samuel Eliot Morison called them "The Great Generation," a bright array of talent in a colony only 169 years after it had been settled in 1607.

Typical of pre-Revolutionary graduates of the college was its president, James Madison, referred to after 1790 as Bishop Madison to distinguish him from his kinsman of the same name who helped draft the Constitution and became the fourth President of the United States.

The college's Madison was reared on an Augusta County farm, son of the John Madison who was the first clerk of Augusta County after it was formed in 1745 from Orange County. John and his wife, Agatha Strother Madison, had eight sons and three daughters. One son, Thomas, married Patrick Henry's sister. Another son and two daughters married children of General Andrew Lewis of Augusta County, kinsman of George Washington and victor over the Shawnees at Point Pleasant. Another brother, George, was governor of Kentucky in 1813.

When James Madison, Jr., second cousin of the college's Madison and future president of the United States, arrived in Williamsburg on January 13, 1778, he was invited to stay in the President's House of the college. He wrote his father ten days later that "at the earnest invitation of my Kinsman Mr. Madison have taken my lodgings in a Room of the President's house, which is a much better accom[mo]dation than I could have promised myself." The day after his arrival he was sworn in as a member of the Governor's Council.

Relations between the two Madisons were obviously close. Williamsburg's Madison often visited his cousin at his home, Montpelier, in Orange County, where Jefferson was also a frequent guest.

Williamsburg's Madison was also a friend of Jefferson, with whom he compared astronomical observations. In the years 1778-1779 when Montpelier's Madison was frequently in Williamsburg, his cousin was often in his observatory near the President's House. Jefferson wrote in 1784 that he and the Williamsburger were "keeping observations for a comparison of climate."

From his observatory Madison watched an eclipse of the sun on June 24, 1778, comparing results with David Rittenhouse of Philadelphia. William and Mary's president wrote Jefferson of the "total Darkness," resulting in "something awful in Appearance which all Nature assumed. You could not determine your most intimate Acquaintance at 20 yds. distance. Lightening Buggs were seen as at Night."

Madison's observations on the eclipse of the moon on November 18, 1789 were read before the American Philosophical Society of Philadelphia, which printed a number of his other papers on astronomical and scientific subjects.

The two Madisons were lifelong correspondents. The nation's president later wrote of his cousin: "He was particularly distinguished by a benevolence, a politeness of mind, and a courtesy of manner . . . [of] intellectual power and diversified learning . . . He was a devoted friend of our Revolution and to the purest principles of a Government founded on the rights of man." Montpelier's Madison believed his cousin was responsible for a "renaissance" of William and Mary after the Revolution.

Once, while the president-to-be stayed with the college's head in Williamsburg, his hat was stolen from an open window of the President's House. As he told it: "Well sir, I was staying at Bishop Madison's in Williamsburg (he was not yet Bishop, by the way), and my hat was stolen out of a window in which I had laid it. It was about a mile from the house to the Governor's Palace, and I was kept from going to the latter for two days, by the impossibility of getting a hat of any kind. At last, however, I obtained one from a little Frenchman who sold snuff—very coarse—an extremely small crown and broad brim, and it was a subject of great merriment to my friends."

On May 1, 1779 the young college president married Sarah Taite of Williamsburg. They lost their first son in the summer of 1781. They had a second son, James Catesby Madison, born in September 1782, and a daughter, Sarah, who married Robert G. Scott of Richmond. Mrs. Madison descended from John Catesby, the naturalist, and was a granddaughter of Dr. William Cocke, physician and widely beloved secretary of state for Virginia, who died in 1720.

After the President's House had been repaired following the 1781 fire, the president and his family moved back to it during July 1786. As their original furnishings had been lost in the fire, they brought what they had acquired while living in the Archibald Blair house, bought with money reimbursed by the French government.

Madison and his faculty were beset in postwar years by the rise of student lawlessness, common to American colleges after the Revolution. Fanned by the radical spirit of the French Revolution, students proved difficult to control. Drinking and gambling increased, and students often brought dogs and horses with them to college.

Landon Carter of Sabine Hall complained to his diary: "My grandson Landon after a 6 weeks' stay at home set off again to the College. I beleive he has only improved his talk for trifling and lounging there. It is a Pity, a fine Genius ruined by a bad example at home;"

Students roomed in the Main Building, but some parents preferred to have their sons lodge with Williamsburg families. Congressman Henry Tazewell arranged for his son, Littleton Waller Tazewell, to live with the Madisons. St. George Tucker's son, Nathaniel Beverley Tucker, described student excesses in 1802 in a letter to his half-brother, Congressman John Randolph of Roanoke: ". . . The disipation which at present prevails, exceeds that of your day. This you may perhaps regard as an impossibility . . . revelry . . . is now exchanging Mint Julip in the Morning, Gin Twist in the middle of the day, & Wine at dinner and at night, with the accompanyment of cards. That I might no longer consider myself as a member of this respectable body, Papa has been so kind as to remove me from the college, and give me Old Coke [Sir Edward Coke's *Institutes on Littleton's Tenures*] to go upon for the present."

The physical decline of the town began to be evident in the years after the seat of government moved to Richmond, followed by the town's two newspapers, both called *The Virginia Gazette,* and many of its lawyers, physicians, tradesmen, craftsmen, and tavern-keepers. The change was reflected in the lowered morale of the college.

New Englanders, coming from thrifty townships, were especially critical of Williamsburg in these years. Noah Webster, the Connecticut lexicographer, came to lecture at the college for a week in 1785, describing it as "large and elegant" but Virginians as having "much pride, little money on hand, great contempt for Northern people, & amazing fondness for Dissipation."

Jedidiah Morse, a New England congregationalist minister, wrote disparagingly of the town in his *American Universal Geography,* published in Boston in 1793. He misunderstood the college's elective system and was oblivious of the upheaval created by disestablishment of the Anglican church in Revolutionary Virginia, which had not been a problem in New England nor in other colonies without an established church.

President Madison would have been dismayed had he read what Morse wrote to President Stiles of Yale after Morse visited the college in 1786:

> Williamsburg is a place of about 200 decayed houses. The College, which is a hugh [sic], irregular pile of buildings—stands at the West and the Capitol, at the east end of a Main street a mile in length . . . There are about 30 Students . . . most of them Law Students . . . The Professors, successively lecture once a day—the Students attend or not as they please . . . no public Prayers Morning nor Evening no recitations, no public speaking—no examinations . . . the whole of the Professors' business is to compose a Sett of Lectures upon his particular Science, and read them over to the Students once a Year . . . The business of the Student, is to attend daily on these Lectures, if he pleases . . . or, if disposed, he may spend it skeiting, in dancing, or in the tavern at the Gaming table without Control.—Doctor Madison is Professor of Divinity, but he never exhibits lectures upon it because there is not one Student.

Morse was obviously unaware that the divinity school had closed in 1779 and that Madison was not divinity professor. His account, embellished upon in his *American Universal Geography,* was not the general view of the college. More typical was the report of a student from Kentucky, David Yancey, in a letter to a friend on June 6, 1795. He wrote that he attended "Mr. Madison's lectures, with which I am enamored, and without which I think no man can boast of a good education . . . Study is our principal amusement but sometimes we go out and take a game of fives against the old house. If a person comes here for improvement he must study hard, but if pleasure be his object, it is a fine place for spending money as ever I saw. . . "

Another student view was given by Benjamin Crowninshield of Massachusetts in a letter of May 30, 1804 to Dr. B. Lynde Oliver: "As I was yesterday walking in the college garden in company with Bishop Madison, a little boy brought me your letter. . . The pleasing manner of this place would be sufficient to keep me here, but the advantages of the college, I should think would keep me here forever."

After having closed its grammar school for thirteen years, the college concluded in 1792 that it was necessary to train applicants for college. Its revival disappointed Jefferson and supporters of his university curriculum. Meanwhile the Board of Visitors did little to find new financial support or to stimulate enrollment, especially after 1789, when Rector John Blair, Jr., was named by President Washington to the United States Supreme Court, in Philadelphia. Madison wrote Jefferson in January 1800 that "the Visitors seem to have abandoned the College. We have not been able to obtain a meeting of them for 5 years."

Clearly James Madison was the most versatile scholar of the college's first century. Besides his administration, teaching, and research, he had studied chemistry and anatomy in London in 1775-1776. He also served as rector of James City Parish from 1777 onward, performed military duty, and was versed in the law. In 1774 he was elected secretary and curator of the Society for the Advancement of Useful Knowledge, of which John Page was President and George Wythe was Vice President. Ten years later he and Professor Robert Andrews ran the boundary line between Virginia and Pennsylvania, by appointment of Jefferson during his governorship.

The disestablishment of the Anglican church in Virginia created Madison's severest problems, both as president of the college and as a clergyman. Madison was active in early conventions of the Episcopal clergy, and he was elected Bishop of Virginia in 1790, an earlier choice, Dr. David Griffith, finding himself unable to go to London for consecration.

Thus in 1790 James Madison went to Lambeth Palace to be consecrated by the Archbishop of Canterbury, returning to Williamsburg to serve simultaneously as president of the college and as first bishop of the Episcopal Diocese of Virginia. In his combined role he retained for the college useful Episcopal support, though some churchmen at first regarded him as "lukewarm."

One of these critics was a young postulant, William Meade, who came from northern Virginia to the President's House in 1811 to sit for his canonical examination by Bishop Madison and then to be ordained in Bruton Parish Church. To zealous William Meade, who would become Virginia's third bishop in 1829, Madison at first seemed a spiritless shepherd. He later concluded Madison had been maligned. "Infidelity, indeed, was then rife in the State," Meade later wrote, "and the College of William and Mary was regarded as the hotbed of French politics and religion."

Student protests of college discipline led to campus riots in 1802 and 1808, after undergraduates had been expelled for infractions. During the 1808 outburst the President's House had to be guarded against threats to break its windows, a trial for the mild president and his wife.

Madison died at the President's House of a heart ailment at sixty-three on March 6, 1812. He was survived by his wife, his son James Catesby Madison, and his daughter Sarah Randolph Madison Scott. Though ailing for months, he met his classes till two days before he died. Like Blair and Thomas Dawson, he is thought to have spent his last illness in the large bedroom of the President's House, overlooking the college yard and Duke of Gloucester Street. He was buried in a vault under the college chapel.

If a man of Madison's caliber could do no more to revive the fortunes of William and Mary, what was to become of it? William Nelson, a judge of Virginia's General Court who was professor of law at the college from 1804 to 1811, succeeding George Wythe and St. George Tucker, asked that question upon Madison's death:

> He performed the arduous duties of an instructor in the College over which he presided, for a period of nearly forty years, and the magnitude of his abilities, together with the zeal of their application, caused him to be regarded as the chief pillar of its prosperity. The support he lent to this ancient seminary of learning is now at an end, and there is cause of serious apprehension that the fabric itself will fall a victim to premature delapidation. May the Guardian Angels of science avert this catastrophe by furnishing a successor who shall possess all those attributes of heart and understanding.

It would be a long time before the President's House would see the equal of James Madison.

# 11

# *The Lure of Richmond*

THE decision of Professor James McClurg in 1783 or 1784 to move to Richmond and the consequent cessation of medical studies led to an issue that was to embroil William and Mary for a hundred years: Why not move the college to Richmond? It was a controversial idea, pitting Richmond against Williamsburg, but Virginia's population was clearly moving inland. To Virginians who desired a university to train doctors and lawyers, moving the college to the capital made sense. There it would be close to the General Assembly, to physicians, and to law courts.

The idea was first mentioned in Madison's presidency, when Edmund Randolph wrote a friend in 1792 that some people in "the high lands" were afraid to send sons to Williamsburg because of "the moisture and heat of its atmosphere." He foresaw some "violent act of legislature" to erect a "university, in the neighbourhood of Richmond."

Similarly, Jefferson in 1813 was to criticize John Bracken's election as president in a letter to William Short: ". . . Wm & Mary College, removed to a central and healthy part of our state, with such a man as Correa [the Portuguese scholar, Correa de Serra, in Virginia at that time] for its president instead of the simpleton Bracken, would afford a comfortable look into futurity . . ."

Bracken's election by the Visitors in 1812 was due either to the Visitors' misjudgment or possibly to the influence of his Burwell connections. The portly, middle-aged cleric was a litigious man who had already troubled the college. He had brought suit against it to regain his job as grammar master, abolished in the 1779 university reorganization, and to recover his lost salary. Yet the Visitors—possibly influenced by his position as rector of Bruton and as chaplain to the House of Delegates—elected him a few hours after Bishop Madison's funeral in March 1812.

Complaints about their choice were numerous. James Semple, a Visitor who had opposed it, complained by letter to Jefferson. He felt that the college, by electing a minister for reasons of precedent, "has sustained a rude shock in the appointment of Mr. Bracken to the Presidency. If the Gordian knot cannot be untied, I woud at once cut it. The best interests of our Country should not be jeopardized for the sake of preserving the words of our Royal charter, nor should delicacy towards an individual who disregards the publick wishes restrain me for a moment . . . The connection between a Litterary Institution and the Church seems to be as preposterous and absurd as the connection between the Church and State." Semple objected that ministers still ran the college despite Jefferson's attempt to secularize it.

Portly, stubborn Dr. Bracken was about sixty-seven when he moved into the President's House in 1812. His wife, the former Sarah (Sally) Burwell, presumably had died, for no reference to her occurs in his two-year presidency or thereafter. He appears to have lived in the house alone, for his children, thirty-three-year-old John Bracken, Jr., and his daughters Julia and Sarah were married.

Bracken was a busy and sociable man, serving outside the college and church in important civic and business roles. The notice of his marriage to Sally Burwell in Purdie's *Virginia Gazette* of September 30, 1776, was evidence of their standing in Virginia:

Could I on airy pinions soar,
Where mighty poets flew before,
How would I, in unpolish'd lays,
Rehearse this happy couple's praise!
My tight-strung lyre should sing the fair,
With whom but few can well compare,
For modesty and sense combin'd,
These valu'd qualities of mind.
Of Bracken too my muse should sing,
His praise should echo from my string;
Religion, virtue, all around,
And morals good, should loudly sound.
. . . .

The Brackens lived well, aided in 1777 by a settlement from Sally's father, Carter Burwell, of more than £713 in the first year of their marriage. They had moved soon thereafter to the fine dwelling on Francis Street now known as the Lightfoot house, which had been the townhouse of William Byrd III before his suicide in 1777. John Bracken sold the house in 1802, ten years after the college had reopened its grammar school in 1792 and rehired Bracken to teach. Bracken and his family probably soon moved into the Brafferton, which he was renting as his residence in 1804 and possibly earlier.

For most of John Bracken's life he had taught, either as grammar master at college, as a private tutor, or as master of a grammar school started in 1784 by Walker Maury in the abandoned Capitol. While the college grammar school was suspended from 1779 to 1792, Bracken in 1787 took over Maury's school and ran it until the college grammar school reopened. Obviously he enjoyed teaching.

Bracken's salaries as president and as Bruton's rector enabled him to increase his wife's inherited fortune. He was a director of the Dismal Swamp Land Company with George Washington, and he was elected Williamsburg's mayor in 1796 and 1800. From 1790 to 1791 he was president of the board of the Lunatic Asylum, and in 1793 he received a doctorate of divinity from the college. Bracken's Pond near Yorktown bears his name.

Little is known of Bracken's birth and education in England until he was licensed by the Bishop of London in July 1772 to be rector in Amelia County. Once in Virginia, he was elected in June 1773 as rector of Bruton after the incumbent, the Reverend Josiah Johnson, had died. However, his election had been contested by the Reverend Samuel Henley, professor of moral philosophy at the college, who thought he rather than Bracken deserved the job.

The two clergymen engaged in unseemly vituperation in the two *Virginia Gazettes* from 1773 to 1774. One reader finally advised the editors "to get your Bruton Parish Disputants, if they intend appearing again in the Gazette, to make Use of Hebrew, or some Language that we common Folks don't understand . . ." Like James Blair, Bracken seemed to enjoy controversy.

Bracken's later life was clouded by his abortive election in 1812 to succeed James Madison as Bishop of Virginia. He was chosen by the church's convention in Richmond by a vote of 22 to 3, but three opposing clergymen publicly declared him too old to rally the demoralized church. After thinking it over, Bracken in 1813 "gave in his resignation as Bishop-elect" at the next year's Episcopal convention.

He apparently agreed the bishop should be younger.

In 1813 Bracken suspended "publick examinations" at the college when its upper rooms were occupied briefly by the 52nd Virginia Regiment after a British naval force had entered Hampton Roads and attacked Norfolk and Hampton in the War of 1812. Hearing that British marines had moved inland and were about to enter Williamsburg—a rumor that soon proved groundless—St. George Tucker wrote in derision that ". . . the whole company . . . made such haste to get out, that men, officers and all, not able to see their way in the dark, stumbled and rolled down the long flight of stairs leading to the ground floor." Williamsburg was spared, but war again scattered the students.

Several times Bracken's stubbornness brought him into conflict with faculty and Visitors. In 1814 the Visitors finally forced him to resign. The aging widower probably moved then to a two story frame house on Francis Street, now called the Bracken house, where he lived until his death in 1818. Bracken was eulogized in *The Richmond Enquirer* as "benevolent in his disposition, just in his dealings, warm in his friendships, and kind to the distressed." He was buried in the Burwell graveyard at Carter's Grove.

A derisive glimpse of Bracken in old age was penned by eighteen-year-old Hardress Waller of Williamsburg in writing his sister about the wedding on February 23, 1815, of a cousin, William Waller, to Mary Griffin of York County. The wedding was to take place at seven in the evening, but when the bridegroom and Hardress reached Mary's house just before wedding time, the Reverend Mr. Bracken had not arrived with the marriage license, which had been entrusted to him. Hardress wrote:

> We started and got to York and lo Mr Bracken alias (the Round Bellied Vicar) could not be found any where [.] Majr Griffin began to be very uneasy and sent off a servant to look for him [.] about Eight oClock he came in all covered with mud and water the greatest sight you ever saw—It seems the Worthy old gentleman with Miss Elizabeth Gatliff in the gigg with him had started from Wmsburg at eleven Oclock in the morning [.] being in his Cups he took the Martens Hundred Road and went to the [Carter's] Grove before he discovered he had lost his way, he then turned back and got almost to Mr Semples farm [.] he there upon a dead level upset the Gigg and broke it and fell on Miss Elizabeth Gatliff and almost killed her. We had grand doings there and Majr Griffin gave us some Wine which he said was the age of his daughter which he had saved for Her wedding.

To replace Bracken, the Board of Visitors went outside the clergy for the first time. In 1814 it chose physician Dr. John Augustine Smith, who had graduated from the college in 1800 and, after medical training in London, had in 1807 joined the faculty of the College of Physicians and Surgeons in New York.

Smith's credentials were excellent, but his interest lay in medicine rather than in academic subjects. Smith taught moral and political philosophy at the college. He was a small, quick, active man who had close ties to the Nelson family of Yorktown. He was the son of an Episcopal minister of Westmoreland County, and his attendance at William and Mary had been paid for by General Thomas Nelson, who had succeeded Jefferson as governor of Virginia. In 1809 Smith had married Letitia Lee of the Stratford Lees, and they had nine children before and during their twelve years in the President's House.

To provide premedical training, a professorship of chemistry was established with Smith's election, and "chemical and philosophical apparatus" was brought from Philadelphia. In 1821–1822 the college reestablished a course in theology, with the Reverend Reuel Keith as professor of "Divinity, History, and Humanity."

Smith complained on his arrival at the college that he found "not a single Lecture-Room properly fitted up . . . & the whole establishment . . . tending rapidly to ruin." Accordingly, he had three classrooms and an apparatus room put in order, a chemistry laboratory built, and the Main Building interior refinished.

The President's House, alive with the Smiths' children, did not "require the expenditure of a large sum, though some reparations to it are necessary," Smith told Visitors. Between 1815 and 1818 he replaced the rotting outside kitchen for $122.06, paid a Philadelphia stonemason $350 for "Stone Steps for the President's House," and "put down" a "Dial Post" or sundial in his front yard. In 1825 the college decreed that "cattle shall not be turned into The Inclosures before or in the rear of the College at night."

In Smith's first year enrollment rose, but possibly because of "a more liberal plan with respect to the conferring of degrees" in 1821—two years for a Bachelor of Arts degree and three for a Master's—William and Mary had only thirty-five students in 1824.

Jefferson's hopes for this alma mater waned as he developed plans for a state university at Charlottesville. In 1813 he had written William Short to deplore John Bracken's election and to prefer as the college's site "a central and healthy part of our state." On his birthday in 1820 he wrote Short enthusiastically of his new university plan, noting that the opposition "of our *alma mater,* William and Mary, is not of much weight. She must descend into the secondary rank of academies of preparation for the University . . ."

President Smith thought the college should be moved to Richmond, and he spent his last years in office trying to relocate it. At a meeting of Visitors on July 5, 1824, he warned that "The University of Virginia, which is just about to go into operation, can not but affect us." He saw one alternative, "& that is a transfer of the establishment to Richmond."

However, the Visitors wanted the school in Williamsburg, as did the townspeople. When the issue was submitted by Dr. Smith in 1824 to the General Assembly, citizens of Williamsburg met at the Williamsburg courthouse to adopt a remonstrance against the move. One observer wrote from Richmond on January 12, 1825, that the subject of the "removal of William and Mary Coledge has produced a great deal of excitement in the Legislature. They have had Dr. Smith the President a very smart fluent little fellow frequently before the Committee . . . The opponents to the removal say the coledge has declined in consequence to Some of his philosophical opinions."

The chief stumbling block to Smith's hoped-for removal was alumnus John Tyler, who served as governor of Virginia from 1825 to 1827. Tyler continued to oppose removal efforts until his death in 1862. These included attempts made in the administration of Robert Saunders from 1846 to 1848 and after the Main Building burned in 1859. The move was again proposed and defeated in 1865 after the Civil War ended.

Like the Blairs and Randolphs earlier, the Tylers were influential in the nineteenth-century college. John Tyler's sister, Anne, was married to Judge James Semple, who taught law there from 1820 to 1824, and two daughters married leading Williamsburg men: Elizabeth to William Waller of the Benjamin Waller house and Alice to the Reverend Henry Denison, rector of Bruton Parish.

When John Tyler and the General Assembly defeated the move in 1825 they destroyed President Smith's last hopes to relocate and revive the school. Understandably, when the physician learned that the College of Physicians and Surgeons in New York would be reorganized, he obtained his former professorship there. In his last report to the Visitors at the commencement program in July 1826, he reported only nineteen students, two "resident Graduates," and the revived grammar school. On his return to New York, John Augustine Smith was eventually elected president of the medical college, which later became part of Columbia University.

Williamsburg found comfort in reports that the university at Charlottesville had its troubles too, chiefly in finding faculty. John Page, Jr., of Rosewell, an alumnus and son of governor Page, wrote from Williamsburg on October 12, 1825, to St. George Tucker, retired as the college's second professor of law and living in Nelson County:

> Perhaps you may wish to know my opinion of the University of Virginia . . . The fact is, that there is much less taught (at this time) in the University than in Wm & Mary College. There are two professorships in that institution which we do not have in this viz. of Medicine and Modern Languages. Without questioning the use of the first, I will offset it by the Professorship of Law in this College . . . With regard to Languages generally I think that you will agree with me, in believing they can never be *properly* taught by public lecture. . . . Here the Ancient Languages are taught by *lesson* and by *application* . . . I am clearly of opinion that if the public were well informed of the actual condition of each, and disposed to patronise Literature equally where ever it was to be found in the State William and Mary would have nothing to fear from the University.

But Page was too optimistic. The choice of Jefferson's college as the state university clearly hurt the three existing Virginia colleges—Hampden-Sydney and Washington College as well as William and Mary. With Virginia's population and wealth moving upland, the school in Williamsburg was fated to decline further. Its future in 1826 was bleak.

# 12

## *Back to the Clergy*

THE Board of Visitors—all of them Episcopalians—were pleased to see the revival of the Episcopal church in Virginia after the Reverend Richard Channing Moore of New York had become the second Bishop of Virginia in 1814, upon the death of Bishop Madison in 1812 and the declination of that office by John Bracken. It was a sign that the pre-Revolutionary Anglican leadership in Virginia was reviving.

Hoping to renew the college's theological courses, President John Augustine Smith and the Visitors in 1821 had engaged the Reverend Reuel Keith as professor of divinity, history, and humanity. However, the Episcopal Diocese of Virginia decided in 1823 to open a seminary in Alexandria, and Keith, who then had only one divinity student at William and Mary, moved to Alexandria as the first seminary professor.

One of the young Episcopal ministers who helped persuade Richard Channing Moore to come to Virginia from New York had been William Wilmer. Wilmer had been rector of St. Paul's in Alexandria since 1812 and an ally of the Reverend William Meade in founding the Virginia Episcopal Seminary there. Like Meade, Wilmer who had been born in Maryland, had worked to revive the church in the Old Dominion. The election of Wilmer as president of William and Mary in 1826 as Augustine Smith's successor was welcomed by Bishop Moore, Meade, and other Episcopal leaders who had been his co-workers.

William Wilmer was forty-four when he moved from Alexandria into the President's House in 1826. Accompanying him and his wife, Anne Brice Fitzhugh, were several of his eight children from his three marriages. He was soon elected rector of Bruton, for he was a vigorous preacher. Among the five faculty chairs, he took over that of moral philosophy.

He found the college once again preponderantly a grammar school. Of sixty-one students at the session ending in July 1826, forty were grammar scholars and only twenty-one collegians. Several of Wilmer's sons attended grammar school, taught by the well-liked Dabney Browne, the grammar master. Under a 1825 statute, the grammar master or professor of humanity was to furnish board and lodging for his students. The Brafferton was turned over to the steward as a dining room for the college students.

Wilmer had been in office a year when he died in the President's House on July 24, 1827. The faculty proposed that he be honored by burial beneath the chapel, but Mrs. Wilmer preferred that it be under the chancel in Bruton. Wilmer had been a popular churchman, but his brief tenure at the college left little impact. One of his sons, the Reverend George Wilmer, later returned to Williamsburg to teach at the college. Another, William Wilmer, Jr., became bishop of Alabama.

To succeed Wilmer, the Board of Visitors chose fifty-two-year-old Adam Empie, who had been born and educated in New York, where he had been ordained and served in the Episcopal ministry before accepting a parish in Wilmington, North Carolina. Apparently a widower when he arrived in Williamsburg, Empie was accompanied by a son, John J. Empie, who attended the college, and a daughter, Susan, who later married Professor Morgan Smead. Empie was elected rector of Bruton and served in that capacity from 1828 to 1836.

Empie's nine years at the college were free of the divisions suffered by John Augustine Smith. Empie collected the *Laws and Regulations of the College . . .* including new statutes passed in 1830, and had them printed. He had the chapel repaired in 1831 and reopened "with as much effect as might reasonably have been anticipated." He was careful to see that prayers were held daily in the chapel before the first lectures. Enrollment during his nine years ranged from 58 to 113, the drop in 1833–1834 to 58 reflecting the suspension of law courses between the departure of Professor James Semple in 1833 and the arrival of Professor Nathaniel Beverley Tucker a year later.

Empie was allowed to "keep his cows in the back yard of the College," though the college steward, residing in the Brafferton across the yard, was required to remove his livestock and "his Stable yard out

Photographs by Thomas L. Williams

*Four nineteenth-century presidents were Thomas R. Dew, top left; Robert Saunders, top right; Benjamin Ewell, bottom left; and Bishop John Johns, bottom right.*

of the College enclosure" to the college farm on Jamestown Road. A familiar painting of these years shows cows grazing on the campus while men in stovepipe hats converse nearby.

A problem of Empie's presidency was the flooding which plagued College Corner after rains. Water collected around the President's House, the Brafferton, and on adjoining roads. On Richmond Road it formed a pond whose bullfrogs disturbed sleepers in the "Frogpond Tavern," as locals called an inn near College Corner.

The stagnant waters around the President's House were suspected of causing undiagnosed fevers for several presidents and members of their families had become ill. The faculty called this to the attention of Visitors in 1830 and in 1831 reporting that: "Some members of the Presidents family having been long & very ill last fall & there being reason to believe that this & the other cases of sickness usual here from year to year have been caused in part by the ponds of water constantly collected on Jamestown, & Richmond roads in the vicinity of the Brafferton and President's House the Society have thought proper to cause these ponds to be drained."

It was an old problem, going back to the first years of the President's House. Some identified it as "summer sickness," which coastal Southerners attributed to heat, humidity, mosquitoes, and foul water during the "dog days" of July and August. Jefferson had questioned Williamsburg's healthfulness in summer, and others had labeled it "feverish." Some tidewater families were reluctant to spend July and August at home and journeyed upland to the springs.

Faulty drainage at College Corner actually dated back to the beginning of the college yard in 1695. To flatten the campus, laborers had filled in ravines which cut through the triangular plateau on which the Main Building had been placed. However, the builders had failed to substitute adequate drainage to permit a runoff of rain water.

Corrective drains were built in 1705 and repaired in 1784 and 1786, but the problem persisted. As one William and Mary president put it, "the President's House was built over a mud puddle," as was the Brafferton.

In an effort to eliminate the problem in 1831, the Board of Visitors asked Empie and Professor Dabney Browne to investigate. They proposed a plan "with a view to promote the health of the tenants of Brafferton & the President's House &c," and the college engaged Mr. Gresham, its steward, to supervise the work. In July 1834 "a partition fence" was built around the president's yard and a gate from the Brafferton was closed and replaced by "a stile or steps." The formality of the campus was being sacrificed to the needs of the times.

In June 1834 a tornado severely damaged the Main Building and other college structures, greatly increasing expenditures for repairs. The President's House suffered a broken window and sash, and two dozen broken window panes. A cellar cap, privy, and attic door were also destroyed.

Students behaved no better as the century wore on. Empie had to put up with the parading of a horse "through the upper passages of the college" [Main Building] in 1832, and another "poor old horse" three years later was forced "up the Steps into the second Story of the college" to be "introduced" into a student's room.

William and Mary grew more sectional in the 1820s as antislavery sentiment in the North rose. During the Missouri Compromise debates in Congress in 1820 and 1821, support for slavery and states' rights hardened in Williamsburg. Hopes for Virginia's emancipation of its slaves were killed when Nat Turner led his insurrection in Southampton County in 1831. After William Lloyd Garrison launched the abolitionist movement the same year, several of Empie's professors repudiated the antislavery principles of Jefferson, Wythe, and St. George Tucker, and by the 1830s William and Mary became a center of states' rights thought.

The most vocal advocates of slavery on Empie's faculty were Thomas Roderick Dew, an 1820 graduate who became professor of history and political law in 1826, and Nathaniel Beverley Tucker, son of St. George, who taught law from 1834 to 1851. A third, who joined the faculty in 1833, was mathematician Robert Saunders, of Williamsburg, a son-in-law of the late Governor John Page. All were articulate speakers who contributed to sectional debate.

Empie's faculty also gained two notable scientists. One was William Barton Rogers, a graduate of William and Mary, who was to charter the Massachusetts Institute of Technology in 1861. The other was John Millington, who in 1835 succeeded Rogers when he went to the University of Virginia. Millington taught chemistry and natural philosophy from 1835 to 1848. While at William and Mary he wrote a popular textbook, *Elements of Civil Engineering,* which gained national circulation.

In the 1840s John Millington's son, Thomas, created the previously mentioned popular lithograph of the campus showing cows grazing on campus. It was often reproduced and became the most familiar of all early depictions of the college.

William Barton Rogers, who taught chemistry and natural philosophy under Empie from 1828 to 1835, was one of the college's notable teachers in its long history. He had graduated in 1828 from William and Mary, where his father Patrick Rogers had earlier held the same professorship. In 1845 the younger Rogers wrote of the college that "the privilege of election of studies is allowed at William and Mary. Within its venerable precincts liberal methods of instruction found a home before they were adopted by the thronged and applauded colleges of New England . . ." Rogers himself later adopted some of these innovations at MIT.

President Empie's ability as a preacher led St. James's Episcopal Church to call him to Richmond in 1836, where he remained until 1858. Then, at about seventy-eight, Dr. Empie retired to Wilmington, North Carolina, where he died in 1860. The faculty lauded him as "always urbane, always kind, eminently qualified for all his Duties." To succeed him in 1836, the Visitors selected thirty-three-year-old Thomas Roderick Dew, professor of history and political law since 1826.

Dew was a tall, gaunt bachelor who was to prove one of the most unusual presidents. He chose to occupy only part of the President's House, sharing it with other professors. For the strenuous years of his administration he devoted himself wholeheartedly to the college, dying in 1846 after ten years in office.

Dew was an innovator on a campus hitherto devoted to the humanities, philosophy, theology, and law. He had been educated at the college, graduating in 1820, and afterward spending two years studying in Europe. He was an economist who advocated free trade and the laissez-faire economics of Adam Smith and the "common sense" philosophers. He championed southern interests and opposed congressional tariff measures to protect New England industry, which he felt enriched northern factories at the expense of southern agriculture.

Dew's views meshed with the pro-slavery philosophy of Nathaniel Beverley Tucker and helped formulate the South's political creed. The college became known for its states' rights teachings, endearing Dew and Tucker to southern conservatives.

Much of life in this period revolved around professors' homes, for the faculty—no longer required to remain single or live on campus—was active in town. The best-known was Nathaniel Beverley Tucker, who was active in Whig politics as a friend of John Tyler's in the years 1837–1841 when Tyler lived in Williamsburg, just before he became President.

Tucker was also close to his half-brother, John Randolph of Roanoke, a states' rights leader in Congress for most of the period from 1799 to

1827. Other Tucker allies, most of them his former students, were Abel P. Upshur of Eastern Shore Virginia who served in Tyler's cabinet; George M. Bibb, a native of Prince Edward County who was prominent in Kentucky politics; Thomas Walker Gilmer of Albemarle, another of Tyler's cabinet; and William Taylor Barry of Kentucky, who was postmaster general under Andrew Jackson.

The most unusual of Dew's faculty was Charles Frederick Ernest Minnegerode, a bearded German who came from Europe and succeeded Dabney Browne as professor of humanity in 1842. Despite his accent, Minnegerode was an accomplished lecturer. It was to Tuckers' family, living in their house on Nicholson Street, that Minnegerode introduced the German custom of the Christmas tree in 1842.

Minnegerode read theology at home for his Episcopal ordination and was ordained to the Episcopal priesthood. He had left the college and was preaching at St. Paul's Church in Richmond on Sunday, April 3, 1865, when word came from Robert E. Lee to Jefferson Davis, worshipping at the church, that the Confederacy must evacuate Richmond and Petersburg.

It was said of the voluble German that once, arriving late to conduct a funeral, he found another cleric performing the service in his place. As the substitute was intoning, "I am the resurrection and the life," Minnegerode rushed up and took over. "Nein, nein!" he shouted. "*I* am ze resurrection and ze life!"

Mathematics was taught in Dew's day by Professor Robert Saunders, who was active in Virginia's Whig politics and served twice as Williamsburg's mayor. Like Dew and Tucker, he was repeatedly urged to run for Congress but declined. Saunders lived with his wife and children in a capacious house, now called the Robert Carter house, on Palace Green, near the site of the ruins of the Governor's Palace.

Compared to his fellow professors, Roderick Dew was an intense and unworldly scholar. He was one of six sons of Thomas Dew, a King and Queen County planter, and had received his Bachelor of Arts from William and Mary in 1820 at eighteen. After a two-year European tour, largely devoted to German scholarship, he returned for his master's studies at the college and was appointed professor of political law in 1826. His courses embraced history, metaphysics, natural and national law, government, and political economy.

Dew was a prolific writer, whose essays appeared in many periodicals and books. Like Jefferson, he preferred politics and economics to other subjects. His syllabus for his students' use, published as *A Digest of the Laws, Customs, Manners, and Institutions of the Ancient and*

*Modern Nations,* reflects wide familiarity with history. His studies left him little time for social life.

When the future of slavery in Virginia was debated by the Virginia Assembly in 1831–1832, Dew wrote a defense of it which was published in many papers. He cited the rise of the slave-based civilizations of Greece and Rome, the loss Virginia slaveholders would suffer by emancipation, and the profits in slave-breeding. J. D. B. DeBow, the editor of *DeBow's Review* in New York, wrote that Dew's "able essay on the institution of slavery entitles him to the lasting gratitude of the whole South." Like Tucker, whose novel *The Partisan Leader* foreshadowed secession, Dew tried to justify the South's disaffection with national politics.

As Williamsburg feared, the opening of the University of Virginia in 1825 hurt the college's enrollment. William and Mary also was affected by the opening of other colleges in the 1830s. Methodists opened Randolph-Macon College at Boydton in 1832. In the same year Baptists started a seminary which became the University of Richmond. In 1838 Emory and Henry College opened in southwestern Virginia. Virginia Military Institute began at Lexington in 1839. These four schools plus Washington College, Hampden-Sydney, and the University of Virginia created intense competition for student enrollment.

Like John Augustine Smith from 1814 to 1826, President Dew came to believe that the solution to William and Mary's problems was to move the school to Richmond. In the 1840s Dew wrote to his friend William Barton Rogers, then at the University of Virginia saying "I have reason to believe more strongly than ever . . . that if next year is a failure like the present, the Visitors will consent to a removal of the College [to Richmond]." However, Dew underestimated John Tyler, who continued to checkmate any move.

During "the sickly season" in Williamsburg each summer, Dew went to the mountains like many other people. There in the 1840s he met Natilia Hay, daughter of a Clarke County physician and a connection of the Burwells of Carter's Grove and of Carter Hall in Clarke County. The two were married in 1846 and left on a wedding trip to Europe. During the voyage, the scholar became ill and subsequently died of a lung ailment in a Paris hospital on August 6, 1846.

Dew was buried in Montmartre Cemetery, but his kinsmen—descendants of Dew's five brothers who had preceded or followed him at William and Mary—had the remains brought back in 1939 to the college chapel. At the service President John Stewart Bryan recalled Dew's advice to students in 1837 that there was no easy road to wealth or fame. On the contrary, Bryan said, "The great men of the world are the real working-men, and everywhere talent and learning command the admiration and respect of mankind." Dew was a shining example.

Of all William and Mary's early presidents, only James Madison had greater intellectual gifts than Thomas Roderick Dew. Even the severe Bishop Meade gave generous credit to Dew's "tact at management, great zeal, and unwearied assiduity" for lifting the college to "as great prosperity as perhaps had ever been its lot at any time since its first establishment." The praise was too generous, but Dew had indeed helped the college.

# *Book Three*

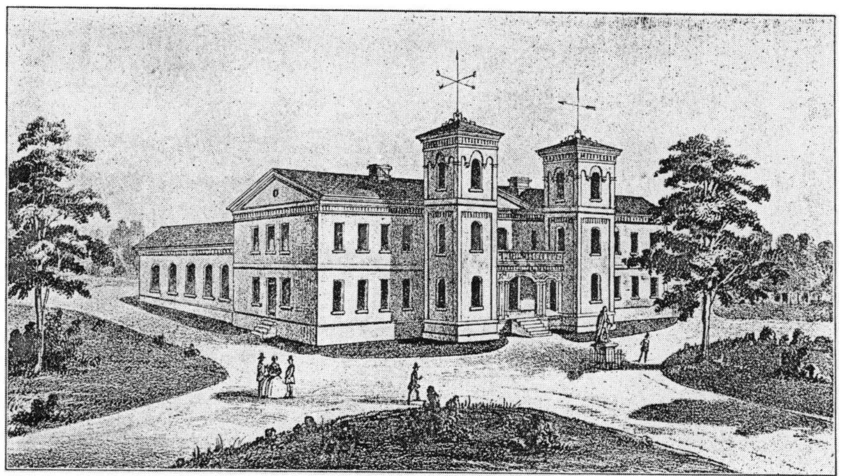

William and Mary College Archives

## Seeds of the Whirlwind

### 1846–1919

The president's house . . . caught fire . . . from sparks from a burning chimney, and narrowly escaped destruction. The fire broke out in two places at once, and owning to the steep French roof and no ladder, it was difficult to control. The students and citizens worked faithfully and prevented a disaster. Among the most conspicuous workers was Mr. R. A. Lively, whose prompt attention with a patent pump arrangement probably saved the building.

*The Richmond Whig*
ca May 1, 1879

# 13

## *Days of Acrimony*

THE decades of the 1840s and 1850s were the most prosperous in Virginia since the Revolution. Railroads had begun, and turnpikes were being built to make travel faster. Academies and colleges had sprouted. Cyrus McCormick had revolutionized wheat harvesting with his reaper, and the James River Canal was cut through almost to the Kanawha River in western Virginia.

Not much changed in Williamsburg, however. The town had no factories, and it was too far from cities to attract a turnpike or railroad. Except for the college and asylum, it had little to draw visitors except sittings of the James City County Court. An elm blight in 1843 left the campus almost denuded. Boredom showed in querulous exchanges between the Board of Visitors and faculty.

After President Dew's death in Paris in 1846, the Visitors offered the presidency to Robert Saunders, Jr., of Williamsburg, professor of mathematics since 1833. Saunders served on a pro tem basis from October 1846 until October 12, 1847, when the Visitors officially named him president.

Saunders had been born in Williamsburg in 1805, the son of a prosperous lawyer, and he had attended the University of Virginia when it opened in 1825. Before and after his Charlottesville sojourn he was schooled at William and Mary, where he studied law. However, he chose to teach mathematics, which he continued to do at the college through his presidency.

In 1828 the handsome, dark-haired scholar had married Lucy Burwell Page, daughter of the deceased Governor John Page of Rosewell, and by her he had five children. Upon his father's death in 1835 Saunders inherited his comfortable house on Palace Green. There Robert Saunders, Jr., and his family lived throughout his brief presidency of William and Mary—possibly the only one of its twenty-four presidents never to live in the President's House. Except for the Civil War years, when Saunders was an officer in the Confederate Quartermaster Corps in Richmond, he lived his life in Williamsburg.

Saunders had hardly become president when the issue of moving the college was raised again. Contention spread from faculty and Visitors to townspeople and even to students. John Millington, professor of chemistry, wrote a friend in January, 1848, that he and other professors were promoting the removal of the college to Richmond. At first, he added, "Messrs Saunders[,] Minnegerode and Holmes were also very warm about it." However, George Frederick Holmes resigned in March 1848, complaining that there was "no conceivable probability of unanimity among the Professors, or of cordiality between the Faculty as a body and the Students." He was later a professor at the University of Virginia.

Millington did not resign then but he confided to his friend, Professor Joseph Henry of the Smithsonian Institution, on May 30, 1848, that: "Since the death of our late esteemed president Mr. Dew, a great change has taken place in the affairs of our College—acts of Nepotism have disturbed our former peace—a schism exists between the Faculty & the Visitors and as a means of checking this, the Visitors have requested the whole faculty to resign which request has been complied with."

Accordingly, President Saunders and the remaining faculty—except for Professor Nathaniel Beverley Tucker, who was allowed to continue his law classes—resigned as requested. Classes were suspended for one academic year, to give time for "the excitement and prejudices . . . to subside, & for the Buildings to be put in habitable condition," as the Visitors later explained.

The faculty dispute apparently arose over the appointment of Archibald Peachy, an alumnus related to a Visitor, as professor of moral philosophy. When the appointment was criticized as nepotism, Peachy sent a challenge to one critic to a duel. The student delivering it was dismissed, creating hostility between President Saunders and Professor Peachy. When the furor spread to students and townspeople, the Visitors met and closed the college. President Saunders went to Europe and joined the daughter of General Nathanael Greene, his father's Revolutionary commander, on a visit to Lafayette's family.

After Saunders returned to Williamsburg in 1849, he resumed his community activities but never went back to the college. Instead, he represented the Peninsula as a state senator from 1852 through 1856, and served in the 1840s and 1850s as mayor, president of the board of the asylum, and vestryman of Bruton Parish.

Saunders died September 11, 1868, after returning with his family from Richmond where they had resided during the Civil War. He was buried in the family cemetery behind his Palace Green house. The Saunderses' graves were later moved to Bruton churchyard.

Observing the college from a distance, one applicant for a professorship in 1849 thought it needed an experienced educator at the helm. He was William F. Hopkins, a professor at Masonic University in Clarksville, Tennessee, who wrote to a Visitor on May 31, 1849:

> There may be a clergyman who is a man of business & a disciplinarian, but I never saw one, and the permanent & real success depends more on the discipline than on the éclat of any man's name. That is a point upon which Virginia has made, in politics as in other things, most ugly mistakes. I am told (there are some graduates of William and Mary here) that the little town is completely divided into "Saundersites" and "Peachyites" and that every newcomer will be compelled to take one side. If this is true it will not be either comfortable or of good omen to the College. But I'll try hard to keep peaceable and neutral. They *shall* not come into my laboratory or house to talk small politics.

Hopkins was not elected president but became professor of natural philosophy and chemistry in 1849. Instead, to repair the buildings and reopen the school, the Visitors chose Benjamin Stoddert Ewell, a handsome mathematician who had taught at West Point and Hampden-Sydney and was then professor at Washington College in Lexington. James Heath, a William and Mary Visitor and Ewell kinsman, sounded out Ewell in a letter from Richmond, offering a " . . . $1000 salary an excellent house in the College yard which they have ordered to be repaired at an expense of $500 and a spacious garden."

Notifying Ewell of his election, Corbin Braxton of the Board of Visitors wrote him in July of 1848:

> I put you in nomination for the mathematical chair, and no other gentleman was named, so you received the entire vote, with the

Photograph by Thomas L. Williams

*Maggie, Marianne, and Lelia were daughters of Robert Saunders, president in 1847-48. The 1838 painting hangs in President's House.*

> exception of one vote for Mr. Saunders.—I distinctly stated to the board that you did not wish the Presidency . . . but some of your friends had spoken of your peculiar fitness for, and tact at the management of young men, that my objection was overruled. You may be disappointed in the duties of the President here. I understand they are light and requiring but little from him . . .
>
> I presume you will visit the ancient city and see and know more about it by ocular observation before you finally decide your course of action. Under all the disadvantages under which the college labored last course, there were 50 odd students there, and I should hope that now, under the new organization, this number would be larger, by double.

Ewell accepted the professorship but would agree to act as president only temporarily. He moved from Lexington into the President's House in October 1848, the normal opening time for the fall term. Apparently he had left his wife and daughter in Lexington. Because the college was closed for all but law classes, Ewell concentrated on repairs and on finding a new faculty while the Visitors sought a president.

Unlike Robert Saunders, Ewell later wrote "that the President of the College ought to occupy the President's house, in part at least. When I came to the College in 1848, I found that this house had not been occupied, at all, for two years, and that it had been, previously, rented by President Dew, for years. *Since that time,* saving from 1862 to 1865 it has, continuously been tenanted by members of the College Faculty—the President being, invariably, one of its occupants."

As a graduate of West Point, Ewell knew drafting and construction, and he believed in devoting "proper attention to neatness and to the comfort of those residing on the College Grounds." Using a local carpenter and brick mason, he spent $4,903.28 to repair the three buildings and to lay walkways, clean out wells, install pumps, and build a covered way between the President's House and its kitchen.

The President's House was painted and the interior "refitted." The major change Ewell made to the house was "taking down old portico on building" and adding a porch, built by carpenter James T. James to Ewell's design for $90. It remained until the building was restored by John D. Rockefeller, Jr. Ewell had some $2,000 spent in repairing or replacing chemical and philosophical apparatus.

To serve as president after Ewell, the Visitors approached Bishop John Johns, assistant to the widely known Bishop William Meade of the Diocese of Virginia since 1842. They offered him the presidency and the professorship of moral philosophy. With Meade's approval Johns agreed, offering to serve for a nominal salary and the use of the President's House, provided that the Reverend Silas Totten would take the professorship and its salary.

The college reopened in October 1849 with Johns as president and only Benjamin Ewell and Nathaniel Beverley Tucker remaining from past years. The new professors were Totten, who was to take charge in President Johns's absence; Morgan Smead, ancient languages; William F. Hopkins, chemistry and natural philosophy; and Henry A. Washington, philosophy and political economy.

Before moving in, Bishop Johns wrote Ewell from Baltimore that he had bought three mantels for the dining room and two parlors of the President's House for $105, plus a mantel and grate for the president's study for $30.50. Johns also had the first floor wallpapered at an average of $14 per room. Fine features of the 1786 rebuilding were effaced, and woodwork was stained in the Victorian style.

The masterful Johns raised attendance impressively during his five years as president. An imposing figure with a narrow head, long nose, and humorous eyes, he was "bright in intellect and genial in disposition." He had stood first in his class at the College of New Jersey at Princeton in 1815 and was adjudged by one fellow cleric "the greatest preacher, not even excepting Bishop [Alfred Magill] Randolph, that the Church in Virginia has ever had."

After the one-year college closing which followed Saunders's presidency, attendance rose from fifty-five students in 1851-1852 to eighty-five in 1852-1853. The Richmond *Daily Republican* reported on February 27, 1852:

> When the present Faculty was appointed, the operations of the College had been entirely suspended for one year. The new Faculty commenced with about fifteen students, and now, having completed the second term . . . there are fifty collegiate students without counting the law class, which, under the instructions of Judge Scarborgh [Judge George P. Scarburgh] the able successor of the lamented Tucker . . . will probably add fifteen or twenty more names . . . There are both Whigs and Democrats in the faculty, but politics are not taught directly or indirectly. Nor is the instruction in any degree sectarian. The students are required to attend prayers at the College . . . and to attend church on Sunday, but the choice of churches . . . is left to themselves.

*The Virginia Gazette* of February 23, 1854, notes that seventy-four students were then in attendance and more expected, adding that "the same College buildings which stood long before the Revolution, still rear their massive walls, and bid fair to survive the flight of centuries."

To allow himself more time for ecclesiastical duties, Bishop Johns resigned, to take effect March 31, 1854. Upon William Meade's death in October 1861, he became the fourth Episcopal bishop of Virginia.

The outgoing president recommended the Reverend Richard Wilmer, an Episcopal minister and son of former President William Wilmer, to succeed him. However, the Visitors preferred to go back to Benjamin Ewell. They had been impressed by his handling of college affairs, and this time Ewell accepted. From this point on, his thirty-four-year tenure as president, extending through the Civil War until 1888, was the longest in college annals after James Blair's fifty years and Bishop Madison's thirty-five.

Ewell's long service was beset by an unhappy marriage. His wife, Julia McIlvaine Ewell, left him and their baby daughter Lizzie in 1851 to return to her parents in York, Pennsylvania. She stayed away until after Ewell's death thirty-seven years later, while the daughter visited each parent in turn. Apparently her instability and incompatibility with her serious-minded husband, ten years her elder, led to the couple's alienation.

Ewell's widowed mother, Elizabeth Stoddert Ewell, often came from her home in Prince William County to look after his daughter, Lizzie, when she was in Williamsburg and to entertain for the president. She was an able, strong-minded woman, and her letters illuminate her son's presidency.

In Ewell's tenure the President's House not only sheltered him but also a succession of professors and students. In 1858 a total of eleven people lived there, including Ewell and his mother and daughter, six grammar school students housed on the third floor, and a new professor, Robert J. Morrison, and his wife, who had rooms on the second floor. One of the third floor students had become homesick earlier while attending Miss Gabriella Galt's school and had gone home to Petersburg. On his father's plea, Ewell accepted the boy into the college grammar school and found room for him in his attic. He was a kindly man who took in many roomers.

Each July President Ewell held a party in the President's House for the graduating class. The center of merriment was piano music played by his mother or sister. The piano had been made by Clementi of London in the eighteenth century and given to Ewell's mother by her father, Secretary of the Navy Benjamin Stoddert, who had served in John Adams's cabinet from 1798 to 1801.

Absent from the Ewell's 1858 graduation party was Lucian Minor, professor of law. Professor Minor was ill and asked to be baptized by a Baptist minister in a tub on the front porch of his house on Prince George Street, along with his friend, General Hartwell Cocke of Bremo, who was at college for graduation. Ewell's mother, Elizabeth, described the situation in a letter on July 9, 1858, to her son Richard Ewell, later a famous Confederate general. ". . . he [Professor Minor] has been sinking ever since, the day before yesterday he was taken out of bed[,] carried onto the front porch & immersed in a bathing tub borrowed from the asylum, General Cocke . . . was immersed at the same time, he is near 80[,] looks like a pine knot[,] has been married 3 times, is ready for a 4th and was baptized once before[,] altogether it is a strange proceeding or rather a droll one[,] Mr. Minor died suddenly yesterday." After the college cemetery was laid out in 1859, Professor Minor was re-interred there, where Ewell's mother was soon to be buried. Ultimately the president and his sister were also buried there.

Occasional college functions were held at the Raleigh Tavern until the old hostelry burned in 1859. Proprietor Parkes Slater apparently kept to some of its high colonial standards in 1854, for he advertised in *The Virginia Gazette* in July of that year:

> The Proprietor of this well known establishment, is now prepared to accommodate his patrons. . . . His rooms are in good order and well furnished. The table will be constantly supplied with everything in its season which the market will afford. In winter he is prepared at all times to serve up Wild Ducks and Turkies, Partridges, Venison, fresh York River Oysters, &c &c. Crabs and fresh Fish, in their season. His Wines and other Liquors will always be found of a superior Quality.
>
> PARKES SLATER, Proprietor

Because of Ewell's preference for teaching and in response to the Visitors' desire for a clergyman president, in 1858 the Board offered the presidency to the Reverend Robert Barnwell of South Carolina College at Columbia. Barnwell was a Harvard graduate who had studied at Heidelberg and Berlin, and he was teaching sacred literature and moral philosophy in his native state. His election had the blessing of Ewell, who still did not relish the presidency.

Shortly before Barnwell's consideration for the presidency Ewell started to look for a farm in James City County to which he could move before the new president's arrival in Williamsburg. Ewell had bought 400 acres in 1857 on the Richmond stage road west of Williamsburg, in

James City County. After the Visitors offered the presidency to Barnwell, Ewell decided to build a house, which he completed in 1859.

On January 22, 1857, *The Virginia Gazette* reported Ewell's acquisition, noting the "The price paid for both [tracts] averaged $6 per acre which we consider very low, for the soil is good, and the location is a very healthy one."

After mulling over the proffered presidency, Barnwell declined it because "he did not wish to leave his native state." Nevertheless, Ewell went ahead with his farm and rented slaves to raise truck crops. He summered there each year from 1859 until the college closed in 1882, after which he lived there full-time until his death. Ewell Hall became a flag stop on the Chesapeake and Ohio when rail service came to the Peninsula in 1881.

Students in the Main Building were awakened suddenly on the morning of February 8, 1859. A fire which had started in the basement or first floor chemical laboratory swept the building, leaving only the exterior and a portion of the interior walls standing. The library of 8,000 books and scientific equipment, including antique instruments described as "relics of the science of the former ages," were consumed. Marble tablets on the chapel walls to Sir John Randolph and Bishop Madison "were calcined by the heat & entirely destroyed."

Only a few objects from the second floor Blue Room could be rushed out of the building by Ewell, Professor Robert Morrison, and a few others. Saved were some records, a few volumes of Congressional Reports, the college's six portraits, and copies of the 1859 college catalogue. Its predecessor, printed in 1855, had been William and Mary's first general catalogue.

Professor Morrison, asleep with his wife in their second floor bedroom in the President's House, was awakened by a servant and saw light "streaming in through the windows of the President's House." However, by that time the fire was too far along to stop.

It was almost as disastrous as the fire which had destroyed the Main Building in 1705. The structure was insured for more than $20,000, but no insurance covered the library or scientific apparatus. The faculty met on the day of the fire and appointed a committee to rent suitable lecture rooms, with classes to meet as soon as possible. Lectures were continued in the Brafferton, occupied by Dr. Totten, and commencement exercises on July 4, 1859, were held in the new classical style Baptist church on Duke of Gloucester Street. There were forty-seven collegiate and law students in attendance in 1858-59. The grammar students were boarded and lodged off campus in the master's house.

The fire renewed demands for the college's removal, but Rector John Tyler and the Visitors were as adamant as before. Expert brick masons examined the walls and found them "strong enough for a warehouse." When Professor William Barton Rogers returned to the campus and saw the ruins of the building wherein his father and he had taught, he wrote to his brother:

> The old foundations and the front wall will be retained, but of course a more convenient interior has been planned. The insurance money, with what has been and will be collected from friends, will, I believe, put the college in a better position than before. I obtained in Williamsburg some lithograph views of the college and surroundings taken by [Professor John] Millington's son some years ago . . . Though a poor specimen of art, it will be precious as reminding us of the home of our dear father, and the spot where we first caught the inspiration of science.

Aided by ex-President Tyler, the college canvassed alumni to collect funds to rebuild. Richmond's *Weekly Gazette and Eastern Virginia Advertiser* editorialized: "The town of Williamsburg is eminently adopted to the requisitions of a 'resort of learning.' It is quiet and orderly; the students, when not engaged in their academic pursuits, may indulge in the improving society of some of the most refined people in Virginia. There is[,] in addition, about the old metropolis, an atmosphere of philosophy and history, which is largely favorable to the pursuits of the student and the thinker."

The appeal for funds met with liberal response, especially in Virginia and in New York. Five Virginia donors gave $1,000 each or more: Hugh Blair Grigsby, Richard Baylor, William Beverly, Philip St. George Cooke, and William Broaddus Harrison. Eight donors gave $500 or more, and others gave lesser sums. Every Visitor made a contribution.

Before long $35,000 had been raised, and plans were drawn for rebuilding. Mr. Exall, a Richmond architect, drew the plans and the new building was started within the walls of the old. Tuscan villa architecture was in vogue, and the Visitors decided the building should be "clad in the unique beauties of the Italian style of Architecture."

Two Tuscan towers were erected to flank the entrance, and the roof line was lowered one story. The building was ready for students at the October 1859 session, only eight months after it burned. When graduation exercises were held in the chapel on July 4, 1860, *The Virginia Gazette* pronounced it "restored and improved." It was a far cry from the Christopher Wren structure it replaced, but the building pleased most contemporaries.

Courtesy Colonial Williamsburg Foundation

*Nathaniel Beverley Tucker wrote that the campus was almost treeless in the 1880s, after a blight in 1843 killed the "venerable old elm trees of noble growth."*

William Barton Rogers, in the midst of planning to open MIT, in Cambridge, Massachusetts, helped replace his alma mater's scientific apparatus with "instruments of the first class in each division," while others helped build a collection of 5,000 books, "selected with great care."

Fires in 1705, 1781, and now in 1859 had destroyed many records of the college founding, and Ewell now tried to replace some of them. He wrote Queen Victoria in March 1861 to ask if she could provide a copy of the college charter of 1693, whose original was recorded "in the Chapel of the Rolls of Great Britain," together with a copy of the 1729 Transfer. Before an answer could be received, however, the college was at war.

Serving as he had as a West Point cadet, Ewell opposed secession as unlawful and fruitless. However, the firing on Fort Sumter in 1861 and President Lincoln's call for state troops to put down secession aroused Southern emotions which overcame even such moderates as he. After the war, he wrote that "There were men on the faculty opposed to secession, believing it to be unwise and inexpedient, and the President was one of these. But when active war was waged, resistance became a matter of self-defense, and all, whatever their views, united."

The president's brother, Captain Richard Ewell, USA, also a West Pointer but who had stayed on in the Army, wrote from his post at Albuquerque in 1861 to ask his niece Lizzie Ewell "what the Southern

States will do?" He added that "Officers are generally adverse to anything like civil war, though some of the younger ones are a little warlike." Events were soon to answer, Richard Ewell becoming a senior Confederate officer and rising to important commands.

On May 10, 1861, after Virginia had voted to leave the union, William and Mary suspended classes, for students were leaving to get into uniform and resist the feared invasion. It began seventeen days later, when Federal forces under General Benjamin Butler began landing at Old Point Comfort and Newport News, thirty miles east of Williamsburg.

Soon the campus was deserted except for Ewell and Professor Robert Morrison. On May 24, 1861, when he was about fifty-one, Benjamin Ewell was commissioned a lieutenant colonel of the 32nd Virginia Infantry. His confederate assignment was to raise troops and protect the peninsula, already threatened by Federal forces at Fort Monroe at Old Point and, after May 27, by Camp Butler at Newport News. Ewell served under Colonel John Bankhead Magruder of the Confederacy, a dashing, handsome cavalryman who had been at West Point with him and also with Robert E. Lee, Joseph E. Johnston, and Pierre G. T. Beauregard.

The Main Building of the college was taken over in 1861 by Confederates and used as a barracks and later as a hospital. It was held until Confederate forces evacuated Williamsburg on May 5, 1862. Professor Robert Morrison had been asked to stay on campus to "superintend the building, and other property of the College, so long as Circumstances may permit him to remain in this place."

To assist in Virginia's defense, the college invested its funds in Confederate bonds. College valuables were hidden or given into the custody of officials. Books and equipment were moved to the asylum.

As a large Federal army assembled on the lower peninsula, Williamsburg shuddered. Home defense forces were organized to resist the Union's anticipated march up the peninsula from Fort Monroe through Hampton and York County. For a year after the college closed, Magruder and Ewell with their troops built three parallel defense lines across the lower peninsula, throwing up earthworks between creeks and marshes from the James to the York. Ewell appealed for "able-bodied free Negroes to assist" his troops and slaves to build defense works. He hoped Williamsburg could be spared another invasion.

Many Williamsburgers fled while they could. The storm was gathering, and Williamsburg was again in the path of war.

# 14

# *The War and the College*

WILLIAMSBURG'S worst ordeal began in April 1862, after the Union's field commander, Major General George B. McClellan, launched his drive from Fort Monroe, the federal stronghold at Old Point Comfort. His 120,000-man army swept through Yorktown to confront General John B. Magruder's 10,000 men, soon joined by 8,000 more. Confederate defenses centered on Fort Magruder, the command post that Virginia's defenders had built on the road from Williamsburg to Yorktown.

In 1862 the optimistic McClellan believed he could soon capture Richmond and end the war. "It was as evident in 1862 as in 1865," he wrote later, "that it was on the banks of the James that the fate of the Union was to be decided."

The Confederates in Richmond had sent General Joseph E. Johnston to oppose McClellan outside Williamsburg and take command. Since Johnston's victory in the first Battle of Bull Run eight months earlier, he had been Virginia's top field commander.

Johnston set up headquarters near the old Williamsburg Capitol in the comfortable residence of William W. Vest, the town's leading merchant, who had moved his family to Richmond. The house, later reduced to its colonial size, is now known as the Palmer house. Johnston put General James Longstreet in field command and as his assistant adjutant general chose his West Point schoolmate, Benjamin

Ewell. It was a wartime reunion of old friends, Johnston then fifty-five and Ewell fifty-two. They remained close until Ewell's death.

From April 2 to May 4, 1862, the cautious McClellan moved up the peninsula from Old Point. To defend their Williamsburg line, Johnston and Longstreet spread their troops from the James to the York.

McClellan struck at dawn on May 5. All day long during the battle of Williamsburg cannon rumbled at Fort Magruder, while wagons bore wounded soldiers into Williamsburg to makeshift hospitals at the college, courthouse, Baptist church, and in homes throughout town.

Badly outnumbered, the Confederates decided to limit their losses to a day's skirmishing. Then General Johnston ordered his army to withdraw under cover of night through Williamsburg, and to retreat westward to the swamps of the Chickahominy toward Richmond. His reasoning being that it would be easier ground to hold. All night long on May 5 until the dawn of May 6 soldiers sloshed in mud through Williamsburg and past College Corner to Richmond Road.

The next morning McClellan's conquering army poured into town. While "Little Mac" moved into Johnston's abandoned quarters at the Vest house, his forces seized the college and asylum. They ran up the American flag on posts which had flown the Stars and Bars and required all able-bodied whites to sign an oath of loyalty.

The college was overrun with Union soldiers. The Main Building became a barracks and a depot of commissary stores, while the Brafferton for a time became the Union officers' headquarters. Some college valuables had been sent to the asylum for safekeeping. Young Lizzie Ewell had gone to stay with her mother in Pennsylvania. After the Confederate evacuation, Mrs. Virginia Southall and her family moved into the President's House, where Ewell had offered to let them live when he went into the service. They remained there until the spring of 1864.

At Robert Saunders's deserted house on Palace Green, marauders took furniture, letters, and books, including correspondence to and from Governor John Page, Mrs. Saunders's father. Some of the manuscripts turned up later in Northern repositories.

While McClellan fought his way toward Richmond, Williamsburg remained a Union nerve center, providing his army with communications by way of Fort Monroe to Washington. To break these lines, the Confederate cavalry made sporadic hit-and-run attacks on Union pickets around Williamsburg. On September 9, 1862, a band of Confederate cavalry under General Henry A. Wise, a pre-war governor of Virginia, recaptured Williamsburg for one day, taking the Federal provost marshal as temporary prisoner.

Striking back later the same day, members of the 5th Pennsylvania cavalry entered Williamsburg and set fire to the Main Building at the college. A witness said soldiers surrounded the structure with drawn swords to prevent efforts to save the building. Once again the old structure was almost consumed, leaving only its walls standing. The blackened ruins were boarded up against further damage. However, coffin plates in the vaults beneath the college chapel were all removed. Ewell described the burning in a memorandum to Congress in 1872:

> After a conflict on the 9th of September, 1862, between the garrison and a body of South Carolina cavalry, the latter took possession of the town for a few hours. After the withdrawal of this force—it had gone before 11 a.m.—returning stragglers of the garrison, in a state of disorder and under the influence of drink, fired and destroyed, late in the afternoon of the same day, the main College building, with furniture and apparatus, surrounding it with drawn swords, and thus keeping the citizens of the town from attempting to extinguish the flames.
>
> At later periods all the remaining houses on the College premises were burned, or wholly or in part pulled to pieces. The buildings not fully destroyed, and the grounds, were held by Union forces from May, 1862, to September, 1865, for depots of stores and for other purposes.

The statue of Lord Botetourt in the college yard, purchased by the college in 1801 from the State of Virginia, escaped damage, but it was moved a year or so later for safekeeping to the asylum, to be returned after the war.

After Mrs. Southall moved out of the President's House, Federal officers occupied it until the war's end. To discourage further Confederate raids, Federal troops fortified the campus and barricaded Richmond and Jamestown roads.

Ewell noted that in the spring of 1865, shortly before Lee surrendered at Appomattox, ". . . a line of defensive works was thrown across the College yard, of which the walls of the Main building [,] the remaining portion of the brick kitchen near it, the Brafferton & the President's house formed a part, some of the door ways and windows being bricked up and loop-holed, the whole being connected and flanked by a strong line of palisades, extending across the two adjacent roads, and further defended at some points by Chevaux-de-frise."

Once a Union intelligence agent found a Confederate mail pouch among the vaults under the chapel, awaiting pickup after dark.

"By means of secret signals," wrote Captain Edward Cronin, the

Union provost marshal in Williamsburg, "messages were exchanged both day and night between the Confederates and their friends in town, who gave prompt warning of any increase of force or apparent movement on the part of the Unionists." Both Union and Confederate spies frequented town.

Ewell remained in service until three weeks before Appomattox, resigning March 20, 1865, on account of illness. He could see the end coming and hoped to reopen his college that fall. After Lee had surrendered on April 9, Ewell made his way back to Williamsburg under safe-conduct pass, even though Federal forces held the campus until September.

Ewell met with his Board of Visitors in Richmond on July 5, 1865. It was the first meeting since 1860. Chancellor and Rector John Tyler had died, but all other Visitors were present. Always optimistic, Ewell reported that the walls of the Main Building were "apparently in as good condition as they were after the fire of 1859, in fact are less warped and cracked." He estimated their damage at $40,000, later raised to $70,000, and set that of the Brafferton as $3,000 and of the President's House at $1,600.

Old Buck, as Ewell came to be known, proposed that the college reopen without using the ruined Main Building. He suggested that the Brafferton be used instead for classrooms; the President's House be used for the library and laboratory; that a wing be built on the President's House for professors' rooms; and that the steward's residence, built on Jamestown Road in 1852, become the College Hotel, containing dormitory rooms and classrooms.

"From what I saw in Williamsburg," he told the Visitors, "it is as quiet and orderly as Richmond. Most of the old citizens are returning." The Board accepted Ewell's proposals and authorized reopening the college in October 1865.

College fortunes had been declining since the Revolution, but from 1865 until 1888, during the Reconstruction period of the South, they reached their lowest ebb. Ewell spent his last twenty-three years trying to revive the college, to recover endowments lost in the collapse of Confederate bonds, and to obtain students amid the postwar poverty. He pinned his hopes on a new generation.

Again the cry arose, "Move the College" to Richmond or Alexandria, but the President and Visitors opposed it. So did the college's Chancellor Hugh Blair Grigsby of Charlotte County, historian and planter. One proposal was to merge it with the University of the South at Sewanee, Tennessee. Another came from the city of Norfolk, which offered it the Norfolk Academy site for its campus and proposed to build "suitable dwellings for the professors in the neighborhood."

When the college reopened in October 1865, it enrolled eighteen collegians and thirty-two grammar students. The wing which Ewell had proposed was being built onto the President's House, and solicitation was underway to rebuild the Main Building. Professor Robert Morrison had died, but Professors Edwin Taliaferro, Thomas T. L. Snead, and Thomas McCandlish had returned, and a new grammar school master, William R. Garrett, was on hand.

From 1865 on, Ewell divided his time between teaching and raising funds. Through acquaintances with officers he had known at West Pont, he obtained some help, but Southerners had little money to give. Most Northerners were at first unsympathetic, but some softened. Surprisingly, an eloquent ally was the celebrated Congregational minister Henry Ward Beecher of Brooklyn, who now preached Northern forgiveness. On April 9, 1867, Beecher sent a letter to potential benefactors in the North. He urged gifts to Ewell's campaign to "refit" a college building destroyed by the war: "I cordially commend his cause . . . Funds contributed will serve the cause of Education, both among the whites and the blacks, raising up schoolmasters of the coming system of Common Schools, which, with the Churches, will restore Virginia to her historic renown, and make the nation as proud of her future as it has been sorrowful for her recent history."

Raising money did not come easy for William and Mary's Board. "Begging is an unpleasant office to a Virginian of our latitude," wrote Chancellor Grigsby from Charlotte County in 1866, "but we should not scruple to emulate our other colleges. Washington College [at Lexington] is becoming enriched by Northern funds, and she lost comparatively nothing by the war. Will you think of this," he wrote Ewell, "and adopt some mode of appeal to the liberality of those who inflicted wantonly our calamities upon us?"

The Main Building was hastily rebuilt in 1868–1869 with what remained of endowments and with gifts from northern donors, including New York investor August Belmont and Washington financier W. W. Corcoran. A contribution even came from the Archbishop of Canterbury. The architect was Alfred L. Rives of Richmond and Albemarle, whose daughter, Amelie Rives Troubetzkoy, was by 1888 a rising novelist. Rives made no attempt to re-create the building as it was before, although original walls were again utilized. The structure was to remain in an altered and reduced form for many years, again without its original third floor.

In 1865 Ewell and the Visitors began proceedings to obtain the principal and interest of an English trust fund, which eventually netted the college more than $8,000. It was the fund left years earlier by Mrs. James Whaley, the former Mary Page of Williamsburg, who had established a free school to memorialize her son, Matthew, who had died in 1705. After Mrs. Whaley died in England in 1742, the unused funds accumulated.

When finally obtained by the college, the $8,480 was used in 1870 to build a grammar school on Palace Green, called the Grammar and Matty School. It offered free tuition to some students, in compliance with the trust, and also replaced the college's erstwhile grammar school. After the college added teacher training in 1888, it was known as the Matthew Whaley Observation and Practice School. It became Williamsburg's first public school.

Impressed by the success of Washington College at Lexington, which had called Robert E. Lee to its presidency after Appomattox, Ewell proposed that William and Mary's Visitors ask General Joseph E. Johnston to head the college. "In his [Ewell's] judgment, the College needed a man of large influence at the helm," a Visitor wrote. However, the Board expressed satisfaction with Ewell.

Because the college's burning had been an unauthorized act of a few vengeful Union soldiers, Ewell sought restitution through Congress. His chief ally was congressman George F. Hoar of Massachusetts, who was not to see reimbursement voted until 1893, when Hoar had become a senator. Speaking for the first bill in 1867, Hoar argued that "To spare, and if possible to protect, institutions of learning, is an obligation which the most civilized nations impose on themselves." However, Congress refused to appropriate funds.

Ewell continued to visit and write to industrialists throughout his presidency, producing sporadic gifts. On May 4, 1869, Thomas Russell addressed a group of prominent Bostonians from the Boston Customs House, where he was collector of customs:

> Dear Sir:
>
> President Ewell of William and Mary College, Virginia, who comes recommended by President Grant, General Burnside, Judge Bond of Baltimore, and other good men, wishes to present the claims of the college to the liberal men of the North. I am sure you will be glad to meet and to hear from a worthy man advocating a good cause . . .

Little came of the visit, Ewell explaining later that "The financial crisis of 1871 and the Boston fire in 1872 deprived the college of not less than $100,000 from the citizens of Massachusetts." About the same time he wrote to *The New York Times* that the college was alive: "Its losses during the late war exceeded those of any other Southern college. The liberality of some gentlemen, W. W. Corcoran of Washington, A. T. Stewart, W. E. Dodge, August Belmont, Robert Barnes, and others in New York and elsewhere enabled the college authorities to begin the work of reconstruction."

Usually it required several visits to obtain a gift. From New York in January 1869, Ewell wrote his daughter Lizzie in Williamsburg, using the letterhead of his kinsman Newton Ewell's bank and brokerage house on New York's Broad Street: "People are fast to say that they feel great interest in the college's restoration but slow to say they can help. Yet I must wait to get answers, whatever they may be."

A few gifts were unexpected, like the books that author Thomas Dunn English sent in 1869 after hearing the college library had been partially lost. From England came gifts from the Archbishop of Canterbury and the Earl of Derby. Among book publishers who contributed were Charles Scribner, Harper and Brothers, D. Appleton, D. Van Nostrand, and A. J. Barnes.

Ewell also corresponded with educators to exchange information on enrollment or to ask about a recommended teacher. A letter from Robert E. Lee at Washington College assured him that William and Mary "must necessarily suffer under the depression incident to the calamities that oppress the State, but they will pass away, and William and Mary will again resume her front rank of the colleges of the country. Time, which brings a cure to all things, will, I trust, remove the difficulties in the way of her progress and her restoration."

Ewell was especially fond of General Francis Henney Smith, superintendent for fifty years of Virginia Military Institute, who had known Ewell at West Point and in Lexington when Ewell taught at Washington College. Noticing the suggestion in an Episcopal periodical, *The Southern Churchman,* that William and Mary should be incorporated into the University of the South at Sewanee, Tennessee, Smith wrote and urged Ewell to oppose "the mad scheme" of removing William and Mary. "Your true interest is to fight out your battle on your own ground. You have to aim and arm yourself amidst great reverses, and I think the worst is over. The Peninsula is going to be the most populous secition of Virginia, and if you hold your ground, you will reap all the advantages of the improvement."

Another Ewell ally was General Samuel Chapman Armstrong, a

Courtesy Newport News Daily Press

*This Civil War era photograph of Brafferton Hall shows unpaved Jamestown Road between the fences that kept livestock from invading college yard.*

Federal officer in the Civil War who had persuaded the American Missionary Society to establish the school for emancipated slaves at Fort Monroe which ultimately became Hampton Institute. Armstrong had friends in the Federal government and wrote them in Ewell's behalf, one letter describing Ewell as seeking

> . . . an appropriation that shall make good the damages done during the war to his college, amounting to $69,000. I most earnestly bespeak your hearty cooperation with the Colonel. He is one of the leading men of this state, and no one has been more liberal and polite and kind to all kinds of Northern people and enterprises than he.
>
> He has especially favored our school, at much sacrifice of his comfort, and the institution he represents really deserves aid.
>
> This grant would do more to bring about good feeling than any measure of the government since the war.

Another bill to reimburse the college was introduced in Congress in

1872, and won unanimous support of the Committee on Elections and Labor. Congressman Samuel Griffin of Williamsburg, who was a member, wrote hopefully that "the Committee was unanimous that the Government ought to restore the building. This is based on the grounds that the Government had taken possession of it and therefore was responsible for its care and that whilst so situated it was carelessly, if not wickedly, destroyed, and, as all institutions of learning have in all wars been held sacred and when destroyed accidentally or otherwise, have been rebuilt, therefore we should rebuild this. This I believe is the opinion of a majority of the House."

But the college was soon shocked to learn that it had enemies in its midst. When the Congressional proposal became known in Williamsburg, critics of the college called a meeting at the Courthouse in February 1872 to oppose it. A roving night patrol of Williamsburg Home Guards spied lights in the Courthouse and broke into the meeting. The anti-college group objected that its right of assembly had been violated, for the captain of the patrol was Richard A Wise, son of General Henry A. Wise and professor of chemistry at the college.

The protestors asked Congress to vote down the reimbursement, calling the college "sectional" and "anti-Union." The distressed president did his best to undo the damage, but the protest had triggered Congressional doubts. Plaintively, Ewell wrote to one of the bill's sponsors:

> Learning that objections are made to the bill . . . allow me to state . . . that the Institution ought not to be held responsible for a body [the Home Guard] over which it exercises no control . . . Whatever the members of this company may have, inadvisably and inconsiderately, done, I venture the opinion that 9/10 would today, if necessary, take up arms in defense of the United States Government . . . [Dr. Wise] indignantly denies having intentionally interfered with any public meeting or designedly manifested disrespect to the U.S. Authorities.
>
> It is my belief that the College is, as a whole, well affected to the National government. The college has, since the war, educated without charge, and does so now, young men and boys regardless of the political opinions of their fathers or guardians. Honorary degrees have been given to Northern men. Does this indicate sectionalism?

Dr. Wise offered to resign because of "the late attempt to the enemies of the petition of the college now before the Congress to injure the cause of the college," but Ewell and the college refused. However, it was clear that the college had lost again. The bill was not passed by Congress until 1893, when sectional hatred had cooled a little. By that time Ewell had retired from the presidency, but he was still alive to see his efforts rewarded.

Enrollment in the 1860s and 1870s seldom rose above seventy even including the Grammar and Matty School. The president and professors did not always get all their salary, but they were better off than most townspeople. A few had other income. Dr. Wise, professor of chemistry, took medical patients. The Reverend Lyman B. Wharton, professor of ancient languages, preached in Bruton. Ewell raised produce at his Ewell farm. Nearly every Williamsburg family had its cow, chickens, and vegetable garden.

To publicize the college's need, Ewell and Grigsby wrote a brief history of the college in 1895 at the suggestion of George F. Hoar of Massachusetts, Ewell's ally in Congress. It emphasized the birth of Phi Beta Kappa at the college in 1776, for the society had been transplanted in 1779 by Elisha Parmele, a Connecticut student at William and Mary, to Harvard and Yale and was flourishing at both. Hoar printed an appeal to accompany Ewell's booklet, signed by President Charles W. Eliot of Harvard, poet James Russell Lowell, and others. "There is a tender feeling here [in New England] for your good old college," Hoar wrote Ewell.

Despite limited funds, Ewell kept open house during his years in the President's House. After his mother died, his sister Rebecca kept house for him until her death in 1867. Thereafter, his daughter Lizzie helped, remaining close to her father even after she married Beverley Scott of Prince Edward County in 1867.

Normally sanguine, in old age Ewell suffered moments of discouragement. Though he had been described by a West Point classmate as "lenient and forgiving, almost to weakness," the old man could be severe. From Union Place Hotel in New York, he wrote to "My dear Lizzie" on January 4, 1868:

> How remarkable it is that as women grow older they become more and more ill-natured, more and more inclined to grumble and find fault. You are not exempt from the common failing; that is, judging from your last letter, which contains quite a supply of it. . . .
>
> If anyone wants to get conceit and vanity taken out of him or her, a trip here [to New York] . . . of a week or so will do much towards it. The perfect indifference with which everybody is regarded is

Drawing by Major Edward Cronin, Courtesy New York Historical Society

*The college building (Wren Building) was burned by Union soldiers in 1862, leading to retaliatory attacks by Confederates, which Union occupiers resisted.*

> wonderful, especially to one coming from a small town where everybody's business is made a matter of comment and discussion by everybody else.

Yet "Old Buck" did not lack spirit. In the archives of William and Mary is a challenge to a duel, evidently averted, between Ewell and Professor Edwin Taliaferro, who taught Latin and romance languages before and after the Civil War. The undated note was copied from an original in possession of the late Professor Peter Paul Peebles, who taught law at the college from 1924 to 1938. Addressed to Captain Bucktrout, a magistrate of Williamsburg, it reads:

> Dear Sir
>
> We deem it our duty as well to the college as to the Commonwealth to inform you as a Magistrate that there is an affair to take place at Old Point as soon as possible between two gentlemen, in whom we are equally interested, Professors Ewell and Taliaferro.

> We would urge upon you all possible haste, as they are to leave immediately.
>
> Friends

Details of the dispute between friends are long lost, but the duel was evidently averted. The college needed all its sons.

# 15

## *"A Truly Remarkable Man"*

A NEW South grew out of Appomattox, and William and Mary had trouble finding its place in it. Slavery was dead, and industrialism was the road to the future. Fields which had grown tobacco and grain reverted to forests. The old South was changing.

Shorn of West Virginia, which had opposed Virginia's secession from the Union, the shrunken Old Dominion became Federal District No. 1, with a military governor in the Capitol which had so recently housed the Confederacy. When a state constitutional convention met under Federal auspices in Richmond in 1868-1869, it was dominated by radical Republicans and blacks. Ex-Confederates were suspect.

Universal education was the constitutional convention's chief hope for creating a more equalitarian society in the onetime slave states. Freed blacks were to be given the vote on the same basis as whites. Public schools were decreed for both races. Agriculture, applied science, and technology were to be taught at the State's new Agricultural and Mechanical College and Polytechnic Institute, chartered in 1872 at Blacksburg. Teachers for public schools were to be trained in normal schools, including a new one for blacks at Petersburg. The capable Dr. William Henry Ruffner, an industrious Presbyterian minister, became Virginia's first superintendent of public instruction, charged with creating public schools in every county and city.

Higher education, heretofore a privilege of wealth, was now a possibility for all Virginians. No longer would colleges offer only classical, philosophical, mathematical, scientific, and religious training. College now was also to train individuals for greater social usefulness and a better income. In a widening democracy it was to prepare men—and later women—for careers in industry, technology, farming, and business. It was a radical change for the old Williamsburg campus, demanding far less classical background but preparing graduates for broader choices than the learned professions which once faced William and Mary's matriculates.

This new vocational emphasis was promoted by the Morrill Land Grant Act, which Congress had enacted in 1862 to expand higher education through proceeds from the sale of public lands. Land grant funds in Virginia and the other states were used to make college less expensive and more accessible to blacks as well as whites, opening up new careers to many who had not before aspired to college.

Virginia allocated her land grant money chiefly to the new institute at Blacksburg, later Virginia Polytechnic Institute and State University, and the new normal school for blacks at Petersburg, later renamed Virginia State University. Other Virginia institutions reduced their tuition charges in response to the land grant colleges' influence, thus increasing competition for students.

William and Mary's enrollment was disappointingly meager after it reopened in October 1865, six months after Appomattox. By July 1871 it had only forty-one collegians and thirty-four grammar students, the latter taught after 1870 in the Grammar and Matty School on Palace Green, "a commodious brick building, 62 feet by 43 feet," near the site of the Governor's Palace. College enrollment "did not meet the expectations of the faculty," a professor wrote. It was an old story.

By 1881 college enrollment had fallen to twelve, and in 1882 it dropped to three. Accordingly, in July of that year Ewell urged the Visitors to ask the General Assembly to take over the college and endow it as a normal school—a course finally taken seven years later. Meanwhile the college suspended classes until funds and students could be increased. Thus the institution slumbered from July 1881 until October 1888. Each year Ewell reported to the Visitors on college property.

To add to the college's woe, a fire in April 1879 had again struck the President's House, though it did limited damage. As *The Richmond Whig* described it, " . . . the house was ignited by sparks from a burning chimney, and narrowly escaped destruction. The fire broke out in two places at once, and owning to the steep French roof and no

Photograph by Thomas L. Williams

*Lyon Gardiner Tyler brought State support and coeducation to the College of William and Mary as president from 1888 until 1919.*

ladder, it was difficult to control. The students and citizens worked faithfully and prevented a disaster. Among the most conspicuous workers was Mr. R. A. Lively, whose prompt attention with a patent pump arrangement probably saved the building."

Ewell wrote Lively, editor of the revived *Virginia Gazette,* that with a "Fountain Pump and Sprinkler you were the means of saving $4,000 worth of property"— evidently the value Ewell placed on the President's House and contents. Insurance covered the damage. In 1884 the outside kitchen and servants' rooms of the President's House were repaired, but Ewell wrote that "the House assigned to the President is in all essentials comfortable."

The decision of Ewell and the Visitors in 1881 to close the college had not been easy. One reason was that the Chesapeake and Ohio Railway was extending its tracks from Richmond through Williamsburg to Newport News. With rail service available at last, prospects for the economic rise of the long-dormant Peninsula were clearly improving.

Realizing the potential of rail service, Ewell had predicted that "When the lines [Chesapeake and Ohio] of improvement from Richmond westward are completed and the products of the west pour into her [Virginia's] lap, she will find additional outlets to Deep Water a necessity for her continued growth and prosperity . . . The Town will, of course, be sought by business men of Richmond as a cheap and quiet home for families."

Simiarly, Chancellor Hugh Blair Grigsby foresaw that the Peninsula "will soon be one of the most accessible parts of the State. In less than 30 years . . . the Peninsula will become densely populated."

But such predictions, even though correct, could not pay bills. After the college closed its doors, Benjamin Ewell kept his office in the President's House but moved his household to his farm. Remaining in the house to safequard it were the Reverend George T. Wilmer, professor of moral philosophy, and Dr. Richard Wise, professor of chemistry, with their families.

Wise, son of Virginia's pre-war Governor Henry A Wise, moved his office in 1882 from the college to the Lunatic Asylum, where he became physician in charge. He was elected to Congress in 1898. Looking back on his association with Ewell, he recalled the amity that had prevailed in the President's House when two professors' families had shared it with the president. "Colonel Ewell was kind as a father to me," Wise wrote, "and I can never forget him."

For six years after 1882 the campus was almost deserted. On weekdays Ewell would come from his farm to town in his buggy, driven by his coachman Malachi Gardner, an ex-slave who was also the college bell ringer. Describing the routine, a friend wrote that Ewell would read his mail in the President's House "and go through the formalities of a college president's day. He was a remarkably fine mathematician. He bore himself proudly, moving with dignity among the dusty books and signs of decay."

Once he had written or dictated his letters and taught two or three teenage boys who were preparing for college, Ewell would don coat and hat and summon old Malachi to drive him back to Ewell Hall.

One of Ewell's grammar students was George Preston Coleman, son of Dr. Charles Washington Coleman and his wife, the former Cynthia Beverley Tucker, of Williamsburg. Coleman became a civil engineer and Virginia highway commissioner in Richmond before serving as

Courtesy Nancy Wilson Mann

*President and Mrs. Lyon Tyler brought their children, John, Julia, and Elizabeth to live in the house in 1888.*

president of Peninsula Bank and Trust Company in the 1920s and as Williamsburg's mayor 1929–1934. Another of Ewell's students was William W. Joynes, son of Edward S. Joynes, onetime professor of languages at the college and later at Washington and Lee. Also an Ewell pupil was Hugh Bird, who in time became a professor and one of the "Seven Wise Men," a phrase which later immortalized some of the 1888–89 faculty who enjoyed long tenure.

Ewell kept the college's spirit alive, hoping it would soon reopen. On the traditional day of the college matriculation each fall he or his servant, Malachi, would toll the bell at the Main Building to proclaim that William and Mary lived. According to *The American Architect and Building News,* published in Ewell's old age, " . . . as each September comes drearily around, the old gray-haired president goes to the bat-inhabited belfry and rings out a peal that wakes no echo save in the histories of those who once inhabited its walls." Dr. Richard Wise explained in 1898 that Ewell guarded the charter by having the bell rung

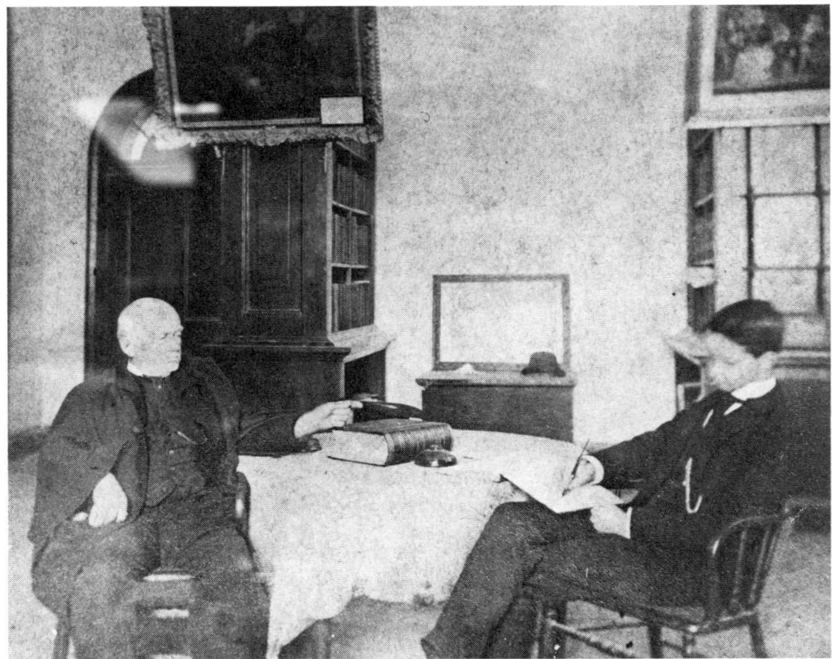

Courtesy Colonial Williamsburg Foundation

*President Benjamin Ewell taught Hugh Bird in the President's House after the college closed for lack of funds in 1882. It reopened in 1888.*

every opening day. He kept up the [college yard] enclosure and did all as far as he could to preserve the corporation. . . . He spent many thousands of dollars of his own money to maintain the credit of the college."

Thus William and Mary slumbered until 1888. Providentially a new member of the General Assembly the preceding fall was Lyon Gardiner Tyler, thirty-four, who had received his M.A. at the University of Virginia in 1875. Tyler had taught briefly at William and Mary in 1877–1878 as professor of belles lettres, but left to become head of a high school in Memphis, where he remained four years.

Returning to Virginia in 1882, he settled in Richmond and practiced law. He was the son of John Tyler, tenth President of the United States, and his second wife, Julia Gardiner, of Gardiner's Island, New York. As a boy, Lyon Tyler had spent the Civil War years with his mother's family in New York.

Meeting with Ewell and with the college's Board of Visitors before the 1888 Assembly convened, Tyler agreed to introduce a bill for the state to appropriate $10,000 yearly to William and Mary to train young men to teach in public schools, as Ewell had first proposed in 1881. The group got the support of the state superintendent of public instruction and then approached members of the Assembly. Judge W. W. Crump, rector, worked on Democratic legislators, while Dr. Richard Wise, a Republican, canvassed Republicans and Readjusters.

Some lawmakers opposed the bill because they felt it would hurt enrollment at the University of Virginia, but Tyler argued that few Charlottesville students were interested in low-paid teaching careers. Having sponsored passage of the Virginia Constitution of 1867–1868, which had created the public schools, most Republicans supported Tyler's bill. Democrats were more divided.

At last the measure was enacted on March 5, 1888. It provided for a new Board of Visitors numbering twenty-one, ten of whom would serve under the college charter and the other ten would be appointed by the governor. The superintendent of public instruction was designated an ex officio member, making eleven public members.

Once the legislation was passed, the Visitors had to find a faculty, for the fall session was to open in five months. Ewell, who was seventy-eight, told Visitors he was unequal to the job but would stay until a successor was chosen. He later said the best move he ever made was "resigning at once and finally as president of the college in 1888 and not letting personal considerations hamper [its] success."

The Visitors first offered the presidency to John Buchanan, Virginia's second superintendent of public instruction. Ewell tried to persuade him to accept, writing to General William Booth Taliaferro, rector of the college:

> I wrote some three weeks ago to Dr. Buchanan, urging him to become president of the College and endeavoring to remove some of the objections I was told he entertained. He came down [to Williamsburg] for a day a couple of weeks ago, went over the building, and left, favorably impressed, as far as I could judge. I trust he will come. The success of the "new departure" is largely dependent on his acceptance.
>
> I have not left the premises as yet, for I felt sure that there would be serious trespassing on the College property, but have held myself prepared to do so at 48 hours' notice.

Buchanan declined, declaring the college too "broken down and deserted" to be revived. With the reopening only three months away, Lyon Tyler then swallowed his pride and offered himself. At thirty-five, he lacked the father image that characterized elderly presidents of his day, but he had other claims to the presidency. The Visitors wisely elected him, and Ewell accordingly drove into Williamsburg in July 1888, for his last meeting with the Visitors. As always, some members from out of town stayed at the President's House. Ewell's closest friend on the Board was Hugh Blair Grigsby, who wrote the younger man: "I believe I have been your guest for fourteen years past, so that more than one fourth of your life I have been receiving acts of kindness and courtesy from you; and I hope that the next fourteen will tell the same tale, though I shall then be an octogenarian and yourself a septuagenarian . . . I rode on horseback eighteen miles to the commencement at Hampden-Sydney last week."

Tyler's first act as president-elect was to notify the press that William and Mary would reopen on August 23, 1888. Then he searched for the traditional "six masters or professors," for his faculty, aided by a prostrate Virginia economy which offered few competing opportunities to scholars. William and Mary's salaries of $1,000 to $1,500 a year were eagerly sought.

Tyler himself was to teach moral philosophy, embracing ethics, political economy, and government. He had taught for four years in Memphis after his brief 1877-1878 professorship at William and Mary, and he was committed to education and to Virginia's renewal. In Richmond he and a fellow attorney had established the Virginia Mechanics' Institute, at which he taught for four years. He had also begun publication of his two-volume *The Life and Times of the Tylers,* the first of his historical writings.

Tyler's second in command, who was to be William and Mary's first dean, was thin, myopic, John Lesslie Hall, professor of English and history. Trained in German universities, Hall held a doctorate from Johns Hopkins. A Richmonder, he was the grandson of Richard Channing Moore, who had become Virginia's second Episcopal bishop in 1814, on the death of William and Mary's James Madison. Although eccentric in method, Hall was a sound scholar and teacher, who helped Tyler rebuild the college.

Thomas Jefferson Stubbs, born in Gloucester, taught mathematics. An ex-Confederate with the beard and bearing of Robert E. Lee, Stubbs was stern but fair. Amiable and attractive Van Franklin Garrett, the physician son of Williamsburg's Civil War surgeon Robert M. Garrett, taught natural science and prepared students to enter medical school. The Reverend Lyman B. Wharton, called "Lima Beans" by students, gave up his interim rectorship of Bruton Parish to resume teaching ancient and modern languages.

As professor of pedagogy, to produce school teachers, Tyler chose young Hugh S. Bird, whom Ewell had taught pre-college courses in the President's House while the college had been closed. Bird was also secretary of the faculty and in 1903 was made supervising principal of the "model school," as the Grammar and Matty School was designated. Many of Virginia's early teachers, principals, and superintendents trained under him.

Filling out the faculty in 1892 was Charles Edward Bishop, a Presbyterian minister and graduate of European universities, who taught Greek grammar and French. Thereafter, the president and most of his professors remained the core of the faculty well into the twentieth century.

With Tyler's help, Ewell's long pursuit of Congressional reimbursement finally bore fruit. It came in March 1893, as William and Mary prepared to celebrate the 200th anniversary of its chartering. After repeated efforts by Massachusetts Senator George F. Hoar, Congress honored the claim which William and Mary had submitted nearly thirty years earlier, which partially indemnified the college for its Civil War losses.

However, the $64,000 check was no longer adequate to rebuild the Main Building as Ewell had thought it would be in 1866. The hasty rebuilding of 1869 remained an unsatisfactory makeshift, but the college needed the money more urgently for other things. Ewell's portrait from this period shows a gentle old man with a gray beard, the quiet force that had kept the college alive.

When Mrs. Francis Smith, wife of Virginia Military Institute's elderly superintendent, asked her husband after he had visited Williamsburg, "Does Mr. Ewell look old?" "Yes," General Smith mused, "as old as Methusaleh, and I was ashamed to be welcomed among his contemporaries!" Only after Ewell died in 1894 did his estranged wife come from Pennsylvania to live in Williamsburg. The breach which separated Benjamin and Julia Ewell went with them to their graves.

Lyon Tyler recorded his predecessor's death in June 1894 in his new *William and Mary Quarterly:*

> DIED, Tuesday, June 19, 1894, BENJAMIN S. EWELL, LL.D., Fellow of the Royal Society, President Emeritus of William and Mary College, and late Colonel of the Thirty-second Regiment,

> Virginia Volunteers, C.S.A. He was truly a remarkable man. Though eighty-four years of age, he retained almost to the last his brilliant powers of conversation and inexhaustible fund of cheerfulness and wit. The College was put in mourning for his loss, and his body was deposited in the College burying-ground. . . . Chiefly through Col. Ewell's exertions, the *Historical Catalogue* of the College was prepared in 1859. I believe it is the first of the kind in the United States.

The elitism of "their Majesties' Royal College" was declining by the time of Ewell's death. A new institution was about to emerge as Lyon Tyler and his family moved into the President's House.

# 16

# *The Railroad Comes to Town*

BENJAMIN Ewell did not exaggerate the benefits that rail service would bring to Williamsburg. After 1881 the Peninsula no longer had to depend on riverboats or on the stage wagons that lumbered past the President's House and College Corner. Its pace quickened with the arrival of the iron horse.

The new industrial age began October 16, 1881. In a field in James City County, close to Ewell's plantation, workmen drove spikes which anchored the rails to wooden ties forming the roadbed. They worked under pressure, for Collis Huntington had promised congressmen that they could travel over his new Chesapeake and Ohio tracks to attend the Yorktown Centennial of October 16–19, 1881, and that climactic moment was at hand.

Optimism was typical of Huntington, who had made a fortune in the California gold rush and had become one of the nation's great railroad builders. By early October, most of the Peninsula track was in place, with a spur projecting from the main line at Lee Hall in York County to the centennial at Yorktown. All that remained to be done on October 16 was to connect the tracks at Ewell—the farmhouse of Benjamin Ewell in James City County—so that gaily-decorated Congressional trains could arrive from Washington.

To celebrate the juncture, the C&O invited citizens to come out after church on October 16 to see the driving of "the golden spike." As journalist E. H. Lively of Williamsburg described it: "At 2:30 this day the two working parties met in the Magazine field. The locality bears the marks of the [Revolutionary] ravaging party under Lieutenant Colonel Tarleton, while Washington was holding Tarleton's chief, Cornwallis, in a state of siege at Yorktown. The Rails from both directions came together at 2 o'clock and kissed, and I thought to myself that the morning and evening stars sang in happy euphony in honor of the occasion."

So pleased was Williamsburg to have a railway that its City Council, under Mayor John Henley, had permitted the C&O to lay temporary tracks down Duke of Gloucester Street. Meanwhile, a permanent rail line was being built around the north end of town, skirting the Grammar and Matty School and the site of the Governor's Palace.

A broadside issued in Richmond that October 16 hailed the event:

> The men worked dexterously and untiringly to consummate this result that there might be no drawback on the Centennial at Yorktown—the completion of this work being one of the grand auxiliaries to the successful celebration of the one hundredth anniversary of American Independence, when on the 19th of October, 1781, the English Lion trailed his defeat on the sward above the tidal wave of the noble York. . .
>
> To Mr. Hungtington, the President of the Chesapeake and Ohio Railway, our people feel gratefully indebted for the construction of this road . . . The waters of the Chesapeake and Ohio are now linked with "hooks of steel."

Excursion trains from Washington began rolling through Williamsburg on Monday, October 17, 1881. It was odd to stand on College Corner and see a steam engine puffing by. Yet, though residents shook their heads in disbelief, it was merely the first of many industrial changes that would revolutionize the college and the town.

Williamsburg had lost its most famous hostelry when the Raleigh Tavern burned in 1859. Its role through the Civil War was taken over by the Raleigh Hotel, which incorporated remains of the earlier Market Square Tavern. A comfortable, frame Colonial Inn, built onto an earlier nineteenth-century structure, faced Market Square Tavern across Duke of Gloucester Street, on the eighteenth-century site of Chowning's Tavern. It was to be enlarged and refurbished by 1907 to house visitors to the 300th anniversary celebration of Jamestown's settlement. An advertisement in an 1886 *Williamsburg Gazette and James City County Advertiser* proclaimed it as "large and airy, furnished in the most modern and comfortable style."

In 1881 the City Restaurant and Boarding House advertised 15 cent lunches, 25 cent dinners, and rooms at $1 a day and $3 a week. "Ice cream served every afternoon and evening at 5 and 10¢ a dish . . . Dinners sent out for 25¢ each," proclaimed the host, one O. J. Anderson.

Boundary Street was Williamsburg's western limit until 1902, when the college campus was placed within the town's limits. Until World War I, the land behind the college remained in farmlands and forests, dotted by an occasional house. However, rail service had begun to attract a few houses to the west end of town. Occasional Victorian style structures arose along Scotland Street, between Henry and Boundary Streets, to which Judge Richardson Henley's peafowl attracted the name, "Peacock Hill."

In the Williamsburg where Lyon and Annie Tyler settled in 1888, black families lived in cottages and lean-tos along and in back of city streets, a holdover from slavery. The town's only Negro church was the Baptist, being built in 1855 on Nassau Street on land given by Robert P. Cole. A few old-fashioned house servants continued to worship at Bruton, as their mothers and fathers had before them.

Stimulated by its new rail service, Williamsburg tried to find businesses to add to the small lumber mills, truck farms, and brickyards which shipped their wares from Williamsburg, Ewell, and Toano—the latter renamed when "Burnt Ordinary" proved too long for the railway signboard. The town envied the growing industries of Richmond and Norfolk.

Lyon Tyler wrote a pamphlet after he came to town, promoting its advantages, at the request of the Business Men's Association. In 1893 *The Virginia Gazette* came to life again after sporadic printings following the Civil War, still using the name of the weekly which William Parks had launched in 1736. Soon a knitting mill, a bank, a planning mill, an ice factory, and a cannery were opened in or close to town.

Even so, Williamsburg remained little more than a county seat and market town. Farmers from James City and York drove tumbrel carts and wagons on weekdays to Market Square, an open area near the Powder Magazine. Sometimes these were drawn by oxen, which continued in use on Peninsula farms until after World War I. The fish man sold his catch at Market Square from a horse-drawn fish wagon, loudly blowing a conch shell as he drove. Cooked crabs and deviled crabs were hawked by street vendors and eaten on sidewalks.

Saloons were common. Early in his presidency, Tyler went to City Council to protest the sale of whiskey to students by Williamsburg tavern-keepers and grocers. "It was the day of free drinking," he wrote,

> and the ill effects of liquor in the College made themselves felt. I thought it was my duty to take the lead in attacking this great curse. Williamsburg and the surrounding counties were converted to the cause of local option . . . On several occasions when the Commonwealth's Attorney declined to prosecute cases in the infraction of the liquor laws selling to students, I acted as attorney in his place. The measures taken in 1900 which resulted in the temporary abrogation of all the liquor licenses in town were followed by the repeated local option victories in Williamsburg and the counties of James City and York, which cleared immensely the moral atmosphere of the College and helped to spread temperance sentiment throughout the State.

One of the residents whom the Tylers met when they moved to town was John S. Charles, who had been born in James City County in 1851 and received schooling from Benjamin Ewell in the President's House, later attending the college. In 1928, Charles wrote his recollections—dictated to his granddaughter—of a town impoverished by long years of neglect and war.

In John Charles's youth Jamestown Road had been known as "Mill Road" from Boundary Street westward, and used by farmers to haul corn and wheat to the water-powered mill at Jones's Millpond, part of it later called Lake Matoaka. Near the road's intersection with Boundary Street stood the College Hotel, whose seventeen rooms after the Civil War housed occasional college classes, along with student and faculty roomers. It was razed in the 1900s to make way for a college dining hall.

Richmond Road was known as "the Stage Road." Douglas Freeman wrote in 1931 that even in the 1880s it retained the ruts dug into it by McClellan's artillery as it had sloshed through Williamsburg in 1862, chasing General Joe Johnston's Confederates westward after the battle of Williamsburg.

The road's most familiar landmark, apart from the college, was the hostelry known as "Frog Pond Tavern." It sat at the corner of Boundary Street, across the road from the President's House. "In front of it and in the middle of the road," Charles recalled, "was a big mudhole, which seemed then to defy all efforts to refill it; so there it remained practically all the year, and produced fine crops of frogs that furnished entertainment for Tavern guests and to the neighbors during the summer months."

Many structures had been razed by Union soldiers during the Civil War for firewood. Others had been dismantled by Union engineers and reerected at Fort Magruder, after the Union army captured that Confederate outpost in the battle of Williamsburg in 1862. Also removed was the "neat picket fence" which had enclosed the college yard before the Civil War. Gone also were the wide single and double gates, each supported by brick pillars, which once separated the college yard from Main Street, as Duke of Gloucester was then called by all except old-timers.

The tallest structure in town was the tower building of the Lunatic Asylum on Francis Street, built before 1846. The original central asylum had been destroyed in 1885, three years before the Tylers arrived. From the tower building, twelve-year-old John Charles had watched the 1862 battle of Williamsburg with spyglass. The burned structures were replaced after 1885 by nondescript buildings which stood until most of the institution was removed a half-century later to Dunbar Farm in James City County.

In Tyler's time the churches in Williamsburg were the Episcopal, Baptist, and Methodist, all on Duke of Gloucester; and the Presbyterian Church on Palace Green, not far from the former home of Robert Saunders. John Charles recalled that "he owned many slaves and an extensive plantation on York River," until "he died not long after the War and was buried in the garden of his home under a big weeping willow tree."

The town's most irreplaceable loss in the Civil War was the Williamsburg and James City County court records. Removed for safekeeping from the clerk's office, which then stood on Market Square near the Powder Magazine, they were sent up to Richmond and stored near the Capitol. These burned during the fire accompanying the Confederate evacuation in 1865. Lost were irreplaceable records of Jamestown and Williamsburg, although the records for York County, in which a part of Williamsburg stood, have survived since 1633. Among the documents then lost in 1865 were the wills and inventories of those who died in the President's House.

So badly treated in the war was Williamsburg's District Courthouse, built shortly before the Civil War, that it was sold after the war to become a hotel for a brief time. The Williamsburg-James City Courthouse had suffered less damage, though for a time court had to convene in the basement of the Baptist Church near Market Square. The church had recently served as a Confederate hospital in the battle of Williamsburg, and its basement later housed a freedmen's school. John Charles described its teacher as a Boston man who was engaged in "savory and altruistic work" educating ex-slaves.

In 1888 Williamsburg men still resorted to the duel to resolve affairs of honor. Common in Tyler's presidency were bare-knuckled fights in the "Pugnaculum" behind the college cemetery. After slugging it out, students usually shook hands and made up. "Classes were too small to have a lot of fellows refusing to speak to each other," wrote Robert M. Hughes, a former student. Ex-soldiers in college introduced hazing as a means of controlling freshmen, or "ducs," as grammar school or introductory students were known.

The interiors of the President's House and its neighboring structures were altered to provide bathrooms. No longer did students call the Main Building "Paradise" or the privy behind it "Purgatory." The back campus was used for football and baseball, which in the 1890s were beginning to stir collegiate rivalries. The hollow that is now the Sunken Garden was called Player's Dell and was also used for theatrical performances by the Ben Greet troupe of Shakespearian actors.

A shocking outburst of wounded vanity in 1901 suddenly threatened to destroy all that Lyon Tyler was trying to achieve. The complainant was the rector of Bruton, and he divided Williamsburg into factions. "The Roberts Affair," embittered many Williamsburg people before it subsided.

It began in November of 1901, when delegates from Virginia's counties and cities gathered in Richmond to revise the State Constitution. Encouraged by college growth since 1888, Tyler and the Board of Visitors asked the Constitutional Convention to revise the laws so that Virginia could take over the college as a full state institution, analogous to the University of Virginia, Virginia Military Institute, Virginia Polytechnic Institute and the normal schools.

But the rector of Bruton, the Reverend W. T. Roberts, objected to the proposal. Since his arrival at Bruton in 1894, he had come to dislike the college, its president, and some of its faculty. To the presiding officer of the Constitutional Convention, the Reverend Mr. Roberts on November 20, 1901, typed a six-page letter, attacking State funding of William and Mary as "a wrong on the taxpayers of the State." He called the college a "once honorable but now dishonored seat of learning," and signed himself "W.T. Roberts, rector of Bruton Parish."

In the uproar which followed, it developed that the minister had sought Tyler's support of his appointment to the Board of Visitors, but without success. Injured pride had led him to seek revenge.

Tyler conceded that when the college had reopened in 1888 it had been necessary to accept some unqualified men, but the caliber of students had greatly improved by 1901. "The college during its first five years [1888-1892] was a little more than a high school," he wrote later: "but gradually the standards were advanced, until now it has the regular four years work of the most advanced college . . . The great educational awakening of the public school system in the State was made possible by the leadership of men trained at William and Mary."

Bruton's rector further attacked the college's proposal to make its president an ex officio member of the State Board of Education. He called William and Mary the "smallest and least efficient College in the State," unworthy of "equality with the great Educational Institutions owned and operated by the State." He said the proposal was "a shrewd piece of work. . . . altogether unworthy of Constitution makers."

Roberts charged that Tyler had supported the social equality of Negroes by sending his eldest daughter, Julia, to Wellesley College, where Booker T. Washington's daughter was then a student. Recalling the recent furor when President Theodore Roosevelt had invited the black educator to dine at the White House, Roberts asked the Convention chairman: "Was it a crime against society for the President of the United States to sit down at the dinner table with Booker Washington? Then it must be equally criminal for the daughter of the president of William and Mary College to sit down in the classroom and at the dinner table with the daughter of Booker Washington."

The minister expressed confidence that the Convention would not "endorse such monstrous things" as "Mixed Schools, Social Equality and Miscegenation." Playing on the spirit of Jim Crow, which was evident in antiblack segregationist measures then before the Convention, Roberts asked the Convention Chairman, "Is it any wonder that the College, year by year, is dwindling in numbers and influence?"

Roberts's outburst inflamed the town. At the President's House, Lyon Tyler stayed up late to type an eight-page response to the Bruton vestry, to whom the rector was answerable. At a meeting of that body the next day held at the parish house, adjoining the churchyard, the letter was read aloud by the register, Henry Denison Cole, who operated a souvenir shop facing Bruton Church.

"It is simply inconceivable to me that such poisonous thoughts could find lodging in the brain or the heart of any human being!!" Tyler exploded. He reminded the vestry that since 1888 the State had appointed half of the Visitors, and he denied that William and Mary was "an alien and outside institution" or was "not owned or controlled by the State." He declared its enrollment of 154 was greater than that of

Hampden-Sydney, Randolph-Macon, or Emory and Henry and about equal to that of Richmond College and Washington and Lee. "It is wonderful how well the College has done with such an enemy as W.T. Roberts in our midst," Tyler fumed, "who, it can be proved, has advised students not to come to this institution."

In his defense, Tyler pointed out that his daughter Julia had entered Wellesley before Booker T. Washington's daughter had. He called Roberts's statement that the girls dined together at college "an infamous falsehood." He asserted that the Negro educator's daughter boarded off the Wellesley campus.

In conclusion, Tyler asked why Roberts had never before complained of conditions at William and Mary. He attributed the attack to Roberts's resentment that Tyler had not supported his efforts to be appointed a Visitor. "I regarded him as a firebrand, as a marplot, as a headstrong, passionate, vindictive man, as a fanatic who would throw everything into confusion," Tyler told the vestrymen. He urged that Bruton disassociate itself from Roberts's charges.

Sentiment in the college was bitterly against Roberts, but a few townspeople took his side. Particularly irate were Professors John Lesslie Hall, Van Garrett, and Lyman Wharton, who were active in Bruton. Students at the college showed their feelings by entering the minister's stable at night and painting his horse green.

Throughout 1901 and 1902 "the Roberts affair" was fought out in Bruton's vestry and in newspapers. Five of the nine Bruton vestrymen, led by Van Garrett and Henry Denison Cole, demanded Roberts's removal; the four others favored a reprimand. However, the minister hog-tied his vestry by asserting his canonical right to vote on the question, thus tying the vote. Only after a new anti-Roberts vestry was elected in the spring of 1902 could the angry cleric be removed.

At last, on May 10, 1902, *The Virginia Gazette* announced "Mr. Roberts to Leave." To replace him, Bishop Alfred Magill Randolph of the Diocese of Southern Virginia proposed William Archer Rutherfoord Goodwin, a young cleric who was rector of St. John's Church in Petersburg and was also teaching at the Bishop Payne Divinity School for blacks, for which he had been raising money. Will Goodwin's arrival in 1903 helped to heal the breach between the church and the town. As for the college, it was permitted by the General Assembly to become a full-fledged state institution, contrary to Roberts's entreaty. An act of the Assembly on March 7, 1906, transferred all William and Mary property to the Commonwealth. The new Board of Visitors was to consist of eleven members; the superintendent of public instruction and ten gentlemen to be appointed by the governor for four years each.

By 1907, when Virginia celebrated the 300th anniversary of Jamestown's settlement, the college had grown to 250 students. A new macadam road from Williamsburg took visitors to the island in the James. College buildings and grounds had expanded. The Welsbach Street Lighting Company was providing gas streetlights, but for economy's sake they went unused on moonlit nights. Twenty-four stores dotted city streets, together with wheelwright and blacksmith shops, restaurants, and saloons. Tyler irately called the saloons "grog shops," though City Council had respected his request to rule them off limits to students. Eventually Tyler promoted a local referendum, in which citizens voted to close the saloons.

For much of its rise, the town could thank the coming of the C&O in 1881, generating new life and advancing the fortunes of the college. President Tyler summed up the progress of William and Mary after it was taken over by the state in this 1907 account:

> . . . In 1888 the funds of the institution, after payment of debts, did not exceed $20,000 all told, and, because of its inability to support a faculty, the doors of the college had been closed for seven years. The buildings were only five in number . . . At the present writing (1907), the endowment fund reaches the sum of $154,000, and the college receives annually $35,000 from the state. During the past session the college had almost twice as many students as it ever had in its most prosperous days. There are ten buildings, all in fine condition, well equipped, lighted with electricity, and supplied with the purest sort of water from an artesian well. The college grounds have been surrounded with new fences, and granolithic walks have taken place of the old dirt paths. The library has grown from 7,000 volumes in 1888, to 15,000. The corps of instructors numbers 25, when at no time previous to 1888 did the number exceed ten. The college maintains an observation and training school, which is attended by upwards of 133 children. A sewer system has been put in, and a new library building will soon be erected.

In retrospect, the 1880s brought better times to College Corner, and the President's House was a center of the revival. Once the C&O reached Williamsburg in 1881, town and college began to change. From then on, their path led upward.

# 17

# *New Life in an Old House*

AFTER Lyon and Annie Tyler moved into the President's House in 1888, its rooms bubbled with children and laughter. The couple had been married ten years earlier, and they had abundant youth, good looks, and enthusiasm for life. He was six-feet three-inches tall and towered over his five-foot two-inch wife, who called him "Lony." The thirty-one Tyler years at the college were to be constructive ones.

Tyler was thirty-five—a spare, handsome, erect, and mild man with a vision of a South to be upbuilt. His grandfather and father had attended William and Mary, as had his wife's. Many of his family connections—Armisteads, Wallers, Tazewells, Taliaferros, Douthats—had also attended the college, and some had been teachers or Visitors. The college was his life.

Equally at home there was Annie Baker Tucker Tyler, his thirty-four-year-old wife. She was the great-granddaughter of St. George Tucker, who had come to the college from Bermuda in 1772 and settled his family in Williamsburg in 1788. Mrs. Tyler's father, St. George Tucker, of Charlottesville, had been a Confederate officer and had died in Charlottesville in 1863 of illness contracted during the Civil War.

One of her many cousins was Cynthia Beverley Tucker, daughter of the late Professor Nathaniel Beverley Tucker of William and Mary. Cynthia first married Professor Henry Augustine Washington of the college and, after his death in 1858, Dr. Charles Washington Coleman.

The Colemans lived in the Tayloe house on Nicholson Street with three sons and a daughter. The Colemans and Tuckers were intimates of the Tylers.

But what a mess the couple found in the President's House! Husband and wife had to undress on their bed their first night in residence because of the carpet of fleas on the floor. The president was awakened that night by what he thought were burglars mounting the stairs. When he lighted a candle and went to see, he found rats bringing potatoes up the basement steps, thump by thump.

After the Tylers had moved their furniture into the house, they had its parlor stove polished. When Colonel Ewell drove up with old Malachi in his buggy, he asked Tyler where he had found money to buy a new stove. Soon Annie Tyler had things spic and span.

After beginning the publication of *The William and Mary College Quarterly,* President Tyler stored his files and printer's plates on the President's House third floor. There he kept back issues, at first doing most of the writing, proofreading, mailing, and bookkeeping himself. The children were forbidden to play there.

The President's House was one of the five college buildings in 1888, along with the Brafferton, the College Hotel on Jamestown Road, the steward's house, and the Main Building which had been rebuilt for use in 1869 after the 1862 fire. Tyler made many campus improvements. He had gullies filled, palings replaced around the college yard, and chairs purchased for classrooms to replace old benches.

The horses were still stabled well back of the college buildings, and cows continued to be tethered on the back campus in verdant seasons, browsing on grass that grew on what became the playing field, and in the Player's Dell.

"Most of the furniture has arrived and is being put up," Tyler wrote on September 25, 1888, to General William Taliaferro, C. S. A., a Visitor who farmed and practiced law in Gloucester. "I have my hands full. You may not agree, but I like it. I hate having nothing to do. I think the grounds will look very nice when you come in. The Brafferton looks quite presentable, and I am having the walks fixed up."

With the president and his wife came their three children. The eldest, Julia Gardiner, named for her paternal grandmother, was seven. Then there were Elizabeth Gilmer, five, and John Tyler, named for his grandfather, who was two. They were to have a happy upbringing in the President's House.

Remembered among children's parties in the Tyler household was Annie Tyler's birthday party for a young neighbor, Mary Cary Moncure. Her husband wrote a ditty for the invitations:

Mary Cary's growing up,
Very sweet and hearty.
Mary Cary's going to
Have a birthday party.
Mary Cary wishes you
Would don your little bonnet
And help her cut her birthday cake
With 'leven candles on it.

President Tyler wrote to Woodrow Wilson after he became president of Princeton in 1902, for guidance in his relations with faculty and Visitors. Tyler had graduated from the University of Virginia in 1875 and Wilson, a Princeton graduate, studied law there in 1880-1882. Tyler was aware of Visitors' misgivings about his occasional absences from campus for outside meetings, for he served on educational boards whose business took him out of town. Wilson's reply was simple: the president must be his own man, doing what was necessary for college's welfare.

Tyler sadly concluded that some elderly Visitors regarded him as little more than a custodian of college property. "Under the democratic ideas prevalent in Virginia," he later recalled, "the college president was for most of the time treated by the Board as little more than a chairman of the faculty . . . President [Edwin] Alderman broke the democratic traditions at the University of Virginia, and I to a certain extent broke them at the College of William and Mary. Very often in my applications before the Legislature I exceeded the authority given me by asking for larger sums." Over the years, as the college grew, the president was allowed more freedom of decision, but criticism of his outside interests persisted in some quarters.

Although he was a progressive in some respects, Tyler was critical of President Lincoln's handling of the South's secession and of his conduct of the Civil War. Tyler felt that at the least, Lincoln was "pliant and pragmatic." When the Virginia House of Delegates adjourned for Lincoln's birthday one February in the 1920s, Tyler complained to the *Richmond Times-Dispatch:* "I think the action of the House was a great mistake . . . Lincoln's attitude on every important question suffered constant change." He printed a booklet, "Repeal the Resolution of Respect to Abraham Lincoln the Barbarian," noting that Lincoln had ordered Confederate officer John Y. Beall hanged against the rules of war, and had committed many other breaches.

In a new era of historical writing that demanded more systematic research, Tyler advocated that Virginia should better preserve county and state documents. He encouraged Cynthia Tucker Coleman of Williamsburg and Mary Jeffrey Galt of Norfolk, who formed the Association for the Preservation of Virginia Antiquities in 1889, and approved their efforts to preserve the Magazine and the Capitol site in Williamsburg. In 1892 he began publishing his *William and Mary College Quarterly,* which his successors at the college continued.

After finding colonial deed books rotting on the floor of the York County Courthouse in 1892, he persuaded the General Assembly to appropriate $5,000 yearly to preserve seventeenth- and eighteenth-century records. It was the start of a State archival reform.

His optimism was contagious as William and Mary approached its 200th anniversary in 1893. "Bicentennial Day" was celebrated during finals in the college yard on June 21, before a large crowd. Charles Washington Coleman, Jr., college librarian, read an epic poem he had written, and student J. Allen Watts of Roanoke delivered an oration. The climax was Congress' long-awaited reimbursement of $64,000 for the burning of the Main Building in 1862. On hand was ex-President Ewell, then eighty-three and within a year of his death.

As Lyon Tyler grew older, his absentmindedness worsened, though his wife Annie and his secretary, Miss Mary Jane "Patty" Morecock, tried to absorb details that he often overlooked. "Where are the children?" asked Annie Tyler one day when her husband returned from Richmond. "Oh, my Lord," he was said to have gasped. "They're waiting for me in Richmond!"

A Tyler student, J. Gordon Bohannan of Surry, remembered another case of Tyler's "magnificent forgetfulness":

> His class in psychology was scheduled for final examination and was assembled in the college chapel. Dr. Tyler had forgotten it. The faithful [college sexton] Henry Billups was dispatched to remind him that his students were waiting. I can see him now, striding down the aisle of the chapel and up to the platform. Hands behind his back, he strolled up and down, lost in thought. It was a warm spring day, and amid the buttercups of the campus a cow was placidly grazing.
>
> He lifted his head, and through the open window spied the cow. He walked to the blackboard and wrote ". . . I see a cow" and then continued his walk, while the class gazed in wonder. And then, as if inspired, he wrote an examination, the first section of which dealt with the relation between the physical and mental aspects of

William and Mary College Archives

*The "Seven Wise Men" after 1888: Professors Wharton, Bird, Tyler, Stubbs, Garrett, Bishop, and Hall pose at the Wren Building*

> perception. And the cow, wholly unconscious of the fact that she had been the subject of a psychology test, continued her placid grazing among the buttercups.

Life on the all-male campus was informal except for occasional dances. Professors had wide latitude to lay out and teach courses. Committees and meetings were few. The college honor system, first mentioned in college statutes in 1817, assumed the integrity of each student and left each man's deportment up to him except for clear breaches of honor. Tyler traced the honor system back to the 1779 reorganization. He and his faculty subscribed to the credo which Professor Nathaniel Beverley Tucker had written in 1834:

> It has been the study of its [William and Mary's] professors to cultivate at the same time the intellect, the principles, and the deportment of the students, laboring with equal diligence to infuse the spirit of the scholar and the spirit of the gentleman. He comes

> to us as a gentleman. As such we receive and treat him, and resolutely refuse to know him in any other character. He is not harassed with petty regulations; he is not insulted and annoyed by impertinent surveillance. Spies and informers have no countenance among us. We receive no accusation but from the conscience of the accused. His honor is the only witness to which we appeal . . .

Through his involvement in public life, Lyon Tyler attracted patronage to the college and brought governors, legislators, and scholars to the campus. Slowly, Assembly appropriations to the college rose from $35,000 from the State in 1907 to $54,000 in 1919. Tyler later said that the endowment grew from $20,000 to $154,000, while campus facilities expanded to a value of more than $1,000,000.

As in the past, the President's House was the center of college and community events. There Annie Tyler entertained the King's Daughters charity meetings, the Garden Club, and her church circle. A King's Daughters "silver tea" on January 8, 1894, was recorded in the minutes as "Perfect success. Made $9.10."

Tyler's faculty grew from "a President and Six Masters" to twenty-five teachers, freeing him from the classroom to devote his time to administration. The five college buildings of 1888 had increased to ten in 1907 and to fourteen by 1919, the 15,000 books had grown to 18,000. A new library near the President's House was created with the aid of $50,000 from Pittsburgh philanthropist Andrew Carnegie. Instead of salaries of $1,000 to $1,500 a year, professors by 1919 were getting as much as $3,000.

Though forced to be a man of affairs, Lyon Tyler remained primarily a scholar. As his pupil, J. Gordon Bohannan, observed:

> Dr. Tyler found his pleasure in the classroom in the teaching of American history, the revelation and interpretation of its truths, and the exposure of errors and falsehoods. He taught history not as a bare recitation of facts, of battles won and lost, of movements of troops, and dates and events. To him history was, in the words of Carlyle, "the essence of innumerable biographies" and of events in the lives of men who had cast their shadows across its pages, and, in his teaching, those who had lived in history seemed to walk the earth again.

Despite managerial duties, Lyon Tyler continued in his spare time to research and write accounts of Virginia and the college, working on the third floor of the President's House. His chief undertaking was the editing of the *William and Mary College Quarterly,* to which he contributed much of his own research. He also wrote such books as *The English in America, The Cradle of the Republic,* and *Williamsburg, the Old Colonial Capital,* in which he included a history of the college. His son-in-law, James Southall Wilson, recalled of him that: "He battled bravely for Virginia 'firsts' and for Southern values and yet in many respects he was more a liberal than a reactionary. One of the first men in the country to champion women's rights, his voice was eloquent in behalf of women's suffrage."

The President's House in the Tyler years was usually alive with young people, pets, and out-of-town guests. Annie Tyler and her good-natured cook, Mattie, stood ready on short notice to convert a family meal into a feast for visiting statesmen, educators, beaux of daughters Julia and Elizabeth, or cousins. Once when the family's oyster stew had to be expanded for unexpected company, Annie Tyler had trouble at her end of the dinner table catching enough oysters in her silver ladle for the last serving. Mattie, watching over her shoulder, pointed excitedly, "Dar he, Miz Tyler! Dar he!" It became a Williamsburg byword.

Before World War I French Ambassador and Mrs. Jules Jusserand came to Yorktown, where he spoke on Yorktown Day. They decided to remain for lunch the next day with the Tylers. Annie was not well, so a discreet call for help went out to neighbors. Cousin Mary Haldane Begg Coleman stitched up a French tricolor on her sewing machine to fly with the American flag at College Corner. Meanwhile, neighbors quietly filled the Tyler's kitchen with covered dishes. The lunch was a success.

When word reached the Tylers one July Sunday in 1916 that President and Mrs. Woodrow Wilson were coming ashore from the presidential yacht at Jamestown, Lyon and Annie Tyler met their car at College Corner and showed them through the college and Bruton Church. The two women were old friends, Edith Bolling and Annie Tucker having spent their girlhood days in Wytheville. Wilson returned the next year, on the eve of America's entry into World War I, to speak at the college. He was welcomed to the President's House by the Tylers, their cook Mattie, and three black children who peeked at the President from the pantry door.

The two Tyler daughters had many beaux. Their parents' hospitality also drew cousins and friends to stay with them for Saturday germans and daytime hops, sometimes held at Cameron Hall, at the Lunatic

William and Mary College Archives

*Students and portraits crowd the small library given by Andrew Carnegie during the Lyon Tyler presidency. The photograph was taken about 1900.*

Photograph by E. P. Griffith

*A parade for the fourth annual Peninsula School fair took place in front of the President's House on April 2 and 3, 1915.*

Asylum, and sometimes at the gym. Guests came for college dances, the girls in pinched-waist dresses and the men in dark suits and stiff collars.

In 1910 Julia Tyler, the eldest of the three children, married James Southall Wilson, who taught history at the college. While she awaited the birth of her first child in 1912 in a second-story bedroom of the President's House, she scratched her initials—JGT—and her husband's—JSW—on a windowpane, together with the date, February 1912. Her younger sister Elizabeth married naval officer Alfred H. Miles, while her brother John became a mathematics instructor at the Naval Academy.

A disturbing incident of Tyler's presidency was a rumored manifestation of homosexuality on the campus in 1898, in the wake of Oscar Wilde's widely-publicized trial in England. In January of that year a college dance was marred by a brawl involving intoxicated brethren of one of the social fraternities. President Tyler investigated, and the students were called before a faculty committee. Believing the college was persecuting innocent men, other students protested. Professor Thomas Jefferson Stubbs, who was widely admired for his fairness, was designated by Tyler to meet with the group and sift the facts.

All students were finally exonerated, but three resigned because they felt college was no longer "pleasurable nor profitable." One was James Branch Cabell, a senior from Richmond who had entered college at fifteen and excelled in languages and literature. Incensed that her son would not graduate and would be stigmatized, his irate mother came to Williamsburg with attorney William Preston of Richmond to meet with Tyler. Cabell was readmitted, graduated, and became a famous novelist, though he never showed any enthusiasm for the college.

Less happy was the story of Charles Washington Coleman, Jr., the college's bachelor librarian, who had also been accused in the incident. He was the son of Cynthia Tucker Coleman and her physician husband and thus was a cousin of Annie Tyler's. Mrs. Cabell felt that Coleman's interest in her son's literary efforts was "a bad influence." After the handsome litterateur was cleared by the faculty, he joined the staff of the Library of Congress. Gossip of Coleman's "banishment" circulated widely, as Ellen Glasgow, visiting Williamsburg in 1898, was to write in her autobiography, *The Woman Within*.

Coleman was succeeded as librarian by Miss Emily Christian. Colonel Winder Lane was bursar, and Henry Billups was sexton. Tyler's chief assistant was his secretary, Miss Patty Morecock, who worked at his office in the President's House and occasionally invited children in for refreshments as they played on the campus.

Although a humanist, Lyon Tyler recognized that applied science was needed in Virginia and in the curriculum. "Science—practical science," he wrote, "especially loves the crowded centers, where its activity may receive adequate reward . . . We miss in Virginia what we should miss—the touch of mind with mind, the mingling of soul with soul, leading to great community results." But Tidewater was growing, and Williamsburg lay in the central corridor of urban growth, as Benjamin Ewell and Hugh Blair Grigsby had prophesied.

Enrollment reached 257 in 1917, but it dropped to half that after the United States went to war in that year. The time seemed ripe to Tyler to propose that the college become coeducational, for the enrollment drop worried the Visitors. Throughout the nation women were demanding the vote, and Tyler supported them. Similarly, he advocated equal educational opportunities for women, who were not then fully welcome at any state-supported Virginia institution except the normal schools. He wrote that:

> I had always considered that women had as much right to be admitted to the benefits of the different State institutions as the young men. On various occasions I did not hesitate to champion these opinions in the faculty and Board of Visitors. Therefore, when a bill was introduced in the Senate by Aubrey Strode, [Senator from Lynchburg] I took strong grounds in its favor . . . In my report to the Board of Visitors in 1919 I predicted that when normal times returned, the attendance of the College would be greatly increased, which would render it much easier to obtain appropriations from the Legislature as well as from other sources (numbers seeming to have, in the popular estimation, more importance than any other single consideration).
>
> During the war, Williamsburg, Newport News, Yorktown, and the country around was made a center of military operations, and enormous sums were expended there by the Federal government . . . The country took on new life.

One effect of World War I was felt by Williamsburg in 1918, when the Army built the first hard-surfaced highway up the Peninsula to facilitate troop movements. A two lane road with a median strip was developed up Duke of Gloucester Street from the Capitol site to College Corner. Like the coming of rail service in 1881, it heightened the pace of Williamsburg and brought automobiles and more residents and visitors.

The college was made coeducational on March 15, 1918. It was one of the most important and far-reaching steps in college history, at first violently opposed by students and graduates but later accepted. The college newspaper, *The Flat Hat,* published a protest, but it later withdrew its objection and admitted "We found they [women] weren't so bad, after all."

The college admitted its first coeds in September 1918. The twenty girls, most from Williamsburg and adjoining counties, created a Women's Student Government, administered by a dean of women. Rules were moderate at first, but they were tightened in the 1920s. Housed on the Jamestown Road side of the campus, the girls had to go to the "men's side" on Richmond Road to use the library. Their lights had to be out on week nights at ten o'clock, and the electricity was cut off at midnight.

Despite such restrictions, coeducation took hold. Lyon Tyler, who was sixty-five in 1918, sensed that the school needed a younger president. Ailing Annie Tyler needed to be freed of the constant hospitality which she offered so wholeheartedly. In June of 1919, after the Visitors had chosen his successor, Lyon and Annie Tyler moved from the President's House to their farm, Lyon's Den, in Charles City County. There, in his last years, he began publication of *Tyler's Quarterly Historical and Genealogical Magazine*, completed his multivolume *Encyclopedia of Virginia Biography*, and wrote letters espousing his favorite causes: the advancement of the college, the vindication of President John Tyler, and the justice of states' rights and of the South's conduct in the Civil War.

Never had a wife shared so fully the pleasures and duties of the President's House, imbuing it with warmth and charm. Annie Tyler, "the ideal President's wife," died in 1921 and was buried in Hollywood Cemetery in Richmond. Two years later her widower married Miss Sue Ruffin, siring two sons when he was in his seventies. When he died in 1935 he was buried as his father had been, in Hollywood, close to the tomb of James Monroe on President's Hill. *The New York Times* described him as "a tenacious character" who had sought "to reconstruct the argument for states' rights and the implied right of secession."

Lyon Tyler was that, but he was more. William and Mary knew him as an enthusiast rather than as a controversialist, seeking to restore life to the oldest college in English America after Harvard. Few men had done as much for it. None had infused it with a more gracious presence.

# Book Four

William and Mary College Archives

## The Quest for Excellence

### 1919–1983

When Mrs. Graves and I came to William and Mary in 1971, there had been some discussion toward building a different home for use as the President's residence. The original President's House had never been modernized fully, and as a result it was sometimes a burden for my predecessors just to live there. But she and I agreed that we were not about to be the first of twenty-four presidential families not to live in that historic home. We believed that it would be much more appropriate and indeed more economical to modernize the house, air-condition it, and continue to use it just as it had been used since the eighteenth-century—as a focus of life on the campus, in the community.

President Thomas A. Graves, Jr.,
Address to the Northern Neck
Historical Society, May 21, 1980

# 18

# *The Chandler Revolution*

TO succeed Tyler in 1919, the Board of Visitors split over two men. One was James Southall Wilson, the alumnus and professor who had married Julia Tyler in 1910. The other was Julian Alvin Carroll Chandler, who had also received his M.A. from William and Mary in 1891 at the age of nineteen. In 1896 he obtained his doctorate in history at Johns Hopkins. He settled in Richmond and held positions in schools, colleges, and with a textbook publisher before being appointed in 1909 as superintendent of Richmond schools.

By a narrow margin the Visitors chose the short, stocky Chandler. They liked his no-nonsense manner, his grasp of detail, his enthusiasm, his optimism for its future. In an age of vocationalism, he seemed the right man to expand the college's services and revive its strength.

"Jack" Chandler was an ambitious, iconoclastic New South advocate, with a greater concern for finances than his onetime teacher, the nostalgic Tyler. Like Tyler, he was an historian who sought to restore Virginia to eminence. He was also a businessman.

Chandler and his wife, the former Lenore Duke of Churchland, moved into the President's House in 1919 with two of their four teenage sons, Carroll and J. A. C. Chandler, Jr. The other two—Herbert G. and Alvin Duke—were midshipmen at the Naval Academy at Annapolis. After his wife had died in 1920 and two of his sons had left home, the lonely president lost himself in work.

Lenore Chandler, a former teacher, was a quiet, devoted wife and mother who did not relish the social life of the President's House. She spent most of her time with her sons while her husband was absorbed in work. She recognized that the college was her husband's first love, for he had told her when he graduated in 1891 that he would come back as president.

Williamsburg saw that Chandler was driven by a passion for work that pushed his faculty and staff at an exhausting pace. His single-mindedness always kept him planning, always promoting. "When he entered the room," recalled Douglas Freeman after his death,

> the first impression was that of alert energy. His small, stout figure moved briskly. He smoked his inevitable cigar with nervous vigor. All his words were crisp, punctuated with his characteristic laugh. Quickly, candidly, he would state the case, whatever it was. Then, with a gracious word, he would hurry out to fulfil the next engagement on his crowded calendar. It might be in Williamsburg or Richmond or Norfolk, and it might involve a wrestle with some dark perplexity. That mattered not. He seemed always ready for the next test—seemed, in fact—to be straining like a football player for another plunge at the line. Anyone who knew him casually or saw him only on his daily round would say that President Chandler was essentially a driving, energizing executive, the modern college administrator incarnate.

He had hardly taken office when the new president began to expand the school, responding to the return of men from France. He rented the defunct Female Institute on Scotland Street to house the overflow of the 400 students enrolled in the fall of 1919, for the college then had dormitory rooms for only 215 men and 102 women. He challenged the Board of Visitors to raise $1 million for endowment. He got $25,000 from the General Assembly to repair the President's House and put hot water in all student bathrooms.

In his first year he inaugurated college extension courses in Virginia, soon to grow into the Norfolk and Richmond divisions of the college. Ultimately they would become Old Dominion and Virginia Commonwealth Universities.

So busy was Chandler that he did not pause to be inaugurated as president until October 1921. Then, in the presence of President Warren Harding and a large crowd, he outlined his aims for William and Mary. It should remain a college, he said, not aspiring to become a technical or graduate school. It should stick to the liberal arts, raise entrance

William and Mary College Archives

*In 1923 President J. A. C. Chandler, right, engaged the Reverend W. A. R. Goodwin, second from right, to join the college as teacher and fund raiser.*

requirements, resume the teaching of law (but not of medicine), offer more vocational choices to women, and emphasize government and citizenship. Chandler was soon to overstep his own boundaries, however.

"Who should be the constituents of this college?" he asked further. They should be "all types of students, but there is one type that I am especially anxious to continue to enroll in our student body. It is that sturdy Anglo-Saxon stock found in our state . . . We want the sons and daughters of our farmers, merchants, and artisans who heretofore have not gone to college to any extent to have the benefits of a college education. For this reason, the expenses at this institution should always be kept at a minimum. There is and will not be here an aristocracy of wealth."

Chandler's democratic views appealed to parents, especially those in the Tidewater, where his Caroline County family had centered since colonial times. Senator Carter Glass wrote him that "Under your broad and democratic leadership," the college "has gained my confidence in her future influence and greatness."

Following Lenore Chandler's death in August 1920, after a long bout with cancer, Jack Chandler was often alone with his boys in the house, writing speeches, preparing budgets, and organizing campaigns for state appropriations and private gifts. He found escape in work. When Edward Gwathmey, a new professor, came to pay the usual social call at the President's House in the 1920s, Dr. Chandler met him at the door and asked, "What do you want?"

Simplicity and economy were hallmarks of the Chandler era. By paying low salaries and imposing heavy teaching loads, the president was able to keep tuition charges well below other schools' fees. William and Mary became known to some as a "poor boy's college," to Chandler's satisfaction. It was a different college from the elitist one of colonial times, where privileged young men had followed the fashions of British university life.

When President Harding arrived for Chandler's inauguration, Lenore Chandler was ill. The college president accordingly planned a simple lunch in the president's room of the dining hall before the ceremonies, where he ate most meals. Chandler was pleased when Harding thanked him for serving Smithfield ham and for "letting me eat with the students."

At every session in Chandler's years the college added new courses: journalism, Italian, religion, public speaking, theater, library science, music, and aviation, along with courses preparing for engineering, pharmacy, and medicine. In 1920 the college engaged Oscar Shewmake of Richmond to revive courses in law, which had last been offered in 1861. The following year it began publishing the second series of *The William and Mary College Quarterly,* under the editorship of Chandler and Earl Gregg Swem, a scholarly Iowan who Chandler had persuaded to leave the State Library in Richmond to become librarian.

Despite meager salaries, Chandler was able to lure a few able men to join his faculty. Edward Gwathmey, later president of Converse College, came from the University of Virginia to teach English. Attorney John Garland Pollard of Richmond was hired to create the Marshall-Wythe School of Government and Citizenship, and Colonel LeRoy Hodges, a Richmond administrator, taught business administration.

But Jack Chandler's most useful choice was of William Archer Rutherfoord Goodwin in 1923 as professor of Biblical literature and religious education and to head an endowment drive. He was the same Will Goodwin who had arrived from Petersburg in 1903 to take over the rectorship of the demoralized Bruton Parish Church after the attack by the Reverend W. T. Roberts on the college. After a seven-year pastorate of Bruton, Dr. Goodwin had been called in 1909 to wealthy St. Paul's Parish in Rochester, where he had served until 1923. Now he wanted to come back to Williamsburg to help revive the college and the town.

Chandler saw in Goodwin not only a good teacher but a promoter of William and Mary. Both men were conscious of the success President Edwin Alderman of the University of Virginia was having in obtaining private funds. On June 12, 1923, Chandler informed the Board of Visitors that "Dr. Goodwin has begun his work to raise additional funds, and I am sure that he will have success."

Goodwin obtained $175,000 from Mrs. George Preston Blow of Washington to build a new gymnasium as a memorial to her husband, an alumnus. The board was enthusiastic at this good start. Much more was to come.

For two centuries the college had been able to live on 330 acres purchased in 1695, plus added property across Jamestown Road for the steward's house and College Hotel, built in 1852. Dr. Chandler began to expand the college yard into a campus that eventually exceeded 1,300 acres.

Along Richmond Road he placed the new library and gymnasium, along with men's dormitories. Along Jamestown Road he projected an auditorium and a row of women's dormitories. Buildings rose rapidly: Jefferson Hall in 1921; Monroe in 1924; Phi Beta Kappa Memorial Hall (later Ewell) and Trinkle dining hall in 1926; Rogers, Old Dominion, and Barrett Halls in 1927; Washington in 1928; Brown and an infirmary in 1930; and Chandler Hall in 1931.

Some politicians opposed William and Mary's rise, complaining that it duplicated other state schools and grew too fast. Dr. Henry Hibbs, head of the college's Richmond Professional Institute in 1925 (later incorporated into Virginia Commonwealth University) recalled that Chandler "faced opposition not only in extending William and Mary in Richmond and Norfolk" but also in Williamsburg. "There were strong feelings in Virginia that the State had too many colleges already," Hibbs remembered, and that "William and Mary might not be allowed to grow or to serve more than 150 or 200 students."

Some also felt the college erred in giving its proud name to extension divisions outside of Williamsburg, but Chandler forged ahead.

Fire struck the President's House again the night of April 3, 1922, about nine o'clock in the evening. The college bell alerted the campus. Clyde Bedsaul, a student, recalled that he rushed out of a meeting of the Clayton-Grimes Biology Club to see the third floor of the house in flames: "We college boys rushed over and started carrying furniture out while firefighters were trying to save the building. We had no idea of allowing some of the most valuable antique pieces in the United States to be destroyed . . . We met at the College dining hall next day and signed over our contingent fees to help pay for rebuilding the damaged part of the famous old building." Fortunately, damage was confined to the third floor and roof, and was soon repaired.

After his wife's death, Dr. Chandler hired a tutor for his younger sons, Carroll and Julian. His eldest son, Herbert, and his bride lived awhile on the president's third floor, where their boys, Robert and Herbert, Jr., were born. Chandler sometimes permitted needy students to live in some of his rooms. One of them occasionally carried his fiancée up the stairs piggyback so her footsteps would not be heard by the president from his study. "Is that you, Yel?" Chandler would call out. "Just me, Doctor," Yelverton Kent would reply as his fiancée teetered on his shoulders.

At night Chandler often strolled to the college office and talked with Vernon Nunn and others who worked late. "I'm lonely in that house with Lenore gone," he admitted. He usually talked business at his dining room table but he always had time for his student waiter. Chandler knew most students by name and standing. Sympathetic to their needs in the Depression, he arranged scholarships, loans, and jobs. His help made college possible for dozens, many of whom attained distinction. "He was short-tempered, and he would fire you on the spot if he thought you'd goofed off or let him down," one ex-student recalled, "but usually he'd relent in a day or so and reinstate you."

When Governor E. Lee Trinkle paid a visit in the 1930s, he left his hat at the President's House, and the servant could not find it. Chandler called his grandsons, Robert and Herbert, Jr. "Bobby, did you see the Governor's hat?" the president asked. The little boy took his grandfather's hand and led him to the refrigerator, where he had put it. Chandler beamed. "My little men can do no wrong," he told Trinkle.

Though he was appreciated by many, Chandler took little time to socialize. He had no small talk and offered few endearments to family or friends. As his faculty grew, teachers came to resent his hard bargaining and tight control. Even in the mid-20s, full professors' salaries at William and Mary reached only $3,600, with $600 extra for deans. The president often required professors to teach extension courses in Norfolk or Richmond. Salaries were increased in the 1930s, but Chandler continued to dominate.

To balance the college budget, Chandler strenuously opposed waste.

Courtesy Colonial Williamsburg Foundation

*Julian A. C. Chandler, president from 1919 till his death in 1934, stands beside his 1920s touring car outside his office.*

When he learned that a town student was taking showers in a dormitory, he called the boy in and told him to bathe elsewhere. When students threw flour over the library in 1933, Chandler expelled eleven of them. He insisted that the Honor Council mete out stiff discipline. He forced two women students to leave college for having dates "in improper places." During Prohibition, he urged that students be severely disciplined for drinking even though bootleg whiskey was prevalent in town.

Chandler's impatience to enlarge the college led to criticism in 1933 by Virginia's Auditor of Public Accounts, L. McCarthy Downs, embarrassing the president and his Visitors. Especially embarrassed was Dr. Goodwin, who had obtained many of the earmarked donations Dr. Chandler was spending. It was often quipped that Chandler would lay the cornerstone for a building and then raise money for it, and Auditor Downs made a similar complaint. In a report to Governor George C. Peery, the auditor charged that state money and endowment funds were not always used as the General Assembly or the donor designated, though he exonerated the college of fraud or shortage.

The report came at a time when Chandler, worn out by work, suffered from a bladder ailment. He went to the West Indies in the summer of 1933 for a rest, but his condition worsened. Stopping at Johns Hopkins on his return home, his condition was found to be incurable.

Faculty and Visitors urged him to take a leave of absence but he preferred to spend his remaining time working for the welfare of the college. Friends had planned a testimonial in June 1934 for his fifteenth anniversary, but they moved it forward to April. The ill, pale Chandler smiled wryly at the night's tributes.

"I remember very well when you came to Williamsburg as a student," said alumnus Dr. Killis Campbell of the University of Texas:

> You were younger than most of the rest of us . . . and you had cheeks as red as if they had been touched up . . . We marvelled how a little fellow from the world of Caroline County could be skipping freshman and intermediate Latin—could be through Terence and Tacitus—when the rest of us were desperately contending with Caesar. When I next saw you, you were at the Hopkins; and I remember the same clear-headedness and decision were in evidence there, and that even then you were showing executive ability.

Before Chandler died in a Norfolk hospital, on May 31, 1934, he asked that classes continue despite his death. However, the faculty suspended all activities on June 2, 1934, during funeral services in the college chapel which were attended by an overflow crowd headed by the Governor. He was buried at Hollywood Cemetery in Richmond.

A student at the service, Bruce Kent, a junior from Florida, noticed a familiar figure in the crowd. "I was intrigued," he wrote, "by the fact that Dr. Lyon Tyler, who had retired fifteen years earlier as president, was present at the funeral of the younger man who had succeeded him. Not only was he there but he held an infant son in his arms." The child was Lyon Gardiner Tyler, Jr., one of the two sons born to Tyler and his second wife.

Under Jack Chandler, the college had grown amazingly in response to postwar pressures, swelling from 333 students in 1919 to 1,269 in 1934. College holdings now extended beyond Lake Matoaka to the woods of James City County. The value of campus buildings had grown tenfold, from $450,000 to $4,772,311, not including the Richmond and Norfolk campuses.

Like James Blair, who he resembled in some ways, Chandler was controversial in death as in life. Many people could not accept his changes in curriculum or in student body. Some wished for the old-fashioned men's college they had known before 1919. However, time would show that J. A. C. Chandler had an uncanny perception of the needs of the college and of the role of education in a changing America.

At the graduation ceremonies in 1934, Speaker Ashton Dovell of the House of Delegates extolled Dr. Chandler and his achievements. "If you would know the man, look upon the monument, built by his own hands," he said, paraphrasing a tribute to Sir Christopher Wren.

Jack Chandler had expanded everything at William and Mary. He would be remembered as one of the pivotal men in its life.

As Virginius Dabney was to write later, "he found the college with a small and declining enrollment, and inadequate buildings and facilities, when he became its executive head . . . It should be said, however, that while he was responsible for vast improvement in the physical plant of the college, he did little to improve academic standards or to build a faculty of the highest calibre. Very probably he would have addressed himself more intensively to these problems if he had lived."

# 19

## *The Rockefeller Bounty*

DR. Chandler's enlistment of Dr. Goodwin in 1923 to raise money for William and Mary was the most imaginative act of his presidency. Out of it came gifts from John D. Rockefeller, Jr., and others to help build a college auditorium honoring the founders of Phi Beta Kappa. From that point on the philanthropist's interest expanded to envelop the entire eighteenth-century town. Colonial Williamsburg was to become the best ally the college could have. The President's House was the scene of many meetings between Chandler and Goodwin from 1924 through 1928, when the concept of Williamsburg's restoration was developing.

Although Chandler and Goodwin had disagreements, their work together for the college in the 1920s wrought miraculous changes. Both had been reared on farms, Chandler in Caroline County and Goodwin in Nelson. Both had worked their way through college and graduate school. Both saw clearly what Williamsburg could become to the nation. Though Goodwin was an extrovert and Chandler was taciturn, they shared a love of history. To them the college was Cinderella waiting to be turned into a princess.

Dr. Goodwin's efforts to revive the town began in his first ministry there, twenty-six years earlier. During his ministry of Bruton Parish from 1903 to 1909, he had partially restored the church for the meeting of the Episcopal House of Bishops there in 1907, on the 300th anniversary of the arrival of Anglicanism at Jamestown. Inspired by early memories of a book, *Hidden Cities Restored,* the minister had researched Bruton's history and written two books to document it.

From Lyon Tyler and other Williamsburgers of those earlier years, Will Goodwin had glimpsed the Williamsburg that had been and that could be. In 1922, after fourteen years as minister of St. Paul's Church in Rochester, he wrote Chandler that he would like to return to Williamsburg to teach and help at the college. Chandler was agreeable, so Dr. Goodwin moved back and started work in February 1923. Once in Williamsburg he also began to assist the Reverend Edmund Ruffin Jones, rector of Bruton, succeeding Jones as full-time rector in 1926.

As director of the endowment drive, Dr. Goodwin visited philanthropists in the North to ask help for the college. A total of $5,755,000 was sought for buildings, professorships, scholarships, and pensions. The idea of a memorial hall for Phi Beta Kappa seemed to provide an opportunity to approach northern donors, as Benjamin Ewell had done. With money from Chandler's discretionary fund, the energetic Goodwin boarded the C&O pullman at Williamsburg and headed North to begin his campaign.

A Chandler in-law once heard the president allaying misgivings Dr. Goodwin had voiced. "You just take care of the church, Doctor, and I'll take care of the money," Chandler reassured him. Also working with the two men were Librarian Earl Gregg Swem and Professor John Garland Pollard. Pollard was to leave the college in 1929 to campaign for and win the governorship of Virginia. Pollard often reassured the president, "you just can't fail, Jack."

Goodwin's most fortunate move came in February 1924, when he gave an address at the Hotel Astor in New York concerning the proposed Phi Beta Kappa Memorial Hall on the campus where the society had been organized in 1776. Present was John D. Rockefeller, Jr., a member of the Brown University chapter and heir to the Standard Oil fortune. Mr. Rockefeller talked with Goodwin, who invited him to visit the college. Rockefeller made a substantial contribution to the memorial. Four months later Dr. Goodwin was in New York to solicit campaign contributions and called at Mr. Rockefeller's office to suggest the restoration of the college's three original buildings.

In 1926, following a wait of two years, Mr. Rockefeller found time to see Williamsburg after he had attended a meeting at Hampton Institute. The Rockefeller family met the clergyman by prearrangement on Francis Street, close to Bassett Hall. For a day the minister led John and Abby Aldrich Rockefeller and three of their five sons—Laurance, Winthrop, and the towheaded David—through dusty streets. The restoration of college buildings was the only idea considered at this time.

Mr. Rockefeller was impressed and asked for time to think about the project. Dr. Goodwin agreed to go to New York to discuss plans for restoring the original college and other colonial survivals with Colonel Arthur Woods of Rockefeller's staff. Colonel Woods was then to relay recommendations to Mr. Rockefeller. Thus, armed with photographs and ideas, Dr. Goodwin met Colonel Woods in November 1926, prior to Mr. Rockefeller's second visit to Williamsburg.

When he came to William and Mary on November 27, 1926, for the dedication of Phi Beta Kappa Hall, Mr. Rockefeller admitted interest in Dr. Goodwin's plan. He authorized the minister to have drawings made of the three college buildings and a general layout made of the town. By this time, the college was calling its main structure the Wren Building, based on the assertion of the Reverend Hugh Jones in his *The Present State of Virginia,* published in 1724, that it was "first modelled by Sir Christopher Wren, adapted to the Nature of the Country by the Gentlemen there . . ."

Shortly after the November visit, Dr. Goodwin wrote Mr. Rockefeller of several eighteenth-century houses that might be purchased, including the Ludwell-Paradise house. On December 7, 1926, Mr. Rockefeller wired the clergyman authorization to buy it without revealing the source of funds. He signed his telegram "David's Father" for the sake of anonymity.

Early in 1927 Dr. Goodwin wrote Mr. Rockefeller that he had chosen William G. Perry and his Boston architectural firm of Perry, Shaw, and Hepburn, to prepare the authorized sketches. In May 1927 Mr. and Mrs. Rockefeller again came to Williamsburg, this time to go over Mr. Perry's layout map of Williamsburg in the privacy of Dr. Goodwin's Wythe House office. From that point onward, the project mushroomed to encompass nearly all of the eighteenth-century town, embracing about 173 acres and some 500 buildings.

It was suggested that the restoration be carried out through the history department of William and Mary, but Mr. Rockefeller set up the Williamsburg Holding Corporation to be the administrative organization. For a time the research and architectural work was done under the auspices of Perry, Shaw and Hepburn, and the construction work under Todd and Brown. The Williamsburg Holding Corporation later became Williamsburg Restoration, Inc. The second corporation was Colonial Williamsburg, Inc., to hold special properties, soon taking over title and management of properties; and later historical and educational activities. In recent years the entire organization has gone under the name of the Colonial Williamsburg Foundation. Dr. Goodwin had resumed rectorship of Bruton Parish Church in 1926, continuing his professorship and his pursuit of college funds. He also continued buying property for restoration, concealing Mr. Rockefeller's involvement until he had permission to reveal it. He made the announcement at a town meeting in June 1928.

The Wren Building was the first to be restored. Work was begun in 1928 with part of a $400,000 gift by Mr. Rockefeller to return the three original buildings in the college yard to their 1733 appearance. Though rebuilt three times, the Wren Building contained much of its exterior brickwork, some of which had withstood the fires of 1705, 1859, and 1862, and the alterations after each. It was rebuilt, after extensive research from 1929 to 1931, assuming its 1716-1856 form.

To accomplish such a restoration, it was necessary to bring together scholars and architects to re-create the building techniques of early Virginia. A department of research and record was established by Perry, Shaw, and Hepburn to extract, correlate, and index source material on Williamsburg and the college. Research was pressed in the United States, England, and France. One key discovery in 1929 was an engraving showing Williamsburg's public buildings in the period from 1733 to 1747, found in the Bodleian Library at Oxford University.

As work on the Wren Building approached completion, restoration of the exterior of the President's House and the Brafferton began. The President's House porch was replaced by the simple portico and stone steps which adorned the campus entrance to the house in 1733, as shown on the Bodleian plate.

As restoration of the house exterior approached completion in 1931, President Chandler obtained funds to undertake some interior improvements. Because modern conveniences had to be incorporated, it could not be a complete restoration. However, fireplaces which had been bricked up were reopened, and Georgian mantels were reinstalled in place of the Victorian ones President John Johns had purchased. Of this work, the architect noted: "The original restoration [of 1930–1931] was only intended to comprise the exterior, and plans were made accordingly, but due to the assistance of the President [Chandler], funds were made available from another source, which, though not adequate . . . were sufficient for a restoration of a simple character."

For the convenience of future occupants, the house was altered to admit a "compromise" kitchen and pantry, ending the long dependence on the outside kitchen. The old kitchen was converted into a rental apartment. An early occupant was John Dalton, a senior at William and

Mary and president of the student body. He was to become governor of Virginia twenty-five years later.

Dr. Chandler moved back into the President's House in time to entertain French and British leaders attending the Yorktown Sesquicentennial of October 1931, honoring the 150th anniversary of Washington's military victory there. They included Marshal Henri Petain, Lord Cornwallis, and governors of the thirteen original states, including New York's Governor Franklin D. Roosevelt. During the four days of the sesquicentennial, faculty and visitors also conferred an honorary degree on President Herbert Hoover in a tent on the Yorktown battlefield.

Mr. Rockefeller's 1928 gift stipulated that Colonial Williamsburg would continue to maintain the exterior of the college's three colonial structures, at college expense, to assure authenticity. Gradually some of the Wren Building's interior rooms were absorbed into the Restoration's exhibition building tours.

To enclose the campus, President Chandler had a brick wall built from College Corner to the Richmond and Jamestown Road boundaries of the campus. As the central feature of the back campus, he proposed a sunken garden similar to one he had admired at Chelsea Hospital in London when he had visited it in 1929. Designed by landscape architect Charles Gillette of Richmond, the garden was completed in 1934. Brick walkways were laid, boxwood vistas created, and elms, beeches, hollies, dogwoods, and white pines were planted.

Until his death, Dr. Chandler continued to expand the college, buying property at amazingly low prices in the depressed 1920s and 1930s. Houses adjoining College Corner were bought as residences for professors, fraternities, and sororities. In 1928 the college also bought the Robert Bright farm adjoining the campus on Richmond Road, at first renting out the nineteenth-century Bright house, while developing the farmland into Cary Stadium and playing fields. Close by, on Jamestown Road, the college acquired Jones's Millpond, which backed up behind a dam to form a waterway which the college renamed Lake Matoaka. To protect the campus beyond the lake, the college bought woodland from Mill Neck to Strawberry Plains Road.

Chandler's last purchase was a 131-acre tract north of the C&O tracks to become an airport, where he hoped to train student pilots. It brought his acquisitions for William and Mary to a total of 1,215 acres, which at Depression prices had cost less than $300,000.

During the last years of the Chandler presidency Duke of Gloucester Street was transformed from an undistinguished twentieth-century thoroughfare to its eighteenth-century appearance. Curbs and telephone poles disappeared, and wires were placed underground. Once again the street looked as it did after having been laid out by Governor Francis Nicholson and his surveyor, Theodorick Bland, in 1699.

Partly as an outgrowth of the Yorktown Sesquicentennial of 1931, the United States Park Service created the Colonial National Historical Park to embrace Jamestown, Williamsburg, and Yorktown. Eventually they were linked by a twenty-five-mile scenic and recreational drive enfolding some of America's most historic ground.

Neither J. A. C. Chandler nor W. A. R. Goodwin lived to see the parkway completed, but the ambitious conception had materialized by the time Dr. Chandler was buried in Richmond in 1934, and before Dr. Goodwin was interred five years later near the altar in Bruton Parish Church. Each of the two visionaries had accomplished monumental works. Each could sleep in peace.

# 20

## *"Happy Days Are Here Again"*

J. A. C. Chandler's death in 1934 was a blow to those who knew his ambitious plans. To salvage continuity, the Board of Visitors turned to the man who had served as vice-rector since 1926, under Rector James Hardy Dillard. He was John Stewart Bryan, sixty-two, publisher of *The Richmond News Leader* and active in Virginia life.

Bryan at first said no. He was deeply involved in Richmond business and cultural affairs, and his wife was being treated in a sanatorium for a nervous ailment. His children felt the presidency would be too demanding and the Richmond to Williamsburg circuit too exhausting, but the Visitors persisted. John D. Rockefeller, Jr., added his plea. The college had suffered embarrassing criticism of its financing by the state auditor, and Bryan's name would help to restore credibility.

The publisher at last agreed, provided that his fellow Visitor, insurance executive Charles Duke, Jr., of Churchland, a relative of Chandler's wife, would become business manager and Bryan's deputy. The two were already overseeing the campus landscaping. In addition, Bryan was anxious to raise faculty and admissions standards. He was concerned about low morale among the college's underpaid professors.

Rector Dillard, long active in southern education, hailed the new president as "a distinguished Virginian and statesman—one who sincerely believes in the education of all people." The two had worked together on the Board of Visitors.

Thus in the summer of 1934, amiable Mister Bryan—he insisted that non-medical academics should be "mistered"—moved into the President's House. He turned the third floor over to Business Manager Duke and his wife, the former Virginia Welton, who was to be his gracious and indefatigable hostess for President's House events.

During the Bryan years the college attracted visitors from all walks of life, many of them friends of the president. Bryan was at home in politics, statecraft, business, literature, and the arts. In his eight years in the President's House he brought countless people to the campus. He had verve and style, and students liked him. To many faculty and townspeople, the Bryan years seemed a golden age.

Furnishing the President's House presented a problem for Bryan, for it had no furniture and Bryan's was in his Richmond house, Laburnum. To solve the problem, the college and Colonial Williamsburg enabled the restoration's curator, James L. Cogar, to buy needed furnishings, which were supplemented by reproductions made by Harrisonburg and Norfolk craftsmen. Cogar and Mrs. Duke also purchased draperies, linen, and silver for the house.

To accommodate Bryan's six-foot four-inch frame, he installed an oversized bed in the president's bedroom. Cogar chose a few portraits from the college library collection to hang in the house, and he and Virginia Duke bought some Oriental rugs from an importer in New York. A handsome Virginia-made antique secretary, that Cogar bought for the house from a Petersburg dealer, was found to contain secret drawers. In one of those drawers was a pair of cufflinks engraved "G.W." Could the desk have been George Wythe's? George Washington's? No one knows.

One night at dinner Bryan turned to John D. Rockefeller, Jr., "What is an ideal liberal arts college?" he asked. "And who is an ideal president?" Rockefeller thought a moment and suggested Dartmouth, where his son Nelson had been at school under President Ernest Hopkins. Bryan wrote Hopkins, who deprecated his own effectiveness. "If I have any success with my boys," he replied, "it's because I sit in the bleachers and eat peanuts with them at baseball games."

Hopkins offered to send Dartmouth's Dean E. Gordon Bill to Williamsburg to talk with Bryan, but Dean Bill declined Bryan's invitation to stay at the President's House. "I never enjoy being anyone's house guest," he wrote in reply. "I hope you won't mind my saying that I would rather have an attic room in the local hostelry than a suite in your house!"

The dean made many trips to Williamsburg in Bryan's regime. Bryan credited Dartmouth and Dean Bill with showing him how William and Mary could strengthen its liberal arts and better select its freshmen. The college relaxed its vocational emphasis and moved back towards the liberal arts.

Bryan's chief effort was to raise the caliber of students and teachers. A graduate of Harvard law school, he attracted young Harvard scholars. Outstanding among them were James W. Miller in philosophy, Harold L. Fowler in history, and Charles T. Harrison and Murray Eugene Borash in English. Another Bryan choice was that of classicist George J. Ryan of the University of Michigan.

On the campus the new men joined such incumbents as librarian Earl Swem, historian Richard Morton, psychologist Joseph Roy Geiger, law professor D. W. Woodbridge, linguists Grace Landrum and Jess Jackson, economist Albion Taylor, classicist A. Pelzer Wagener, scientists Robert Robb, William Guy, and Donald Davis, and theater expert Althea Hunt.

Some of the president's faculty favorites were dubbed his "kitchen cabinet," and resented by others who felt excluded.

Of all Bryan's faculty, Swem brought the college widest acclaim with his *Virginia Historical Index,* known as "Swem's Index." Compiled by the meticulous Iowan and assistants over ten years with the support of the Rockefeller Foundation, it was published in two large volumes in 1934. It indexed Henning's *Statutes at Large,* the collected acts of Virginia from 1619 to 1779, three historical and genealogical magazines published between 1858 and 1930, and other historical compilations. It was hailed by *The New York Times Review of Books* as essential to the study of colonial America.

Swem's scholarly repute facilitated the college's acquisition of rare manuscripts and family papers relating to the college and state. Under him, the library amassed a collection surpassed by few colleges in America.

Like Dartmouth's Hopkins, John Stewart Bryan made a point of knowing his students and of mixing with them on campus and at the President's House functions. He also recognized the faculty desire for a greater voice in college affairs. "I feel like a jack-in-the-box who's been let out, now that Mr. Bryan has come," said Professor William Guy, a Rhodes scholar and popular chemistry professor.

To mix students and faculty and to erase the college's "poor boy" image, Bryan instituted elaborate June graduation dances in the Sunken Garden. He also entertained at an annual pre-Christmas party in Phi Beta Kappa Hall to send students home in high spirits. The

William and Mary College Archieves

*In 1918 army reservists staged a fire drill at the President's House. President Roosevelt spoke at John Stewart Bryan's inauguration at the Wren Building in 1934.*

parties were paid for by the president, and all students and faculty were invited.

Never before had the college seen such a gathering as Bryan presided over as "Master of the Revels," his tall frame in colorful colonial garb and handsome wig on his head. As his deputy, the "Lord of Misrule" introduced fraternity and sorority skits presented before a college audience in rented finery. An extrovert, Dean Theodore Cox of the law school, was Bryan's enthusiastic aide in such affairs. After the show the Master of the Revels welcomed guests to an elaborate buffet in the Dodge Room, followed by dancing.

Another innovation was horseback riding, which Bryan himself enjoyed. Civilian Conservation Corpsmen in the 1930s established a camp on college land and laid out miles of hiking and bridle trails around Lake Matoaka, which were used until the outbreak of World War II. The college built a stable adjoining the lake. It was later rebuilt and used as headquarters for the annual presentation of Paul Green's symphonic drama, "The Common Glory," at Matoaka Amphitheater, beginning in 1947.

Bryan set forth his aims at his inaugural in October 1934 on the Wren Building's rear portico. President Franklin D. Roosevelt spoke and recalled his first visit to Williamsburg in 1914, coming by boat to Jamestown and hiring a Negro wagoner to drive him to town.

Bryan was interested in the arts and encouraged the college to utilize the skills of the architects and historians Colonial Williamsburg had brought to town. Out of this grew the college's Department of Fine Arts, the first such undergraduate venture in the South. It resulted from a proposal by Leslie Cheek, Jr., to Bryan in 1935 that Cheek teach architectural history. His success led the Yale architectural graduate to propose other courses inspired by innovative graduate programs at Harvard and Yale.

"Can you organize it?" Bryan asked Cheek. He gave the department the use of Taliaferro Hall, a dilapidated building across Jamestown Road from the Brafferton, and asked Cheek to recommend teachers and a library. Encouraged by the success of a social history course introduced at the college by curator James Cogar of Colonial Williamsburg, Cheek put together a department to teach the enjoyment and techniques of painting, sculpture, architecture, music, and the theater.

An occasional visitor to the department was Abby Aldrich Rockefeller who with her husband, John D. Rockefeller, Jr., spent two months each year at Bassett Hall, their eighteenth-century estate on Francis Street. Mrs. Rockefeller gave the college a painting by Georgia O'Keeffe, a former Williamsburger, and encouraged the college to invite the artist to come back in 1937 for a one-man show and an honorary degree.

The growth initiated by J. A. C. Chandler continued under Bryan until the outbreak of World War II. Marshall-Wythe Hall, later renamed for James Blair, was completed in 1935, along with a new Taliaferro Hall. Put to use the same year was Cary Field, built on part of the 274-acre Bright farm which the college had bought in 1928 for $33,000. The Bright residence was rented at one time to the Kappa Alpha fraternity and later became the Alumni House.

Noticing that fireplaces in the President's House gave off smoke,

Courtesy Colonial Williamsburg Foundation

*John Stewart Bryan welcomed Abby Aldrich Rockefeller to one of his Christmas parties for students and faculty in the 1930s.*

Bryan sought help one day from William G. Perry of the Restoration's architectural firm. When Perry talked with architect A. Edwin Kendrew, Kendrew remembered that screens had been placed over the President's House chimneys in 1931 at Chandler's behest to keep out birds and squirrels. When Kendrew brought an artisan to plumb the chimneys, the expert's plumb line missed the chimney and smashed a windowpane. But Kendrew was proved correct, the chimney screens were removed and the fireplace stopped smoking.

Bryan's wide connections benefited the college. His guest book at the President's House bore hundreds of signatures, from bandleaders to presidents. Franklin Roosevelt signed boldly on one page, followed by Eleanor Roosevelt and presidential secretary Missy LeHand. Other visitors included Edith Bolling Galt Wilson, widow of Woodrow Wilson; Rear Admiral Cary Grayson, Woodrow Wilson's medical aide and an alumnus; and Mrs. Alfred I. du Pont, the Virginia-born Jessie Ball and a benefactor of the school.

John and Abby Rockefeller were often guests. So was John D. Rockefeller 3rd, then Colonial Williamsburg's chairman, and Kenneth Chorley, who succeeded Arthur Woods as the foundation's president.

Alexander Woolcott, writer and bon vivant, had such a good time at dinner, that he burned holes in his napkin and the carpet with his cigarettes.

Another guest was the effervescent Mrs. Archibald "Mollie" McCrea, whose husband restored Carter's Grove, the Burwell plantation on the James below Williamsburg. On a visit in November 1934 she signed "Mollie McCrea, vandal of Virginia"—an allusion to her search for secondhand building materials for her house. Another regular was Douglas Freeman, editor of Bryan's *Richmond News Leader* and popular lecturer at the college and at Columbia University.

Bryan often dictated letters to his secretary, Miss Cora Tomlinson, as he drove his Franklin to Williamsburg over the winding road from Richmond through Bottom's Bridge, Providence Forge, and Toano. His family sometimes came too; his daughter Amanda, Mrs. R. Keith Kane of New York, and his sons John Stewart, Jr. and David Tennant Bryan of Richmond, with their wives.

Bryan added to the staff four Richmonders closely involved in college operations. They were his nephew Thomas Pinckney, Richard Velz, who handled press relations, Mary Tyler Freeman, and Em Bowles Locker. In 1939 Miss Freeman married Leslie Cheek, and Miss Locker became Mrs. Benjamin Alsop.

The president would often phone a faculty couple in the afternoon to come for dinner that night. "I hate to eat alone," he admitted. He enjoyed witty, literate people. "He was a catalyst," said one student, "bringing together all ages and conditions of men." He put guests at ease.

Two visitors in 1935 were Gertrude Stein and Alice B. Toklas, who drove from Richmond with poet Carl Van Vechten for a talk by Miss Stein at the college. Arriving at the President's House, they asked Virginia Duke if the "rose is a rose" poet could rest in the living room. Miss Toklas spread sofa cushions on the floor for Gertrude's siesta while professors who arrived for the lunch waited outside in the hall. Though Miss Stein claimed she disliked chocolate, she ate a slice of Mrs. Duke's chocolate cake and asked waiter William Cumber for more.

Frank Lloyd Wright spoke at the college in 1936 and made headlines by criticizing Williamsburg architecture. The next morning at breakfast in the President's House he was contrite. He signed Bryan's guest book, "Frank Lloyd Wright and wife Algivanne, after a breakfast that justifies 'the restoration.' " The menu included Smithfield ham and spoon bread. In April of 1941 President James Bryant Conant and the Harvard Board of Overseers met for several days at William and Mary as guests of Bryan, a member of the board. "You are spoiling my board," Conant complained to Bryan.

Bryan's friendliness with students grew legendary. In 1935 the president asked the Women's Student Government president Kathryn Chiswell, later Mrs. Whitney Sweeney, Jr., to lead the grand march with him at the midwinter dances. "I'm not much of a dancer," he confessed, "but we can walk around and no one will notice." Mrs. Sweeney recalled that "We danced his way. Everybody noticed for a few seconds, and then nobody noticed. It was marvelous."

Virginia Wilson Halliday, who was a National Youth Administration assistant at the college, found Bryan "as gracious to a country freshman as to his most distinguished visitor. He exemplified Shaw's dictum that 'Good manners are having the same manners for everybody.' " She liked his "old-fashioned Virginia accent—'Cyarter' and 'gyarden', with a Harvard overlay!"

Other students thought the president had a British accent, especially when he put his hands on their shoulders and addressed them as "dear girl" or "dear boy."

A teenaged Norfolk County debater, Josephine Hubbell, stopped at the President's House one night to see family friend Charles Duke. A tall man in a dinner jacket met her at the door and said "Mister

Charles" was out but she was welcome to look around. "We thanked the butler," she recalled, "came in, and had a delightful tour, with the butler pointing out interesting things and showing great interest in us and our debating skills." He politely asked if she thought of coming to William and Mary. "Before we left, the butler offered us chocolates from the biggest box of candy I'd ever seen," the visitor remembered.

Later Miss Hubbell learned that the butler had been Bryan, dressed for a concert. "Over the years I've worked with a number of presidents," she wrote later, "but I remember none the way I remember John Stewart Bryan."

In 1938 the president elevated James W. Miller, a Harvard import who had been recommended by philosopher Ralph Barton Perry, to be dean of the college. He also gave the faculty the voice in academic affairs and the access to the Board of Visitors which many felt Chandler had denied them. Morale was lifted, and standards for admission and graduation were raised.

The new president adapted for William and Mary's purpose student selection and indoctrination methods then in use at Dartmouth and elsewhere. He created the office of dean of freshmen, naming psychology professor J. Wilfred Lambert to the post, with John Hocutt as his assistant. Lambert later became dean of students.

Subsidization of athletics in the Bryan years was to create problems. The president had originally favored the amateurism he had known as a student at the University of Virginia, where he had received his B.A. and M.A., but after William and Mary players had suffered severe injuries in games with subsidized teams, Bryan acceded to Visitor sentiment. "I can't stand to see our boys hurt," he told Charlie Duke. "Let's go after good players." The result was the hiring of Carl Voyles from Duke University in 1939 as director of athletics, with R. L. "Rube" McCray of Tennessee Wesleyan College as assistant.

Visiting New York that year, Bryan met a friend on the street. "I suppose you're up here looking for faculty?" the friend asked. "No," Bryan deadpanned, "Looking for a halfback." His daughter and some professors felt he was letting athletics "carry him too far afield," as Amanda Bryan Kane later put it. She recalled that "We tried to talk him out of it, but he made up his mind, and that was that."

World War II reduced enrollment and interrupted the heady progress of Bryan's first years. In 1941 the Norfolk division of the college was struck by academic scandal. On the complaint of professors there, President Bryan learned that the well-loved Dean William T. Hodges had permitted alteration of student transcripts. Though Hodges was replaced by Charles Duke as dean at Norfolk after an investigation by Bryan, William and Mary was reprimanded by the Association of American Universities. Some Visitors blamed Bryan for the problem, and his relations with some of them deteriorated.

Once the Norfolk crisis was resolved, John Stewart Bryan decided to step down from the presidency. He was approaching seventy, and his health was declining. When he retired during World War II in 1942, he was honored by the Board of Visitors' election to the chancellorship. Even so, recalled Dean Wilfred Lambert, "It always seemed to me that Mr. Bryan left the college with much less enthusiasm, much less peace of mind, than when he came in 1934." He died within two years of retirement after several strokes.

College Corner sadly missed his urbane, gangling figure. Never had the President's House contained such good humor, such joie de vivre. "The whole quality of life in those years was inspired and dominated by Mr. Bryan," said Dean Miller. "He surrounded himself with the best and brightest he could find. Everybody thought William and Mary was on the march."

It was indeed, though it was to have a few detours on the way.

# 21

## *Difficult Decisions*

A CHOICE between the Chandler and Bryan ideals for the college confronted Visitors on John Stewart Bryan's retirement from the presidency in 1942. Which way should the college go? Should it emphasize the liberal arts, as Bryan had advocated, or should it be the hub of an expanding Tidewater university system as conceived and put together by J. A. C. Chandler before he died in 1934?

The two concepts remained at odds for two decades. Some Visitors embraced Chandler's view and opposed what they thought was Bryan's mistaken effort to imitate Ivy League colleges. Others aligned themselves with Bryan. The debate reached the Governor's office and the General Assembly.

It was inevitable, under the circumstances, that the Board of Visitors in 1942 should be divided on the choice of Bryan's successor. Chandlerites favored Morgan Combs, handsome president of Mary Washington College and cousin of E. R. "Ebbie" Combs, a state official and a leader of the Byrd organization. The Bryan group polarized around historian John Pomfret, who was dean of the graduate school of Vanderbilt University.

Pomfret had come to the Visitors' attention as a distinguished academic who was the brother-in-law of John Dana Wise. Wise was serving Bryan as chief executive of his Richmond newspapers after the Bryans had also acquired *The Richmond Times-Dispatch* to add to their

*News Leader* in the 1930s. Wise's sister, Sara, had married John Pomfret, an easygoing, attractive historian who had earned his degrees from the University of Pennsylvania. Pomfret had taught history for twelve years at Princeton before going to Vanderbilt to be dean of the senior college and graduate school.

The Board of Visitors finally chose Pomfret by a one-vote margin after a last minute shift among Combs supporters. He was installed on February 8, 1943, on the 250th anniversary of the college charter. Jack and Sara Pomfret brought their only son, John Dana Pomfret, with them from Nashville. John was away at Episcopal High School and at Princeton during most of his parents' residence in the President's House. He later joined *The New York Times,* becoming executive vice president and general manager.

Williamsburg liked the attractive Pomfrets, although he was a little less outgoing than Bryan had been. They fitted easily into the President's House, entertaining and entering into college functions. As a South Carolinian, Sara Pomfret was welcomed into the Garden Club and other activities of Williamsburg ladies. She had a Southern graciousness and fresh style. She took interest in the plantings of the President's House, whose eighteenth-century garden had been greatly reduced by campus development.

However, President Pomfret soon found that wartime imposed many pedestrian chores on the president. He likened his job to "running a hotel." With students and teachers going off to war, the college was pressed to maintain courses and to keep up buildings. Although accreditation was regained a few months after Pomfret took over, male students and teachers were increasingly hard to find. To keep going, the college took over two wartime military reserve units which helped pay the bills.

Pomfret was amused in these pinched circumstances by the interest of a rich Texas visitor to the campus. The Texan sought out the president and asked him bluntly, "How would you like to have forty, fifty, or sixty million dollars?" "On what conditions?" Dr. Pomfret inquired. "No strings," the Texan replied; he and a friend just wanted to have a "name" college in Houston. They would endow William and Mary and pay to move it if the college would consent. Dr. Pomfret politely declined.

As an historian Pomfret saw opportunity to join the work being done in American history at the college to the research being done by the Restoration. With the support of Colonial Williamsburg and the General Assembly in 1943, he organized the Institute of Early American

History and Culture and obtained funds from the Commonwealth of Virginia and Colonial Williamsburg to support it.

The institution assumed publication of *The William and Mary College Quarterly* widening its range from Virginia to include the other states. Under the editorship of Professor Richard Morton and later of Douglass Adair, it became a leading journal in its field.

A highlight of the Pomfret years was the visit of Winston Churchill and General Eisenhower in 1946, during a postwar visit to Williamsburg and Richmond.

An athletic scandal erupted at the college in 1951, during the eighth year of Pomfret's presidency. School officials were warned that athletes' grades were being raised without justification in college records to permit their eligibility for teams, and Pomfret named a faculty committee to investigate. However, when one alarmed dean notified the press, the Visitors were indignant and chastised the president for not having acted without waiting for a committee. Pomfret resigned.

Colgate Darden, Jr., who was governor and later college chancellor in Pomfret's William and Mary years, criticized the faculty for not coming to Pomfret's defense more strongly. He termed Pomfret's treatment by the Board of Visitors "outrageous" and called the faculty "pusillanimous." The president "was right," Darden insisted. "There never was a more honest, straightforward person than Pomfret." But the harm had been done.

After his resignation, John Pomfret was elected director of the Henry E. Huntington Library and Art Gallery in California, where he served with distinction until his retirement in 1966. Dean James W. Miller, who was chosen by the Visitors as acting president on Pomfret's departure, later praised Pomfret's continuation of "qualitative progress" at William and Mary, begun under Bryan, and his emphasis on teaching and of historical research. "I think Dr. Pomfret made a very good president, though he disliked the nonacademic details," Miller said.

Historian Allan Nevins of Columbia, in an essay honoring Pomfret's retirement from the Huntington Library, attributed his William and Mary difficulties partly to resentment by a few Visitors "in a state sensitive to taxes and hence inclined toward cheesepenny economies in education . . ." It was true that limited funds and stringent budgeting continued to plague the school.

Alarmed by the possibility of further disruption, the Visitors met and decided privately to offer the presidency immediately to Rear Admiral Alvin Duke Chandler, an alumnus and second son of President J. A. C. Chandler. The admiral was on duty in Washington but was known to be

William and Mary College Archives

*King Hussein of Jordan, once aboard Alvin Chandler's Navy ship, visited him in 1959 at the President's House.*

due for a change of command. Accordingly, Rector Oscar Shewmake and Judge Lester Hooker of the Board of Visitors hurried to Washington to convey the offer. When the admiral came to Williamsburg a few days later to discuss it, he was urged by the Visitors to take the oath of office that same day, October 11, 1951.

Chandler did so, even before resigning his naval commission. He thereby incurred the displeasure of the Chief of Naval Operations and of President Harry Truman. When news of his acceptance went out to the world by radio that afternoon, it caught the college by surprise. Some professors were disappointed, for a faculty commmittee was investigating nominees it wished to propose. It felt it had been mis-led.

William and Mary College Archives

*In 1948 President Pomfret (right) conferred degrees on Governor Tuck, Viscount Alexander, Canadian Mackenzie King, and President Truman.*

Some professors felt the admiral was unsuited for the presidency, and they sought to find teaching jobs elsewhere. Alvin Chandler was to feel their resentment throughout his years of service.

The Chandlers moved from Alexandria to the President's House in the fall of 1951, a few weeks after his acceptance. For them it was a homecoming, for during Alvin Chandler's Annapolis midshipman days, his father was president of William & Mary. "Then we would sit on the front porch on Sunday afternoon," said Mrs. Chandler, the former Louise Michaels, of Richmond, "talking with students sitting on the steps."

Now it was a different house. The 1849 front porch and the 1865 professors' dormitory wing had been removed. The exterior was again the symmetrical structure that had been completed in 1733, though the interior had been adapted to twentieth-century living.

Although Admiral Chandler had been in the Navy during his father's presidency, he had ties to the campus. Business Manager Charles Duke was Chandler's first cousin, and Miss Pearl Jones, who had served in his father's office under Kathleen Alsop, was now the secretary to the new president. William and Mary had many family associations for the Chandlers and Dukes.

Louise Chandler hired Helen Canaday as her cook. Helen had worked for the Peachy family, and she arranged for college janitor Arthur Hill to act as a part-time butler. Experienced and relaxed as hosts, the Chandlers had frequent entertainments and guests. They invited student groups for afternoon tea, an eighteenth-century survival which they had enjoyed in London while the Admiral had attended the Imperial Defence College. They gave an annual lunch for seniors with faculty wives serving as hostesses.

Louise Chandler was active in women's historical groups and welcomed them to the President's House. Her warmth and finesse as a hostess is remembered by those who were entertained by the Chandlers, who set a high standard of hospitality in the years before they moved from Williamsburg to Virginia Beach.

Because most students were below the legal age to buy or consume alcoholic beverages, the Chandlers did not serve them during their regime at the President's House. The Admiral's intransigence toward student drinking was to become an issue with undergraduates before he left the presidency.

One of Chandler's World War II comrades-in-arms, President Eisenhower, spoke at his inaugural on May 15, 1953. The head of the student body that day was a thin, dark-haired John Dalton, who lived in an outbuilding in the Chandlers' yard. In 1978 he would become Governor of Virginia.

After Alvin Chandler's inaugural, the Eisenhowers and Chandlers relaxed alone in the President's House. While the President talked by phone with his Secretary of the Treasury in Washington, their wives got acquainted. "I'm an old Army gal," said Mamie, straightforwardly. "You're an old Navy gal. Let's go from there."

At one point President Eisenhower asked Chandler, "Now that you're out of the Navy, what are your politics?"

"My politics are the College of William and Mary," said the admiral.

"That's what I said when I became president of Columbia," the President rejoined.

The Chandlers entertained many Britons whom they had known in London and Washington. Senior officers of Britain's Imperial Defence College twice came to town in Chandler's incumbency, bringing several World War II military heroes. In 1954 England's Lord Chief Justice accompanied the United States' Chief Justice Earl Warren to the campus for the 200th anniversary of the birth of alumnus John Marshall. Another President's House guest was King Hussein of Jordan.

One day Louise Chandler received a phone call from Britain's Third Sea Lord, an old family friend. Could he spend Easter and get into Bruton Parish Church for the Easter service? "You know," he explained, "I find that in America you even queue up to get into church." He was welcomed and got to church.

King Paul of Greece, who had lunched aboard Chandler's ship in the Aegean Sea, visited the Chandlers in the President's House in 1953 with Queen Frederika. Britain's Queen Mother Elizabeth came the next year, following a tour of Jamestown. She was interested in the college portraits then in the President's House and recognized one by Sir Peter Lely. She passed on her enthusiasm to her daughter, Queen Elizabeth II, who was to visit the college three years later.

When Virginia celebrated the 350th anniversary of John Smith's settlement at Jamestown in 1957, the President's House entertained many of its guests. Among them were the master and clerk of the Drapers' Company, one of London's ancient city guilds. The visit led to the Drapers' student exchange program between the college and British undergraduates. It also led to the Drapers' Company's gift to the Great Hall of a portrait of Queen Anne, who in 1708/09 had granted funds to rebuild the college after its first fire.

The climax of the 1957 Jamestown anniversary was the visit on October 16 of Queen Elizabeth and Prince Philip. The Queen's entourage came to the President's House from Jamestown for tea and sherry in the afternoon. It was a rest stop before the monarch and Prince Philip toured Williamsburg and attended a reception in the Governor's Palace gardens and a dinner at Williamsburg Inn.

For all its charms and associations, the Chandlers found that the President's House left much to be desired as a home. It was hot in summer for lack of air-conditioning. Because of the many ravines in the area, its basement was always wet. When C&O trains rumbled through town a few blocks away, the old house shook ominously. Like their predecessors, however, the Chandlers enjoyed the history of the structure and gamely accepted its shortcomings.

Each April Louise Chandler opened the President's House to the public during Garden Week. Hundreds went through it, anxious to see a lived-in Williamsburg residence. Many had links with the college. The re-identification of the college with the early years of America continued. Learning of the house's recent restoration, many gave the college

Photograph by Thomas L. Williams

*Queen Elizabeth II spoke from the Wren Building in 1957, flanked by Rector James Robertson, Prince Philip, and President Alvin Chandler.*

documents or furnishings. Important gifts were received by the college during the Chandler years including portraits of King William and Queen Mary in the style of Sir Godfrey Kneller, which now hang in the hall of the President's House.

Two especially notable donors were Mrs. Jessie Ball duPont of Wilmington, Delaware, and Mrs. Letitia Pate Evans of Atlanta. As each January came round, Mrs. duPont sent President Chandler an envelope for the college containing what she called "sweepings"—odd lots of securities and dividends sometimes running to $50,000. Her gifts made college possible for needy students.

Like his father, Alvin Chandler exerted careful administration over the college and its extensions, and he gave attention to planning and physical facilities. Yet his views in such matters as drinking and uninhibited student self-expression in *The Flat Hat* led to increasing tension between president and many students. Those were years of American unrest, and William and Mary was slowly infected by the student discontent.

Alvin Chandler gave up the presidency in 1960 after nine years in the President's House. He had been chosen by the Visitors to administer the newly created William and Mary complex of colleges embracing Williamsburg, Norfolk, and Richmond, plus two junior colleges created under William and Mary's auspices at Newport News and Petersburg. It was an opportunity to plan ahead, a job which Navy-trained Alvin Chandler felt to be urgent.

Still trying to determine its highest purpose, the college entered a new era. It had not fully resolved its identity, but it was vigorously examining the alternatives. The two Chandlers, father and son, had done much to give the institution opportunity to choose what was best for it. They had also created a complex of tidewater campuses with expanding usefulness. Each had dared to do what he felt the times demanded.

# 22

## *"A Focus of Life on the Campus"*

AFTER the Board of Visitors elevated Alvin Duke Chandler to be chancellor of the College of William and Mary in 1960, it selected Davis Young Paschall, forty-nine, to succeed him as president. Paschall had received his Bachelor of Arts in 1932 under J. A. C. Chandler and his Master's in 1937. He was known universally as "Pat," a man of many friends and legislative connections. He was a popular figure at his alma mater.

The friendly, pipe-smoking Pat Paschall was a natural choice for a college needing strong support from its state and legislature. He had been born in Townsville, North Carolina in 1911. In 1954 he received his Ph.D. in education from the University of Virginia. He was principal of a high school for nine years before serving in the navy during World War II. Entering the Virginia Department of Education in 1946, he became Superintendent of Public Instruction in 1957. In that position he had wrestled with the problem of integration. As an ex officio Visitor he knew the college's needs. Most appealing to the Visitors, his hopes for the college were similar to those of J. A. C. Chandler.

"I'd rather be president of William and Mary than President of the United States," Paschall said. "I have come home again." A few of his teachers, like Richard Morton, Melville Jones, Wilfred Lambert, and J. D. Carter, were still on campus.

The Paschalls moved into the President's House in August 1960 with their seventeen-year-old daughter, Elizabeth, who had been accepted as a freshman before her father's election, and their thirteen-year-old son, Philip. The college grew in size during the eleven years they lived there. Expanded masters' and doctoral programs transformed it into a small university. Though it was afflicted by student radicalism of the Vietnam era, the school moved forward.

Paschall revealed his folksy style at his inaugural in October 1960, two months after he took office. He recalled his student years when he waited tables, labored on the college farm on Jamestown Road, and worked nights as a part-time waiter in the old Colonial Inn. He also remembered growing up on the farm in Lunenburg County. "When we hitched the mules for a long day in the tobacco fields, my father would often say, 'Today we shall walk humbly and plow a straight furrow.' This, with the help of Divine Providence, I shall endeavor to do and earnestly invite the assistance of all who love this ancient college and cherish its mission."

Like other president's wives, Agnes Winn Paschall had her own style. A Kappa Delta sorority member in college (she had graduated a year after her husband-to-be), she had captained the women's basketball team, served as president of the Women's Athletic Association, and competed in women's track and hockey. The Paschalls entertained students at buffets and class teas. "We wanted to know them on a personal, social basis," Pat Paschall said. Undergraduates occasionally stopped in at the President's House for coffee with Agnes Paschall.

The president and his wife opened the house during Garden Week and entertained parents at graduation. When tourists mistook the residence for an exhibition building, Agnes Paschall greeted them at the door and took them on a tour, pointing out portraits of founders. She liked to show them a shelf on the hallway landing, halfway upstairs, where early residents could light candles to see them to bed. Her husband told an interviewer: "At times I seem to awaken during the late hours of the night and hear the faint creak of stairs under the light tread of gracious ladies, who have arrived from the plantation homes on the James . . . From the drawing room below comes the aroma of the pipe and the hearty laughter of men who love life and reflect the finest manners, wit, and culture of the day."

An unusual problem developed during the Paschalls' occupancy. A colony of bees took up residence in the brick walls of the house. Mrs. Paschall was disturbed one day to find honey dripping down a wall and to find dead bees on rugs and steps. The intruders were expelled.

When the Board of Visitors offered to air-condition the house, Paschall urged them to wait until the Wren Building could be similarly

Photograph by Thomas L. Williams

*The Paschall family stood on the President's House steps after his inaugural, with the Reverend Theodore Adams of Richmond's First Baptist Church.*

treated, to save money. Meanwhile, he and his wife gave the interior a more authentic look. Radiators were hidden, eighteenth-century reproduction lighting sconces were installed, and new bedroom draperies and carpets were added. A tall eighteenth-century case clock was bought in England for the hall.

Still surrounding the house were many boxwood planted by earlier presidents, together with jonquils, periwinkle, and flowering shrubs. Shading and framing the house were elms, planted after an elm blight in 1843 had denuded the yard. They had become magnificent specimens by the 1960s.

At the Paschalls' first Christmas in 1960, Colonial Williamsburg asked the president to welcome holiday visitors. The greeting, which Paschall delivered on the campus steps to the President's House, climaxed a community march up Duke of Gloucester Street from the Capitol. The march inaugurated what became known as the "white lighting" or "grand illumination" of the Historic Area. It became a popular Christmas event, later modified for safety's sake.

After two years, the General Assembly in 1962 decided to halt the 1960 restructuring of the college and its branches, which had proved impractical because of the dissimilarity of the schools. The Assembly accordingly decreed the Norfolk and Richmond divisions free to become independent institutions, eventually renamed Old Dominion and Virginia Commonwealth universities. The Newport News and Petersburg colleges, then two-year institutions, continued under William and Mary and its Visitors. Admiral Chandler retired from administrative duties and was named honorary chancellor.

Pat Paschall was deeply attached to the traditions of the small campus he had loved in the 1930s. In his presidency the college continued to hold graduation each June in its front yard, against the facade of the Wren Building, despite growing traffic noise. He revived a Society of Alumni meeting at graduation, instituting a "sunset parade" from the Sunken Garden to the college cemetery, led by the red-uniformed Queen's Guard. At the graveside near Blow Gymnasium, the president paid annual tribute to Benjamin Ewell, and the names of alumni who had died during the school year were read out as a bugler sounded taps.

At the request of Colonial Williamsburg, the college in Paschall's years inaugurated daily tours of the Wren Building for visitors. To illustrate early student life, some classrooms were refurnished in 1967-1968 to the eighteenth-century manner: the grammar school room, the moral philosophy classroom, and the masters' common room. The college exhibited scientific apparatus of the sort demonstrated by William Small and law books used by George Wythe. These exhibits supplemented rooms already popular with visitors—the Great Hall and Chapel on the first floor and the Blue Room on the second.

When the million-dollar Swem Library was opened in 1966 on the newer part of the campus, it contained a gallery housing the statue of Botetourt which the faculty in 1801 had bought for $100 from the state, to spare it from further vandalism in the old Capitol, then falling into ruin. To create a new campus off Jamestown Road, the General Assembly in Paschall's years appropriated more than $40 million.

After eleven years in office, Dr. Paschall decided to retire in 1971, when he and his family moved to their house, Riverwood, in Charles City County, on the Chickahominy. The search for a successor soon narrowed to Blake Newton, Jr., an alumnus who later became president of the American Council of Life Insurance, and Thomas A. Graves, Jr., associate dean of Harvard's Graduate School of Business Administration.

*President Gerald Ford, right, visits William and Mary's Thomas A. Graves, Jr., before a debate with Jimmy Carter in 1976*

Dr. Graves's inauguration, on the 279th anniversary of the college's charter in 1972, was dedicated to excellence. Now that the college was able to compete again for the best students and teachers, he saw the opportunity to raise its standards. Never before had college hopes been higher.

Tom and Zoë Graves moved into the President's House on September 1, 1971, with five-year-old Andrew and three-year-old Eliza. The children were soon playing on a Revolutionary cannon, "Old Spotswood," in their front yard. Their parents also made a playroom for them on the third floor. Andrew and Eliza grew up happily on College Corner, attending Williamsburg schools and later going off to Phillips Exeter Academy.

During John Stewart Bryan's presidency the college had acquired land on Jamestown Road overlooking Lake Matoaka as the possible site for a new President's House. After Graves's election, the Visitors offered to build a larger residence there. The president declined, explaining:

> The original President's House had never been modernized fully,

> and as a result it was sometimes a burden for my predecessors just to live there. But Mrs. Graves and I agreed that we were not about to be the first of 24 presidential families not to live in the historic home. We believed that it would be much more appropriate, and indeed more economical, to modernize the house, air condition it, and continue to use it just as it had been used since the 18th century, as a focus of life on the campus, in the community.

Graves believed that he and his family should be close to the college, accessible to students, faculty, and Visitors. Accordingly, the college renovated the aging house in the 1970s, enhancing the Georgian character of its first floor hall, parlors, and dining room. At the same time, the four bedrooms and two Tyler era baths on the second floor were converted into three bedrooms with three baths, plus a presidential study.

The basement, damp and little used for 250 years, was dehumidified and divided into sitting room, recreation room, and utility room. Students often met with the president in the basement sitting room, while Zoë Graves each Christmas hosted school children in the recreation room with its colorful decor and pingpong table. Through a bulkhead door in the basement food had been brought from the outside kitchen in early years. Still remaining is the eighteenth-century baking oven and oversized kitchen fireplace for hanging cooking pots. In that room President John Stewart Bryan had given Christmas checks to the staff at holiday parties.

A fixture of the Graveses' basement was Andrew's train table, eight by twelve feet, representing a Norfolk and Western coal town. "Thousands of hours have been poured into this N & W train," said Zoë Graves, incredulously. "It is always being worked on!"

Strengthening and air-conditioning of the house in the Graveses' tenure followed an archeological dig of the basement earth. Once completed, the floor was again bricked over, a new heating and air-conditioning system was installed, and decaying basement walls were preserved with an anti-moisture compound. A subfloor was built beneath the wide pine of the first floor to seal off basement drafts. A new phone system and burglar, smoke, and fire alarms were installed.

A family kitchen on the first floor replaced the one built for J. A. C. Chandler in 1931. The attic that had recently provided storage was made into a sitting room, bedroom, bath, and playroom. The house became livable on all four floors.

And indeed the new president's active family needed all of it. Each month Tom Graves met with his President's Aides, a group of about

William and Mary College Archives

*Mrs. Thomas Graves, with Eliza and Andrew Graves, welcomes Prince Charles to the President's House in 1981 when the college made him an honorary fellow.*

fifteen students inaugurated under Bryan, and with his Graduate Students' Advisory Council, which he had founded. "I keep plenty of Cokes, lemonade, and cookies on hand," said his wife. The two also welcomed each class to the house and held a reception for foreign students, who had multiplied since the advent of the Draper Fellows from Great Britain in 1957. In 1983 the college had more than a hundred foreign students from every part of the globe among its 6,500 Williamsburg enrollment.

William and Mary College Archives

*Prince Charles, visiting the President's House in 1981, was greeted by President and Mrs. Thomas A. Graves, Jr., and their children, Andrew and Eliza.*

"Our children took to the President's House immediately," Graves said, "and I think it's been an enormous value to them because they learned to adjust to many new and interesting people. And with time, you get used to the many visitors who pass through on the way to the Wren Building and the cannon in the yard, and the fact that if you don't lock the front door you'll find a tourist there, taking pictures of the Page family portraits inside."

The Graves family enjoyed open fires in their fireplaces. The children liked family cookouts in the kitchen and dinners by candlelight. They learned not to mind visitors who mistook the house as an exhibit or prankish students who knocked at the door at midnight. "It goes with the house," laughed Zoë Graves.

The Graves children brought back the spontaneity of the Lyon Tyler years. They frolicked in the yard and halls. Andrew, who was five when the family moved in, took over the northwest bedroom, where in 1912 Julia and James Southall Wilson had etched their initials on a window. There he raised hamsters, Easter ducklings, and a sooty flying squirrel which had nose dived down a chimney.

An injured pigeon Andrew found in the garden was named Pepper and was repaired by the veterinarian. The bird lived in the wellhouse—the same well that Cornwallis had refused to share in 1781 with President Madison's family during the Revolution. Also reared in the wellhouse were Easter ducks, which sometimes graduated to the pond in Crim Dell and sometimes to the Peninsula Nature and Science Center at Newport News. One duckling was nearly consumed in a vacuum cleaner.

The fertile hamsters numbered three dozen before Andrew Graves went off to prep school. Even there he kept one favorite hamster and brought it home in a shoe box or in his pocket to spend Christmas vacation.

Eliza, who was a favorite of the sororities behind the President's House, practiced ballet and pirouetted through the hall. Sometimes she serenaded the world from a rococo grand piano on the third floor, once the gift of producer Florenz Ziegfeld to show girl Anna Held. Christmas guests at some early Graves parties were Andrew and Eliza's classmates at Matthew Whaley School. Other children came too, to sit around the Christmas tree and sing carols, gobble up gingerbread men, and to listen to stories from Zoë Graves, an enthusiastic ex-kindergarten teacher. When the party grew too big, she had to move it to the Great Hall.

As in Christmases past, carolers from the college and the town paused to serenade the President's House. A Graves guest each yuletide was John S. "Jack" Goodwin, whose father, W. A. R. Goodwin, had often conferred in that house in the 1920s.

The Graveses' years centered around children. Each Christmas, for two weeks before students left for vacation, Tom and Zoë Graves installed a twelve-foot Christmas tree in the President's House parlor. Students provided decorations. Friendly Mrs. Graves made it all a campus project, with the help of volunteers. Mrs. Virginia Hughes, the college "Christmas tree lady," collected homemade student decorations of tiny militia men, mice, angels, and colored balls that were hung by Lyle Wiggins, the college electrician.

The president and his family welcomed holiday visitors in Williamsburg the night after Christmas. The brick of the college yard buildings glowed in the light of pine knots burning in eighteenth-century type cressets in the yard.

After lunch for the work crew, Zoë Graves flung open the doors to student, faculty, and staff, to the strains of Christmas music. The holiday open house continued for two weeks, from 8 A.M. to 4 P.M. daily. Andrew and Eliza, who were hosts with their parents, also had their own three-foot trees in their rooms, each decorated by its owner with handmade or bought baubles.

Halloween was an exciting time for the Graves children. They and their friends made a haunted house out of the President's House hall and staircase, swathing its furniture in sheets and hanging cutout bats and spiders from stairwell and ceiling. Anguished moans came from a concealed tape recorder, close to a skeleton with "blood" flowing from its gloved hands. The prankish president himself hid beneath the table that bore homemade trick or treat candied apples, to reach out and grab the ankle of an unsuspecting guest as he or she reached for a treat.

Stories of a ghost in the house were the children's favorite. As Zoë Graves told it, the ghost was the spirit of a French officer who had died there in the Revolution. Ever since, according to the legend, the spirit had lingered on the third floor stairway.

"I've often heard noises like footsteps going across the playroom floor," she whispered to the children, as they cupped their ears in excitement. "Sometimes Eliza's closet door springs open and———no one is THERE!" According to legend, the skeleton of a man—was it a French soldier?—was once found by workmen repairing a sealed off attic space on the third floor.

To serve as guides during tours of the President's House, wives of college faculty and staff worked with Mrs. Graves to learn the history of the house and of its furnishings. The College Women's Club became involved. The ebullient Claude Jones kept the reception rooms fresh with flowers through the year. Participants in an annual Christmas party were the sixty members of the Wednesday Morning Music Club. Many patriotic, civic, historical, and alumni groups were guests yearly in addition to students, faculty, and visitors.

The President's House in the Graveses' years drew leaders from around the world. On May 2, 1981, Prince Charles of England descended on the campus by helicopter to receive an honorary fellowship. Like his grandmother in 1954 and his parents in 1957, he began his visit to the college with a call at the house that King William and Queen Mary had made possible in 1693.

Dogwood was blooming in the dooryard when the slim prince strode into the house, introduced by the president to Zoë Graves and their children. "He was just like a warm family friend," she said. As for Charles, he thought the house "a lot like home." He recalled that he had been only a boy of eight when his parents had come to Virginia in 1957. "Now I am a prematurely aged thirty-two-year-old, making extraordinarily bad speeches," he said, to laughter.

Like so many other visits, it was another page in the history of America's oldest college residence. Now that the lean years were behind, Williamsburg knew there were more triumphs to come.

# 23

## *The Future of the House*

THE pride that the college took in its President's House touched Tom and Zoë Graves as they and their children settled into it in 1971. Increasingly, however, they were aware of the contrast between the handsome structure and its haphazard furnishings. How could the house more authentically project its very human story to those who passed through its doors?

The solution seemed to them to lie in some such refurnishing as Virginia's Executive Mansion had undergone in the term of Governor Linwood Holton, with the support of Carlisle Humelsine, then president of Colonial Williamsburg, and Harvie Wilkinson, Richmond banker. That project had been headed by Clement Conger, curator of the White House and of the State Department Reception Rooms.

A new policy seemed called for. For nearly 250 years the house had been furnished with the possessions of each president. No standing furniture had belonged to it until John Stewart Bryan's day. Since then, a few fine eighteenth-century furnishings and portraits had set a new standard. Could the college go further with it?

The college made that decision under Tom Graves's leadership. Because of the number of visitors to the President's House, it was decided to display, on its first floor, the gifts in recent years of portraits and furniture; and to supplement these with the acquisition of antique furniture of the type that would have graced the house in the eighteenth and nineteenth centuries.

Accordingly, in 1977 the college began to research and to seek gifts for the house. The effort was timed to coincide with the 250th anniversary of the house's erection in 1732–1733 by Henry Cary, Jr. Dr. Clement Conger of Alexandria agreed to be chairman, and a committee of twenty-four was appointed by President Graves "to begin the voluntary effort to acquire period furnishings . . . for this significant landmark." Support was given by donors called The President's House Friends, headed by Parke Rouse, Jr., of Williamsburg, and who meet several times yearly in the house. They were aided by Mrs. Louise Kale, registrar of the college fine arts collection, and by Mrs. Carol Ten Broeck, administrative assistant.

Goals were set by Chairman Conger. Believing it to be "the most important Virginia Georgian brick house in the Williamsburg area," he directed an appeal to the nation's decorative arts collectors to help furnish the house with objects commensurate with the importance of the house. "Since it has approximately 15,000 guests and visitors a year, including many notables," he wrote, "it seems high time that we should make the furnishings representative of an affluent residence of college presidents in the eighteenth century."

In accepting the chairmanship, the White House curator said "I couldn't resist helping with the President's House because its interior furnishings were really very depressing when we started. It seemed to me that it should be relatively easy to have great Queen Anne and Chippendale furnishings given for such an important building, or at least the money with which to buy them . . . We have made great strides, and hopefully a few more years will see the successful completion."

The Committee to Furnish the President's House has worked six years under Dr. Conger's leadership. Gifts of furnishings and funds have exceeded all expectations, already totaling $1 million. Some pieces associated with the early college have been received, together with other period furnishings to round out the eighteenth-century decorative scheme.

An accessions subcommittee under Dr. Conger screens all offerings for quality, authenticity, and suitability. Meanwhile an interior decorating subcommittee has developed furnishing plans. Obviously, the house is and must remain a private residence, which fills a key role for the college and for Virginia. It cannot be allowed to become a museum at the expense of its family function. "But it can be a beautifully furnished private residence," insists Conger.

In 1982 the two committees launched a 250th anniversary program to mark the 1983 anniversary of President Blair's move to the house in October 1733. The program includes seminars, house tours, and publications. Under the leadership of Mrs. William Bangel of Williamsburg, the celebration planners have received wide support from alumni, art collectors, and friends of the college. It is hoped that continued enhancement of the house and its furnishings can thus be assured.

Meanwhile, research on the history and archaeology of the house continues. Hoping to uncover revealing fragments in the grounds adjoining the residence, an archeological study was made in 1980 when trenches had to be dug to admit air-conditioning ducts into the house. Under archeologist Nick Luccketti of the college's Research Center for Archaeology, fragments of porcelain, stoneware, glass, and metal were dug up. Ranging from the 1730s to the late 1800s, these identified furnishings were from the British Isles, France, Germany, China, and Japan. "The presence of many teawares reflects the status of the site's occupants," wrote Bly Bogley of the Research Center, "for afternoon tea was an important social occasion in eighteenth-century England and Virginia."

In hopes of locating furnishings of the college's earliest presidents, Zoë and Tom Graves corresponded with presidential descendants. A few gave family heirlooms, and others gave information and photographs. Although most of them represented twentieth-century presidents, some few were from earlier occupants.

One gift was a handsome nineteenth-century silver tea urn, used in the President's House in 1851 when the Alpha Chapter of Phi Beta Kappa was revived during the presidency of Benjamin Ewell. It was given by the late Mrs. Mary Heath Keesling, a descendant of John Heath II, of Northumberland County, one of the five founders of Phi Beta Kappa at the college in 1776. The Heaths were among Northern Neck families who sent sons to the college.

The project has stimulated new interest in the twenty-three past presidents, and especially in several who stand out for their accomplishments or length of office. These were James Blair, who served from 1693 until he died fifty years later; Bishop James Madison, who presided from 1777 to 1812; Roderick Dew, the accomplished economist from 1836 to 1846; Benjamin Ewell, who heroically held the reins from 1854 to 1888; Lyon Tyler, who initiated state support and coeducation between 1888 and 1919; and Julian A. C. Chandler, who from 1919 to 1934 expanded the institution to Richmond, Norfolk, Newport News, and Petersburg.

And what of their wives and children? Alas, little has come to light of

Photograph by Thomas L. Williams

*Allan Denny Ivie III and Chairman Clement Conger confer as members of the Committee to Furnish the President's House.*

them before Benjamin Ewell's tenure. Fires and wars have destroyed most pre-Civil War records of the college. Only enough is thus far known to reveal the outlines of presidential family life in pre-Revolutionary years. Perhaps other finds will be made.

However, the names of a few guests in the house suggests the rich tapestry of its history. By the time of the 1739 visit of English evangelist George Whitefield to James Blair, many historic figures had visited in the house. In Blair's presidency they included William Byrd, "King" Carter, and students Peyton Randolph and Richard Bland. The house was later known to Benjamin Franklin, Chief Austenaco of the Cherokees, students Thomas Jefferson, James Monroe, and Benjamin Harrison, and to George Washington when he was in Williamsburg as a burgess of the General Assembly.

The years 1776 to 1781 at the President's House were crowded. President-to-be James Madison visited his cousin there in 1777 and 1778. Cornwallis stayed there in June-July 1781 before Yorktown. Rochambeau hospitalized his officers there after Yorktown. The Chevalier de Chastellux visited the ruins of the house after the 1781 fire and obtained repayment from King Louis XVI.

After the house was rebuilt and occupied by President Madison in 1786, it regained vitality. John Tyler came often as rector, as did Lafayette when he revisited America in 1824 and received a degree from the college. John Marshall, Edmund Randolph, and Winfield Scott were students. The Civil War brought General Joseph E. Johnston, CSA, a West Point schoolmate of Benjamin Ewell, and Union occupying forces came after the town fell to General George B. McClellan on May 5, 1862.

In the decades after Appomattox, the college and Williamsburg struggled to regain their early luster. A student in the 1880s was James Branch Cabell, future novelist. In the twentieth century the college welcomed ten of the nation's presidents: Woodrow Wilson, Warren Harding, Calvin Coolidge, Franklin D. Roosevelt, Harry Truman, Dwight D. Eisenhower, Richard Nixon, Lyndon Johnson, Gerald Ford, and Jimmy Carter. In the afterglow of World War II, the President's House renewed its early British associations with Winston Churchill, Queen Mother Elizabeth, Queen Elizabeth and Prince Philip, and Prince Charles.

Little is known of the house's secrets during several interruptions in its life: of Cornwallis's invasion, the French hospitalization in 1781, the caretaking by Mrs. Virginia Southall during the Civil War, and the subsequent occupation by Federal soldiers until the college reopened after Appomattox. Only after 1865 does the record flow continuously.

A lack of drawings and photographs of early presidents and their families is part of the problem in reconstructing the house's history. No portraits exist of Presidents William and Thomas Dawson, William Stith, William Yates, John Camm, or John Bracken. No presidents' wives survive in portraiture from the time of Sarah Harrison Blair in 1734 until the arrival of Annie Tucker Tyler in 1888. The Committee to Furnish the President's House hopes some may yet come to light.

To further the project, the Committee also continues to look for pieces of eighteenth-century furniture and decorative items needed to complete the work. Gifts of funds and securities have enabled the committee to buy a few items as they came on the market. Generous contributors have included alumnus Roy Charles, Dr. and Mrs. Conger, Mrs. Page Bowie Clagett, and the late Mrs. Maurice Morris of the District of Columbia. Still on the want list are furniture, carpets, chandeliers, and other objects that would convey the taste and elegance of eighteenth-century Virginia at its peak.

"I feel that we have made great strides," says Chairman Conger. "I was particularly pleased to find two great eighteenth-century original brass chandeliers—a pair—for the two drawing rooms. We have also acquired a very early cut glass English chandelier for the dining room. The John Jay Hopkins Foundation has provided the money for its purchase."

Such is the new career of the "commodius brick house" which Henry Cary, Jr., and his workmen completed on College Corner 250 years ago. The fortunes of the college are flowing again after centuries of ebb tide. The President's House is a happy symbol of that faith which has kept alive America's second oldest institution of higher learning.

# Acknowledgements

This book grew out of a suggestion of Zoë Wasson Graves, who has graciously presided over the President's House since her husband, Tom, became president of the College of William and Mary in 1971. They have provided information, suggestions, and contacts with alumni and friends to enable the author to write this account.

I am grateful to all alumni and friends of the college who have submitted anecdotes, photographs, and other material.

I am particularly grateful to Mrs. Mary Randolph Mordecai Goodwin, retired historian of Colonial Williamsburg, for her intensive study of college records and of its presidents, recorded in Colonial Williamsburg research reports. She also worked with this author on the manuscript, suggesting valuable additions and changes.

For information on Benjamin Ewell, president from 1848 to 1849 and again from 1854 to 1888, I am indebted to Mrs. Anne Chapman, whose research has been most helpful.

Several former presidents have submitted to interviews. David Tennant Bryan, son of President John Stewart Bryan, has provided data on his father's Williamsburg years. Mrs. James Mann, Jr., granddaughter of Lyon Gardiner Tyler, has provided memories of her childhood visits to the house, part of them included in appendix 14 & 15.

I have talked with Dr. Janet Kimbrough, descendant of the Tucker and Coleman families; with Mrs. Cara Garrett Dillard, daughter of Professor Van Garrett; with Mrs. Gladys Bennett Guy, widow of Professor William Guy; and with Leslie Cheek, Jr., who organized the Fine Arts Department under John Stewart Bryan.

I derived help from the collection of oral history transcripts compiled for the college by Miss Emily Williams in the years 1974 to 1976. Among reports used were those by the late Colgate W. Darden, Jr., governor and chancellor; James W. Miller, former dean and acting president; J. Wilfred Lambert, former dean of students; the late John Hocutt, former assistant dean of students; Mrs. Amanda Bryan Kane, daughter of President Bryan; and ex-president Paschall.

Records in the college archives were made available by Ms. Kay Domine, archivist, and Miss Margaret Cook, curator of manuscripts and rare books. A copy of the journal of a European trip kept by President Thomas Roderick Dew was kindly lent by a collateral descendant.

The author is indebted to John Jennings, former director of the Virginia Historical Society; J. Wilfred Lambert, former dean of students; Mrs. Carolyn Richardson McMurran, an alumnus of the college; Dr. Janet Kimbrough; Edward M. Riley, former director of research of Colonial Williamsburg; and Mrs. Anne Chapman, all of whom read the manuscript. I thank Thad Tate for helpful guidance.

I record my thanks to Mrs. Jane Abbott Tyler for typing the first draft of the manuscript and for editorial assistance. To my wife, Betsy Gayle Rouse, I owe special gratitude for constant help.

Many Williamsburg people have answered questions, including Mrs. Virgnia Welton Duke Phelps, Vernon Nunn, A. Edwin Kendrew, Wilford Kale, Dr. Carlton Casey, Jr., Ross Weeks, Jr., Mrs. Elizabeth Stubbs, and the Hon. Robert Armistead.

At William and Mary I have received invariable cooperation. Among respondents have been Duane Dittman, Dean Olson, Mrs. Louise Kale, Mrs. Carol Ten Broeck, Miss Brenda Rexrode, Mrs. Joan Gordineer, and Mrs. Jacqueline von Ofenheim. At Swem Library I have been aided by Dr. Clifford Currie, Ms. Kay Domine, Miss Margaret Cook, Mrs. Hope Yelich, Mrs. Dortha Skelton, Ms. Teresa Munford, Ms. Mickey Anas, and the late Herbert Ganter. I appreciate the work of Mr. Wilford Kale to complete the list of rectors of the Board of Visitors, published as an appendix.

Other help has come from Francis Berkeley of the University of Virginia; Howson Cole of the Virginia Historical Society; George B. Eager, Jr., of Princeton University; Miss Sarah Rouse of the Library of Congress; and Ms. Louise Merriam, Miss Susan Stromei, Miss Lou Powers, John Ingram, Miss Suzanne Brown, Ms. Patricia Laland, Norman Beatty, and Richard Stinely of Colonial Williamsburg.

I appreciate permission from Cary Carson, Director of Research at Colonial Williamsburg, to quote from its transcript of the memoirs of John S. Charles, and from Edward Chappell, Director of Architectural Records, for permission to reproduce drawings from Marcus Whiffen's *The Public Buildings of Colonial Williamsburg*. And finally, my warmest thanks to Anita Kordela for her conscientious editorial assistance.

# Appendices

1. Chancellors of the College
2. Virginia Governors Who Attended the College
3. Rectors of the College
4. Professors and Deans of Law
5. Deans of the Faculty
6. Presidents of the Student Body
7. Editors of the William and Mary Quarterly
8. Directors of the Institute of Early American History and Culture
9. Fellows of the Institute of Early American History and Culture
10. Thomas Jefferson Awards for Faculty Service
11. Thomas Jefferson Awards for Teaching
12. The Reverend Henry Ward Beecher to President Ewell, 1867
13. Woodrow Wilson on a College President's Duties
14. Woodrow Wilson Visits the President's House
15. Dining at the President's House with Lyon Tyler
16. The "Seven Wise Men" of the College

---

## Appendix 1

### Chancellors of the College

Henry Compton, Bishop of London. 1693-1700
Thomas Tenison, Archbishop of Canterbury, 1700-1707
Henry Compton, Bishop of London, 1707-1713
John Robinson, Bishop of London, 1714-1721
William Wake, Archbishop of Canterbury, 1721-1729
Edmund Gibson, Bishop of London, 1729-1736
William Wake, Archbishop of Canterbury, 1736-1737
Edmund Gibson, Bishop of London, 1737-1748
Thomas Sherlock, Bishop of London, 1749-1761
Thomas Hayter, Bishop of London, 1762
Charles Wyndham, Earl of Egremont, 1762-1763
Philip Yorke, Earl of Hardwicke, 1764
Richard Terrick, Bishop of London, 1764-1776
George Washington, President of the United States, 1788-1799
John Tyler, President of the United States, 1859-1862
Hugh Blair Grigsby, Historian, 1871-1881
John Stewart Bryan, President of the college, 1942-1944
Colgate W. Darden, Jr., Governor of Virginia, 1946-1947
Alvin Duke Chandler, President of the college, 1962-1974

## Appendix 2

## Virginia Governors Who Attended the College

Thomas Jefferson, Albemarle, served 1779-81
Benjamin Harrison III, Charles City, 1781-84
Edmund Randolph, Henrico, 1786-88
Beverley Randolph, Cumberland, 1788-91
James Monroe, Albemarle, 1799-1802; 1811
John Page, Gloucester, 1802-05
William H. Cabell, Amherst, 1805-08
John Tyler, Charles City, 1808-11
Peyton Randolph II, Richmond, 1811-12
Wilson Cary Nicholas, Albemarle, 1814-16
James Patton Preston, Montgomery, 1816-19
Thomas Mann Randolph, Albemarle, 1819-22
James Pleasants, Jr., Goochland, 1825-27
John Tyler, Jr., Charles City, 1825-27
William Branch Giles, Amelia, 1827-30
Littleton Waller Tazewell, Norfolk, 1834-36
Wyndham Robertson, Richmond, 1836-37
John Munford Gregory, James City, 1846-50
William Munford Tuck, Halifax, 1946-50
Mills E. Godwin, Jr., 1966-70; 1974-78
John N. Dalton, Radford, 1978-81

## Appendix 3

## Rectors of the College

| | |
|---|---|
| 1693-95 | The Reverend James Blair, Williamsburg |
| 1695-96 | Miles Cary, Warwick |
| 1696-97 | John Smith, Gloucester |
| 1697-98 | The Reverend Stephen Fouace, York |
| 1698-1702 | Unknown |
| 1702-3 | William Byrd I, Henrico |
| 1703-4 | Lt. Gov. Francis Nicholson, Williamsburg |
| 1704-5 | Miles Cary, Warwick |
| 1705 | Lt. Gov. Francis Nicholson, Williamsburg |
| 1706 | Unknown |
| 1709-10 | William Randolph, Henrico |
| 1711-12 | Lt. Gov. Alexander Spotswood, Williamsburg |
| 1712-13 | The Rev. James Blair, Williamsburg |
| 1714 | Unknown |
| 1715 | Lt. Gov. Alexander Spotswood, Williamsburg |
| 1716 | Philip Ludwell II, James City |
| 1717-28 | Unknown |
| 1728-29 | The Reverend James Blair, Williamsburg |

| | |
|---|---|
| 1729 | Richard Kennon, Charles City |
| 1730-35 | Unknown |
| 1736 | Henry Armistead, Williamsburg |
| 1737-57 | Unknown |
| 1757 | William Lightfoot, Charles City |
| 1758-59 | Peyton Randolph, Williamsburg |
| 1759-60 | Lt. Gov. Francis Fauquier, Williamsburg |
| 1760-66 | Unknown |
| 1766-67 | Dudley Digges, York |
| 1767-69 | James M. Fontaine, Gloucester |
| 1769-70 | Gov. Norborne Berkeley, Baron de Botetourt, Williamsburg |
| 1770-78 | Unknown |
| 1779-81 | John Blair II, Williamsburg |
| 1781-89 | Unknown |
| 1789-90 | St. George Tucker, Williamsburg |
| 1790-1812 | Unknown |
| 1812-13 | Robert N. Nelson, Williamsburg |
| 1813-14 | Robert Saunders, Sr., Williamsburg |
| 1814-15 | William Browne, Williamsburg |
| 1815 | Robert G. Smith, Richmond |
| 1816-17 | Unknown |
| 1817 | James Semple, Williamsburg |
| 1818-19 | Unknown |
| 1820- | Burwell Bassett, Williamsburg |
| 1821-25 | Unknown |
| 1825 | William Browne, Williamsburg |
| 1826-27 | Unknown |
| 1827-28 | John Tyler, Charles City |
| 1828-29 | John Page II, Williamsburg |
| 1829-36 | Unknown |
| 1836-37 | Edmund Ruffin, Prince George |
| 1837-39 | Thomas Martin, James City |
| 1938-40 | Robert McCandlish, Williamsburg |
| 1840-42 | John Tyler, Williamsburg |
| 1842-44 | Thomas G. Peachy, Williamsburg |
| 1844-45 | Robert McCandlish, Williamsburg |
| 1845-46 | John B. Christian, Williamsburg |
| 1846-48 | Robert McCandlish, Williamsburg |
| 1848-62 | John Tyler, Charles City |
| 1862-65 | No incumbent |
| 1865-69 | Bishop John Johns, Alexandria |
| 1869-71 | William H. MacFarland, Richmond |
| 1871-83 | James Lyons, Richmond |
| 1883-90 | W. W. Crump, Richmond |
| 1890-98 | Gen. William B. Taliaferro, Gloucester |
| 1898-1905 | Dr. John W. Lawson, Isle of Wight |
| 1905-18 | Robert Morton Hughes, Norfolk |
| 1918-40 | James Hardy Dillard, Charlottesville |
| 1940-46 | J. Gordon Bohannan, Surry |

| | |
|---|---|
| 1946-48 | A. Herbert Foreman, Norfolk |
| 1948-52 | Oscar L. Shewmake, Richmond |
| 1952-62 | James M. Robertson, Norfolk |
| 1962-64 | Sterling Hutcheson, Boydton |
| 1964-66 | J. Brockenbrough Woodward, Jr., Newport News |
| 1966-68 | W. Brooks George, Richmond |
| 1968-70 | Walter G. Mason, Lynchburg |
| 1970-72 | Ernest Goodrich, Surry |
| 1972-76 | R. Harvey Chappell, Jr., Richmond |
| 1976-78 | John R. L. Johnson, Jr., Chadds Ford, Pa. |
| 1978-82 | Edward E. Brickell, Virginia Beach |
| 1982- | Herbert V. Kelly, Newport News |

NOTE: In the years 1892-1906, the principal officer of the Board of Visitors was designated President of the board instead of Rector. The second-ranking officer or Rector in those years was Col. William Lamb, of Norfolk.

## Appendix 4

### Professors and Deans of Law

George Wythe, 1779-90
St. George Tucker, 1790-1804
William Nelson, 1804-11
Robert Nelson, 1811-18
James Semple, 1818-33
Nathaniel Beverley Tucker, 1833-51
George P. Scarburgh, 1852-55
Lucian Minor, 1855-58
Charles Morris, 1858-61
No incumbent, 1861-1921
Oscar L. Shewmake, chairman, 1921-23
William Hamilton, dean, 1923-29
Theodore A. Cox, dean, 1930-47
Dudley W. Woodbridge, dean, 1947-62
Joseph Curtis, dean, 1962-70
James P. Whyte, dean, 1970-75
Emeric Fischer, acting dean, 1975-76
William B. Spong, Jr., dean, 1976-

## Appendix 5

### Deans of the Faculty

John Lesslie Hall, 1906-22
Kremer J. Hoke, 1922-38
James W. Miller, 1938-43
Sharvy Umbeck, 1946-49
Nelson Marshall, 1949-51
Charles F. Marsh, 1951-58
W. Melville Jones, 1958-64
*Harold L. Fowler, 1964-74
*Jack D. Edwards, 1974-81
*Zeddie Bowen, 1981-

*Deans of the Faculty of Arts and Sciences

## Appendix 6

### Presidents of the Student Body

| | |
|---|---|
| Robert Morton Hughes, Jr. | 1899 |
| Robert McGuire Jones | 1901 |
| Henry Jackson Davis | 1902 |
| Oscar L. Shewmake | 1903 |

James Hubard Lloyd 1905
William Ralph Wrigglesworth 1906
George Oscar Ferguson, Jr. 1907
Herbert Heldruf Young 1908
Edwin Francis Shewmake 1908
Clarence Edgar Koontz 1909
Roscoe Conkling Young 1910
Frank Erskine Graves 1911
William H. Neblett 1912
Wilbur R. Dameron 1913
John Lewis Tucker 1914
Clarence Jennings 1915
Robert M. Newton 1916
Zelma Talmage Kyle 1917
Floyd Franklin Jenkins 1918
James Thomas Jones 1919
Walter Finnall Cross Ferguson 1919
Walter Hughart Cheatham 1920
Herbert Lee Bridges, Jr. 1921
Floyd Berl 1922
Ottowell Sykes Lowe 1923
Alva Hobson Cooke 1924
Frank Nathaniel Watkins 1925
Andre Goetz, Jr. 1926
Henry B. Frazier, Jr. 1927
James Allan Cooke 1928
James M. Robertson 1929
F. Samuel Wilcox, Jr. 1930
Richard D. Mullowney 1931
Charles H. Dunker 1932
Andrew Christensen 1933
Gerald L. Quirk 1934
John A. Mapp 1935
George Mason 1936
John Trueheart 1937
Carl Buffington 1938
Franklin P. Ryder 1939
John Hudson 1940
Charles Gondak 1941
Douglas R. Robbins 1942
H. Wescott Cunningham 1943
David McNamara 1944
Mary Wilson 1944
William L. Williams 1945
Fritz Zepht 1946
Frances E. Clark 1947
Howard Hyle 1948
C. Warren Smith 1949
John Dayton 1950
Jim Rehlaender 1951
Dave Wakefield 1952
John Dalton 1953
Cary Scates 1954
Ron Drake 1955
Hykel James Abdella 1956
Alex Fakadej 1957
Walt Leyland 1958
Gabriel Wilner 1959
Dick Neely 1960
David Bottoms 1961
Thomas Johnson 1962
Jerry Van Voorhis 1963
William R. Corley 1964
Craig B. Carlson 1965
Jim Armentrout 1966
Larry White 1967
Brad Davis 1968
Tim Marvin 1969
Nancy Terrill 1970
Winn Legerton 1971
Kay Rorer 1972
Andrew Purdy 1972
Cornell Christianson 1973
Chris Owens 1974
Sharon Pendak 1975
Dean Strickland 1976
Laurie Bond 1977
Dave Ness 1978
Bill Mims 1979
Dave Garland 1980
Carla Shaffer-Moreland 1981
Randolph Beales 1982
David White 1983

## Appendix 7

### Editors of *The William and Mary Quarterly*

Lyon G. Tyler, 1892-1919
J.A.C. Chandler and E. G. Swem, 1921-33

John Stewart Bryan and E. G. Swem, 1934-41
J.E. Pomfret and E.G. Swem, 1942-43
Richard L. Morton, 1944-46
Douglass Adair, 1947-55
Lester J. Cappon, 1955-56
Lawrence W. Towner, 1956-62
Lester J. Cappon, 1963
William W. Abbott, 1963-66
Thad W. Tate, 1967-71
Michael McGiffert, 1972-

Visiting Editors:
Whitfield J. Bell, Jr., 1953-54
Jack P. Greene, 1956-62
John E. Selby, 1871
Stephen Foster, 1977

## Appendix 8

### Directors of the Institute of Early American History and Culture

Carl Bridenbaugh, 1944-50
Lyman Butterfield, 1951-54
Lester Cappon, 1955-68
Stephen Kurtz, 1969-72
Thad W. Tate, 1972-

## Appendix 9

### Fellows of the Institute of Early American History and Culture

| | |
|---|---|
| 1945-8 | Arthur Pierce Middleton |
| 1948-50 | Brooke Hindle |
| 1951-3 | Charles Page Smith |
| 1955-8 | Wilcomb E. Washburn |
| 1956-9 | Michael G. Hall |
| 1958-60 | Leonard Louis Tucker |
| 1959-62 | M. Eugene Sirmans |
| 1961-3 | Winthrop D. Jordan |
| 1962-5 | Ira D. Gruber |
| 1964-6 | Gordon S. Wood |
| 1965-8 | Stephen S. Webb |
| 1966-9 | Bernard W. Sheehan |
| 1968-71 | Sung Bok Kim |
| 1969-72 | Norman S. Fiering |
| 1971-3 | John J. McCusker |
| 1972-4 | Richard Middleton |
| 1973-5 | Kevin P. Kelly |
| 1974-6 | Russell R. Menard |
| 1975-7 | Allan Kulikoff |
| 1976-8 | Drew R. McCoy |
| 1977-9 | Charles Royster |
| 1978-80 | William K. Breitenbach |
| 1979-81 | Rachel Klein |
| 1980- | Thomas M. Deerflinger |
| 1981- | Philip D. Morgan |
| 1981- | Daniel F. Vickers |

## Appendix 10

### Thomas Jefferson Awards for Faculty Service

1963 Dudley Woodbridge
1964 William G. Guy
1965 William S. Gooch
1966 W. Melville Jones
1967 Davis Y. Paschall
1968 Vernon L. Nunn
1969 Harold L. Fowler
1970 Cecil McCulley
1971 Carl Roseberg
1972 W. Warner Moss
1973 J. Wilfred Lambert
1974 Frank A. MacDonald
1975 Alfred Armstrong
1976 R. Wayne Kernodle
1977 Jack D. Edwards
1978 Stanley B. Williams
1979 William F. Swindler
1980 William B. Spong, Jr.
1981 W. Samuel Sadler
1982 Frank T. Lendrim
1983 Vinson H. Sutlive, Jr.

## Appendix 11

### Thomas Jefferson Awards for Teaching

1970 Thomas Hearn
1971 Bruce Goodwin
1972 John Conlee
1973 Hans Van Baeyer
1974 Elsa Diduk
1975 Gerald H. Johnson
1976 Alan Fuchs
1977 James J. Thompson, Jr.
1978 Trudier Harris
1979 Allen R. Sanderson
1980 Terry L. Meyers
1981 Craig N. Canning
1982 Jean C. Wyer
1983 Morris McCain

## Appendix 12

### Henry Ward Beecher to President Ewell

Brooklyn, N.Y.
March 25, 1867

. . . I am sorry that you are discouraged. . . . You know how much of the spirit of giving depends upon the state of public feeling. That feeling, through the North, is not yet settled to any defined form. Everything in relation to the South is yet a matter of uncertainty. Politics, you know, is feverish at the best times. How much more now, a long war just closed, a reconstruction policy uninitiated, two parties struggling for the mastery of the Republican camp, and a third party, Democrats, watching for mistakes and the chance to regain power.

I certainly wished that you might fish in such troubled waters as luckily as Peter did, finding a piece of money in the fish's mouth, but I am not surprised that you catch few fish and money.

But I pray you neither to lose courage for the future nor to allow any feeling of irritation to take possession of you. I, too, am waiting. Not half my Church and Congregation go with me in the sentiments which I entertain respecting the settlement of the Country's affairs, and in the temper which I feel toward the South. What then? I wait. Time is the Great Physician, and if the patient can only keep alive, time will cure him.

I hope, therefore, that you will return to Virginia not feeling "the North will not help its Countrymen in the South." But, simply saying, as I think the truth would warrant: A divided and agitated state of the public mind is not favorable for the work of such endeavors.

If you can keep alive one or two years, I feel sure that you will then amply succeed.

I do not believe that you will fare as well in Philadelphia as here . . .

Henry Ward Beecher
*W & M Archives*

## Appendix 13

### Woodrow Wilson on A College President's Duties

After Lyon Gardiner Tyler became president of William and Mary, in 1888, he sent President Woodrow Wilson of Princeton a questionnaire on presidential duties. Wilson replied, writing his answers to the typed questions in longhand:

Q. Do you attend the meetings of your Board?
A. I am a member of the Board, and, in the (usual) absence of the Governor of the State, its President.

Q. Are you a member of the Executive Committee?
A. There is no Executive Committee but I am ex-officio a member of every committee of the board.

Q. What are your duties in relation to soliciting money for the University?
A. I am ordinarily in charge of all such duties.

Q. Do you make reports to your Board?
A. Annual, published reports. I am charged by the charter with "the immediate care of the education and government" of the students.

Q. Do you make up the budget of expenses . . . ?
A. No. This is done by the Treasurer for the Financial Committee of the Board.

Q. What are your relations to the Faculty . . . ?
A. President of the Faculty. Make all nominations to the Board. Am executive and directing head, but the Faculty has legislative power, subject to the approval of the Board.

Q. Do you execute general supervisions of the Institution . . . ?
A. Yes.

Q. What is the custom in regard to your leaving College? Do you have to get the permission of the Board or Executive Committee for absenting yourself on College business?

A. I do not. Our constitution in all these matters is largely unwritten, confirmed by precedent.

(signed) Woodrow Wilson
*W & Mary Archives*

## Appendix 14

## Woodrow Wilson Visits the President's House

In March 1917, President Woodrow Wilson was feeling pressure from every quarter for the United States to enter World War I on the side of England and France. He decided to prepare the nation for a declaration of war with a series of lectures, among them one at William and Mary.

My grandmother, Mrs. Lyon Tyler, was instructing Mattie, the cook, concerning lunch, which would be Brunswick stew with cornpones and wine jelly with chocolate cake. Late in the afternoon, there would be a reception before the dinner and lecture to be held in the Wren Building. At lunch there would be President Wilson with college president and Mrs. Tyler; my mother and father, Professor and Mrs. James Southall Wilson; and my uncle and aunt, Captain and Mrs. Alfred Miles.

I remember being much excited by the thought of meeting the President. Father had told us how, when he received his Ph.D. at Princeton, Woodrow Wilson had made a point of inviting him to his office as "another Wilson from Virginia." Father was a great admirer of Wilson, and another admirer was Professor Dick Crawford.

At 11:30 A.M., we saw Professor Crawford's Dodge rounding the corner from Palace Green into Duke of Gloucester Street, passing Bruton Parish Church. Mr. Casey and others came out of their stores to watch the car coming. Grandpa Tyler and Father were in the back seat, with Mr. Crawford and President Wilson in front. The reason for the informality was that the President of the United States had slipped away for a weekend in Gloucester, Virginia, without many people knowing where he had gone. Without TV and radio this was possible in 1917, although it seems incredible today. From Gloucester he had come to Williamsburg. Now, everyone was waving.

Suddenly, from behind the Wren Building, a brigade of khaki-clad students marched down the campus sidewalk, dividing at the statue and the cannon, and proceeding past the mulberry tree into the circle of bare ground where Duke of Gloucester Street began. They stood at attention. One carried the American flag.

The Dodge arrived and its passengers got out. They greeted the soldiers and headed toward the President's House. We four children, Lion Miles, Helen Keeble, and Alida and Nancy Wilson, fell in behind Father and Mr. Crawford.

President Wilson had only one bag, which Father carried up the steps. We were all introduced to the important guest. Since Woodrow Wilson had been born in the South, he recognized that black Mattie, who stood in the dining room door, was waiting to meet him. He removed his hat, handing it to Mr. Crawford, and held out his hand to her. She stood in her blue uniform, smiling broadly. She apologized for the three little black children peeping from the kitchen. They just had to see what the President of the United States looked like.

Later, they were heard discussing his nose, because there were pictures of President John Tyler (my grandfather was very proud of his father) all over the house, and they thought all presidents had to have long, curved noses. Woodrow Wilson's was quite straight.

My grandmother, small and lively, must have led the way to the third floor, where printing blocks for the *William and Mary Quarterly* were kept. On the second floor were four-poster beds in several rooms, one with a stepladder!

Sometimes one bedroom was turned into a library, lined with books, where Lyon Tyler wrote his many historical works. They explain his absent-mindedness, for he had them on his mind even when he was with people, and he was always eager to get back to writing them or to working on his genealogies, which encompassed most of the families of Virginia.

Wilson refreshed himself in one of the "modern" bathrooms, and came down to dinner. He found the house interesting, but his mind was on America entering the war.

Nancy Wilson Mann, 1981
Granddaughter of President Lyon Tyler

## Appendix 15

## Dining with President Lyon Gardiner Tyler

During the early 1900's, meals at the President's House were brought from the kitchen in a wing of the house, later torn down. The Tylers' son, John, and other students lived in this wing. He and his father were over six feet, so it took much food to satisfy them!

Breakfast consisted of eggs, but always of salted herring with roe. Baking powder biscuits, corn muffins with country sausage, or bacon were served. Pancakes or waffles appeared on Sunday.

Midday lunch, then called dinner, was often Brunswick stew, cooked slowly until thick. It had to be eaten with a spoon, but it was not as thin as soup. During the last hour of cooking, the cook added butterbeans, corn, chunks of fresh tomato, okra, and sometimes black-eyed peas. As a base, a hen was simmered until the meat was about to fall away from the bones. The bones were then removed and the meat left in large pieces. The stew was seasoned with onions, celery, salt, pepper, and bay leaves. Cornpones, always eaten with this, were made of white cornmeal, salt, and water, molded into two-inch ovals and printed with three fingers, then baked until brown.

For Sunday dinner, most Southerners, including my Grandmother Tyler, had roast chicken with green peas and mashed potatoes, or black-eyed peas and sweet tomatoes. The latter were made with alternating bread crumbs, tomatoes and brown sugar. Each layer was dotted with butter. Then the mixture was baked forty minutes in a hot oven. Butter-beans or limas were served with the tomatoes.

Mattie the cook used to make up a breadbox full of Parker House rolls, another of macaroons, crisp outside and soft within, and another of tart shells—regular pastry baked in muffin tins, to be used for quick desserts. They were thinly spread with raspberry jam, with meringue on top. Delicious! If the macaroons became stale, they were rolled out with a rolling pin to sprinkle atop homemade vanilla ice-cream or custard. Wine jelly was usually red from scuppernong wine or sherry, but it could be made with white wine. The jelly was served in a cutglass bowl, and it was broken up so the points would reflect in the glass.

Our favorite in summer was blackberry roll, with hard suace made of brown sugar and butter. The dough was rolled in a large piece, filled with berries, butter and sugar; then, tied and wrapped in a clean cloth. Afterwards, it was suspended in boiling water (for an hour, I think) and served. The sauce melted as you ate it and mixed with the juice. Of course, other desserts were blanc mange and pies, as well as chocolate or lemon soufflé.

In spring we had roast leg of lamb with new potatoes and asparagus. For receptions and holidays, there was a turkey at one end of the table and a Smithfield ham at the other, decorated with cloves and thinly sliced. Pickled pig's feet, brandied peaches, and watermelon pickle were on the sideboard. On the table were platters of stuffed eggs, open tomato sandwiches, and beaten biscuits. These biscuits always appeared at parties, along with cheese sticks. Children did not like them, and servants grew tired of the beating by hand that they required. The biscuits were white, dry, and very smooth.

Salads that were chopped did not come into fashion until the 1930's, so lettuce with vegetables or fruit on top was the rule. Homemade mayonnaise was popular. The dessert that children preferred to most others was floating island: a boiled custard, medium thick, with syllabub and whipped cream floating on top. Then there was tipsy pudding: stale cake of any kind soaked in sherry or bourbon (but not too strong) and decorated with blanched almonds and covered with custard.

Mornings in Williamsburg brought old Ashby, the fish man, blowing his conch shell to wake people up when he brought in his wagon of fresh seafood. Scalloped oysters were a favorite. Oyster stew with milk was a good supper dish.

Nancy Wilson Mann, 1981

## Appendix 16

### The "Seven Wise Men" of the College

The faculty under President Tyler worked towards a high standard of scholarship. The professor who led in this fight and who was willing even to be charged by the students with being harsh in his dealings was Dr. John Lesslie Hall, professor of English and history. Dr. Hall was the finest type of scholar and master teacher. He was recognized for his scholarship, and students who failed at times to reach the high standard that he required in his department realized that his approval meant meticulous work.

Dr. Hall was an interesting lecturer, often interspersing his lectures with entertaining stories. In his zeal for training of English, he rendered a great service. He also established the custom of celebrating Jamestown Day each May 13. On that date he led the students on a pilgrimage to the island, where poems were read and orations delivered by members of the body. He was educated at Randolph-Macon College and Johns Hopkins University, where he received the Ph.D. degree. Dr. Hall served the college for forty years—a longer period than any of the seven. He died in 1926.

The member who was respected and loved by the entire student body was that grand old man, who for twenty-seven years was head of the math department, Dr. Thomas Jefferson Stubbs. Students often entered his room with fear and trembling but soon recognized him as a friend and counselor. He was ever the friend and champion before the faculty of the student in trouble. He had a masterful power of controlling his classes without effort, and imparted information in a simple and direct manner.

Dr. Stubbs was a native of Gloucester County, educated at William and Mary and the University of Virginia, a Confederate soldier, and a member of the Presbyterian church. He taught at the College of Arkansas and was a member of the Arkansas legislature before coming to William and Mary as head of the department of mathematics. He was a faithful and conscientious worker, and his valuable advice promoted the growth and development of the institution. He died practically in office, passing a short while after attending his morning classes in November 1915.

Dr. Lyman B. Wharton, professor of ancient and modern languages, had taught at William and Mary before 1881. He was a member of the Episcopal church and did not entirely give up that work, although his duties as a professor demanded much of his time. He was a thorough scholar and conducted courses from beginner's Latin to Sanskrit. Dr. Wharton was the oldest member of the faculty. His eyesight was not of the best and therefore he was unable to keep up with the "pony races" that were frequently conducted on the rear seats. The "riders" were those students who failed to prepare their assignments before class time.

Dr. Wharton was also a humorist, as evidenced by his address before the William and Mary Ugly Club. He is remembered for his conservative counsel, sincere friendship, and the inspiring influence of his spotless life. His end came suddenly in the Chesapeake and Ohio depot in 1907 where he, in Confederate uniform, was awaiting the arrival of the train to take him to a reunion in Richmond.

Every old student remembers that best-loved member of the faculty, mild-mannered and of gentlemanly bearing, Dr. Van F. Garrett, professor of chemistry and natural science. Dr. Garrett was an alumnus of William and Mary and of the Philadelphia College of Medicine, and he practiced his profession in Williamsburg before he was elected to a professorship at the college.

All of chemistry, physics, and biology were under his care. He was so thoroughly conscientious himself that he was often imposed upon by students who gave excuses for not preparing their work. His services covered a long period before he retired on account of failing health. He died in 1933.

The young man of the faculty was the director of teacher training, Professor Hugh S. Bird. Born in Petersburg and trained for his professions at Peabody College in Nashville, he was especially adept in demonstrating how subjects should be presented to pupils in the public schools. To his students he was the ideal teacher of these subjects, and many of his graduates applied his method in the schools of the State.

Professor Bird resigned his position to direct a Williamsburg business enterprise. When this was discontinued, he returned to the teaching profession, filling a position in the Fredericksburg Normal School [Mary Washington College] and later as principal of a high school.

While at the college he entered into a competition with one of the students for the hand of one of Williamsburg's fair sex and came off conquerer.

The roll of the Seven Wise Men was completed by the election of Dr. Charles E. Bishop as head of the Department of Modern Languages. Dr. Bishop received a part of his education in Europe and brought to William and Mary a measure of foreign methods. Picture him lecturing to his classes from the pen that he erected for himself in one corner of his classroom.

He was a minister in the Presbyterian church, making two ministers among the seven. He finally resigned from William and Mary to accept a similar position in the University of West Virginia at Morgantown. He visited William and Mary only once after he resigned, when he represented his university at the dedication of Phi Beta Kappa Hall in 1926.

Herbert Lee Bridges, in *The William and Mary Alumni Gazette*
vol 3, no. 9 April 30, 1936

# Bibliography


Correspondence and Oral Histories

Letters of the presidents of William and Mary: Faculty/Alumni files of James Blair, William Dawson, William Stith, Thomas Dawson, William Yates, James Horrocks, John Camm, James Madison, John Bracken, John Augustine Smith, William H. Wilmer, Adam Empie, Thomas Roderick Dew, Robert Saunders, Benjamin S. Ewell, John Johns, Lyon Gardiner Tyler, Julian A. C. Chandler, John Stewart Bryan, John Edwin Pomfret, Alvin Duke Chandler, Davis Young Paschall, Thomas A. Graves, Jr., College Archives, Swem Library, the College of William and Mary.

William and Mary College Papers, 1721–1818, Library of Congress.

Oral History transcripts of Davis Young Paschall, Colgate W. Darden, Jr., W. Melville Jones, James W. Miller, Wilfred Lambert, John E. Hocutt, Amanda Bryan Kane, and others. Interviews by Emily Williams, 1974–1976; College Archives, Swem Library, the College of William and Mary.

Books

Billington, Ray Allen, ed. *The Reinterpretation of Early American History: Essays in Honor of John Edwin Pomfret*. San Marino, Calif: The Huntington Library, 1968.

Chapman, Ann West. *The College of William and Mary, 1849–59: The Memoirs of Silas Totten,* M.A. Thesis, The College of William and Mary, 1978.

Colonial Williamsburg Foundation: *Official Guidebook and Map*. Williamsburg, 1980.

Crenshaw, Ollinger. *General Lee's College: The Rise and Growth of Washington and Lee University*. New York: Random House, 1969.

Dabney, Virginius. *Mr. Jefferson's University, A History*. Charlottesville: University Press of Virginia. 1981.

Goodwin, Mary Mordecai. *The President's House and the Presidents of the College of William and Mary, 1732-1976,* 2 vols. Williamsburg: Mary R.M. Goodwin. (mimeograph). 1965.

——— *William & Mary College Historical Notes,* 3 vols. Williamsburg. Colonial Williamsburg Foundation. 1954.

Jester, Annie Lash. Newport News, Virginia: 1607-1960. City of Newport News. 1961.

Journal of the Meetings of the President and Masters of William and Mary

College. *William and Mary Quarterly Historical Magazine,* 1st ser. 1: 130-137, 214-20.

Meade, Bishop William. *Old Churches, Ministers, and Families of Virginia.* 2 vols. Philadelphia: J. B. Lippincott Company, 1906.

Morpurgo, John E. *Their Majesties' Royall Colledge: William and Mary in the Seventeenth and Eighteenth centuries.* Williamsburg: The College of William and Mary, 1976.

Morton, Richard L. *Colonial Virginia.* 2 vols. Chapel Hill: University of North Carolina Press, 1960.

Parrington, Vernon Louis. *The Romantic Revolution in America.* New York: Harcourt Brace and Company, 1927.

"A President and Six Masters." Address delivered by W. Melville Jones, on the 268th anniversary of the granting of the Royal Charter. Williamsburg: College of William and Mary, 1961.

Rait, Robert Sangster. *Life in the Medieval University.* Cambridge: University Press; and New York: G.P. Putnam's Sons, 1912.

Rouse, Parke Jr. *James Blair of Virginia.* Chapel Hill: University of North Carolina Press, 1971.

———*Cows on the Campus: Williamsburg in Bygone Days.* Richmond. The Dietz Press. 1973.

Waterman, Thomas Tileston and John A. Barrows. *Domestic Colonial Architecture of Tidewater Virginia.* New York: Charles Scribner's Sons, 1932.

Whiffen, Marcus. *The Public Buildings of Williamsburg: Colonial Capital of Virginia,* 1958. Williamsburg: Colonial Williamsburg, 1958.

Woodfin, Maude H., ed. *Another Secret Diary of William Byrd of Westover, 1739-1741.* Translated and collated by Marion Tinling. Richmond: Dietz Press, 1942.

Wright, Louis B. and Marion Tinling, eds. *The Secret Diary of William Byrd of Westover, 1709-1712.* Richmond: Dietz Press, 1941.

## Articles and Booklets

Bridges, Herbert Lee. "The Seven Wise Men," *William and Mary Gazette,* Vol. 3, No. 9, April 30, 1936.

Chapman, Anne West. "Graduation, 1850s Style," *William and Mary Alumni Gazette,* Vol. 48, No. 8, May 1981.

——— "Silas Totten: A Yankee Professor at William and Mary," *William and Mary Alumni Gazette,* Vol. 44, No. 11, May 1977.

Coleman, Elizabeth Dabney, and W. Edwin Hemphill. "Founding Virginia's First College." *Virginia Cavalcade Magazine,* Vol. 7, No. 1, July 1957.

"Hon. John Blair, Jr." An address by Henry T. Wickham, Esq., of Virginia at a special session of the U.S. Circuit Court of Appeals, Philadelphia, May 6, 1913.

"Two Hundredth Anniversary of the Charter of the College of William and Mary—1693-1893." College of William and Mary, Williamsburg, 1893.

Tyler, Lyon G. "The College of William and Mary: Its Work, Discipline, and

History, from its Foundation to the Present Time." *Bulletin of the College of William and Mary* (May 1917), 38 pp.

"Vital Facts: A William and Mary Chronology, 1693–1963." Williamsburg: College of William and Mary, 1963.

*Virginia Magazine of History and Biography*. Richmond: Published quarterly by the Virginia Historical Society, Richmond, 1893-1983.

*William and Mary College Quarterly Historical Magazine,* 1st ser., 26 vols., Williamsburg, 1882-1919. 2d ser., Williamsburg. 1921-44.

# Index

**Y**